THE OLD MAN

John Brown at Harper's Ferry

THE

Charlestown, Va., 2, December, 1859. I John Brown am now quite certain that the crimes of this guilty, land: will never be purged away; but with Blood. I had as I now think: vainly flattered myself that without very much bloodshed; it might be done.

John Brown's Last Statement

OLD MAN

John Brown

at Harper's Ferry

TRUMAN NELSON

Originally published in 1973 by Holt, Rinehart and Winston, New York
© 1973 Truman Nelson

This edition published in 2009 by Haymarket Books
P.O. Box 180165
Chicago, IL, 60618
773-583-7884
www.haymarketbooks.org
info@haymarketbooks.org

ISBN: 978-1-93185-964-6

Distributed to the trade in the US through Consortium Book Sales and
Distribution (www.cbsd.com) and internationally through Ingram
Publisher Services International (www.ingramcontent.com).

This book was published with the generous support of Lannan Foundation
and Wallace Action Fund.

Special discounts are available for bulk purchases by organizations and
institutions. Please call 773-583-7884 or email info@haymarketbooks.org
for more information.

Cover design by Ragina Johnson. The cover image is from a daguerreotype
made of John Brown in 1856, taken in Hudson, Ohio by an unknown
photographer.

Printed in the United States.

Entered into digital printing August 2020.

The 1973 edition of this book is catalogued by the Library of Congress
under card number 72–78120.

10 9 8 7 6 5 4 3 2

For Garrison and Abigail,
Elizabeth and Johnny,
Shyla and Ethan
and Peter Lenz

Also thanks to the Louis M. Rabinowitz Foundation for providing the means for researching and meditating this work.

Contents

1

The Coup

He proposed, with twenty five to fifty men, colored and white mixed, well armed, and taking with them a quantity of spare arms, to beat up a slave quarter in Virginia, and making a dash at Harper's Ferry arms manufactory, destroying what he could not carry off. He argued, that were he pressed by the U.S. troops, which, after a few weeks might concentrate, he could easily maintain himself in the Alleghenies and that his New England partisans would in the meantime call a Northern Convention, restore tranquility and overthrow the pro-slavery administration.

Hugh Forbes, New York *Herald*,
October 27, 1859

At daybreak, October 17, 1859, John Brown had taken control of the Federal Arsenal at Harper's Ferry, and "beat up a slave quarter in Virginia," as he had proposed to Colonel Hugh Forbes in August of 1857. He had gone in the night before with eighteen men, black and white, seized the important buildings and forty-odd hostages, including almost all the town notables. Harper's Ferry is a tongue-shaped gap in the towering heights of the Blue Ridge Mountains; then it was a manufacturing town of two thousand inhabitants, with a few cobbled streets and huge, gaunt factories, compressed between beetling cliffs, dark, shaggy ravines, and the white-watered junction of two massive rivers, the Potomac and the Shenandoah.

In *Coup d'État, a Practical Handbook,* Edward Luttwak, the most recent authority on the subject, states that a good coup country is one in which 1) politics are well organized, but polarized into bitterly hostile factions; 2) the country itself is completely independent of outside political pressures; 3) the social and economic conditions of the target area confine political participation to a small faction of the population; and 4) the target area has a high political significance.

Conditions one and two explain themselves. As to three and four, Brown's choice of the federal arsenal at Harper's Ferry, just on the dividing line of Virginia—and what is now West Virginia—carried out these requirements perfectly. The white, nonslaveholding citizens of the mountain counties of western Virginia were so out of sympathy with, and badly represented in, the Richmond government that a few months after Brown's action, they met in convention at Clarksburg, denounced the state government for passing the ordinance of secession from the United States, and set up a separate state, loyal to the Federal Union. John Brown was fully aware of the political importance to southern power of Virginia, birthplace of the early presidents. It was no accident that Richmond became the capital of the Confederacy. Every feature of Brown's assault went against the dignity of the Richmond government.

The Old Man was carrying out a classic coup, as distinguished from both insurrection and revolution. The coup does not depend upon masses of men or large sections of military force. It seizes power within the existing system. Brown had specified in his "Provisional Constitution" that "The foregoing articles shall not be construed so as to in any way encourage the overthrow of the United States and looks to no dissolution of the Union, but simply to amendment and repeal. And our Flag will be the same as that our fathers fought under in the Revolution."

The leverage of the coup comes from a small but critical segment of the state apparatus, used to displace the government from the control of the remainder. John Brown thought he had the support of that segment of congressmen, senators, and governors who had taken a positive antislavery position through the years and had won their offices because of this. Many of them had known since 1858 that he was planning to attack Harper's Ferry and that he was armed with two hundred Sharps rifles given him by the Massachusetts State Kansas Committee.

They had learned this through Hugh Forbes, a European revolutionary and expert on guerrilla warfare who had been hired by

Brown to instruct his recruits. Forbes had tried to talk Brown out of the Harper's Ferry plan in favor of a series of tightly controlled slave raids along the North-South border, a standard guerrilla operation developing into a long and bloody process of eroding the social and political infrastructure of the slave states.

Brown had argued there was no time for this: the slaves were going to attempt to free themselves any day now, but they were so much under surveillance, whipping, and chains that they could not assemble effective weapons or move about enough to organize on the massive scale necessary for success. His plan of involving a limited number, arming them with simple weapons of defense, and providing them with the leadership he had hired Forbes to train, would eliminate the disastrous uncertainties of an uncoordinated insurrection. Once he had aroused the country by taking the arsenal and then moved southward to a base in the Virginia mountains, Brown felt the slaves would not be left to fight and die alone; the white abolitionists of the North would be compelled to join them in a common strategy, bearing arms or using mass political means to help them achieve their own liberation. This could be done, Brown had insisted, "without very much blood."

Forbes had disagreed violently, insisting that Brown's move would trigger a massive slave insurrection which would "leap beyond control . . . the slaves would be slaughtered and the country turn against all the blacks." Brown replied that he did not expect the slaves to come to him in great numbers, nor did he wish it. He wanted no more than could effectively govern themselves under a "Provisional Constitution" in the mountain territory they could wrest from slavery.

Forbes had then broken with the Old Man and rushed to Washington. He had become convinced by the absolute confidence and certainty exuded by Brown that he was planning his move in concert with a powerful group of radical Republicans. In May, 1858, Forbes confronted William Seward, Senator from New York, a party leader and the declared front-runner for the Presidency. Forbes informed him that Brown intended to attack a government arsenal in the South and that the Massachusetts State Kansas Committee had given him two hundred rifles. In addition, two hundred revolvers, camping and fortifying materials, as well as large sums of money, had been given him by a secret committee of six abolitionists, three of them highly distinguished Americans well known to Seward as to the country: Theodore Parker who was, along with Henry Ward Beecher, one of the country's best-known preachers; Gerrit Smith, a former Congressman and a millionaire whose father had been the partner of John Jacob Astor; and Samuel Gridley Howe, a philanthropist of Boston best known for his work in restoring the deaf, the blind, and the mentally impaired to a useful function in society.

"I went fully into the whole matter in all its bearings," Forbes said. "He [Seward] expressed regret that he had been told and said that in his position he ought not to have been informed of these circumstances."

The defecting Forbes also informed Senators Charles Sumner and Henry Wilson of Massachusetts, Senator John P. Hale of New Hampshire, Governor Salmon B. Chase of Ohio, and Governor Ryland Fletcher of Vermont. Although the entire hierarchy of the Republican Party knew, a year before it took place, of a plot against a federal arsenal, none of them informed the proper authorities and only Senator Wilson attempted to block it in any way.

Although a defector, Forbes wanted the Old Man to understand that he was still a dedicated revolutionary and that his disagreement was over tactics, not a betrayal. Insisting that he had disclosed the plan only to sympathizers, he dispatched copies of all the letters he had sent these Republican leaders, saying, "I feel that none of these letters were suffered to be seen by the Secretary of War."

The Old Man took the situation calmly and went on developing the plot as if Forbes's action did not matter. In fact, the revelations given to these men of power, without adverse action on their part, seemed to him a tacit assurance of support. He even kept the letters revealing this complicity in a carpetbag at his base camp across the Potomac in Maryland. This was not a conscious entrapment of powerful supporters but simply a lifetime habit of filing his letters, writing "answered" or "no answer needed" on every one he received.

He knew that the alienation, impotence, and frustration of elected Republicans was profound. The Democratic Party was in control of every department of the Government and had a formidable popular majority behind it. Seward himself had said that without the consent of proslavery politicians, a Republican President-elect "could not appoint a minister, or even a police agent, negotiate a treaty or procure the passage of a law, and could hardly draw a musket from the public arsenal to defend his own person."

The Old Man could not see how true Republicans could feel loyalty to such a government, or "usurpation," as he called it. He nourished the hope that Seward and his colleagues had been inadvertently convinced by Forbes that many influential Americans were indeed ready for a Northern coup against the "slaveocracy." He was known to them as the most ruthless and revolutionary partisan of the Kansas Wars: they could be sure he would do exactly what he said, and none had raised a voice against him.

If his plan worked, he felt that the small group of radical Republicans in the government, men who said over and over again that the party's strength lay in its moral repudiation of slavery, would have to uphold him—peacefully if they could, forcibly if they must. Failure would bring certain death for him and his men, but if he succeeded, it meant the liberation of the slaves and the total reorganization of the government.

So the Old Man went ahead, developing recruits, selecting a target area, keeping the timing flexible to defeat security leaks, all the while constantly anticipating and implementing every significant requirement of the modern coup. The same claim can be made for the details of his strategy—setting up the blocking areas, interdicting arms supplies to the enemy, seizing symbolic buildings associated with political power (thereby giving visual evidence of the reality of the coup), and holding certain individuals as hostages to prevent their influence or charisma to be used by the opposition. John Brown had discovered and implemented every significant requirement of the classic coup, provoking a lurid sequence of public scenes of almost unbearable tension, upheaval, and crisis. Between the anvil of Harper's Ferry and the hammer of Brown's attack, the America of Abraham Lincoln and the day of emancipation were forged.

When the residents of Harper's Ferry woke that morning, both

Harper's Ferry

the bridge over the Potomac, connecting the Ferry with Maryland, and the one over the Shenandoah, linking it with the towering mountains to the south, were occupied by blocking teams, instructed to prevent passage with a minimum of violence. Other teams were occupying a rifle works a half mile from the target area and a storage building containing more than fifteen thousand stands of arms. The town was completely under the control of abolitionists and freed slaves. The active phase of the coup was over; Brown's problem now was to send out his first communiqué and let the country know what had happened. The telegraph lines had been cut when he moved into position the night before. The reality and power of the coup now had to be conveyed to his "New England Partisans, to call a Northern Convention, restore tranquility, and overthrow the proslavery administration."

A mail train of the Baltimore and Ohio, on the west-east run, had been standing at the depot since midnight. In the excitement of the take-over, Brown had forgotten that it was still there. He decided to let it go through and spread the news, without trying to justify the action or attach to it any particular political orientation. Every railroad depot had a telegraph operator, part of a system installed in the previous decade and stretching along the east coast from Richmond to Maine, westward to Canada and the edges of the Kansas and Iowa prairies. The train, released and sent on, stopped at the next easterly depot, and the excited conductor gave his version of the coup to the telegrapher. Crackling like the ignited twigs and branches of a raging forest fire, the news spread north and west, tapping through the constituencies of antislavery congressmen and senators who had been voted in for two decades because they had spoken with horror and compassion about the suffering slave. Northern and western New York, the "northern tier" counties of Pennsylvania, the Ohio "Western Reserve," the northern third of Illinois, Wisconsin, Michigan, almost every free state "had its New England in it," and so had been plowed and seeded by evangelical abolitionists who held that slavery was the sum of all sins and all tyrannies and that resistance to tyranny was obedience to God. Now the Old Man's invitation to men of good will was being sent across the country as every operator along the way picked up the

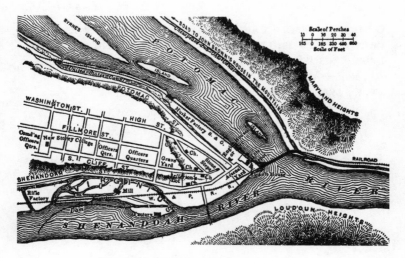

Bird's-Eye View of Harper's Ferry

alarm and cleared the wires for its transmission to the end of the line:

NEGRO INSURRECTION AT HARPER'S FERRY, VIRGINIA—SEIZURE OF THE UNITED STATES ARSENAL BY THE INSURRECTIONISTS—EXTENSIVE NEGRO CONSPIRACY IN VIRGINIA AND MARYLAND—BRIDGE TO HARPER'S FERRY FROM MARYLAND FORTIFIED AND DEFENDED BY CANNON—TRAINS FIRED INTO AND STOPPED—TELEGRAPH WIRES CUT—CONTRIBUTIONS LEVIED ON CITIZENS—SEVEN HUNDRED AND FIFTY BLACK AND WHITE ABOLITIONISTS HOLD ARSENAL AND GUN WORKS—EVERY LIGHT IN TOWN IS EXTINGUISHED AND THE HOTELS CLOSED—ALL ROADS LEADING THERE ARE BARRICADED AND GUARDED—WAGONLOADS OF MUSKETS BEING SENT TO THE MOUNTAINS IN MARYLAND—ADDING NEW FLAMES TO THE FIRES OF EXCITEMENT THE NAME OF THE LEADER IS OSAWATOMIE BROWN—BROWN EXPECTS REINFORCEMENTS OF FIFTEEN HUNDRED MEN BY TOMORROW MORNING—THE BAGGAGE MASTER OF THE MAIL TRAIN

COMING IN FROM THE WEST WAS TAKEN PRISONER AND
CARRIED INTO THE ARMORY WHERE HE FOUND SIX HUN-
DRED NEGROES AND TWO OR THREE HUNDRED WHITE MEN
IN ARMS—ALMOST ALL THE LEADING CITIZENS OF HARPER'S
FERRY ARE HELD AS HOSTAGES—

2

The Conspiracy

I believe a conspiracy has been formed, extending not only over a portion of the United States, but also into England; that money has been contributed at both places; that it has been the work of years; that a military leader was sent from England here to participate, first in the Kansas troubles, and then in this raid upon Virginia.

Jefferson Davis
Senate, December 8, 1859

The Old Man arrived at Harper's Ferry on the Fourth of July with a well-matured plan. With his sons Owen and Oliver, and his bodyguard, Jeremiah Anderson, he made himself familiar with his ultimate target area, that part of the town called "The Point," the passageway to the depot, the arsenal, and both bridges, a remarkably compact area to control.

He had had a secret agent named John Cook working there for the past year. Cook's reports were that many of the citizens of the Ferry were mechanics from the arsenal at Springfield, Massachusetts, and the rest were mostly indifferent, neither warlike, nor defenders of slavery. Nor were they well armed. Cook told his captain that there were no more than a dozen old shotguns and squirrel rifles in private hands and that no important firepower could be delivered against an invader.

Since the Harper's Ferry residents represented no danger, Brown planned on occupying nothing but the enclosure within which stood the government buildings. Just outside the enclosure was a large, three-story building in which, it was rumored, were stored forty or fifty thousand rifles that the southern Secretary of War was planning to have removed secretly to the Deep South. Along the banks of the Shenandoah to the west was another cluster of factories called Hall's Rifle Works. It was a half mile from the Point and would have to be occupied to keep the rifles there from being used against him. John Cook had also discovered that there were no armed guards at the government buildings, only civilian watchmen on patrol to watch fires and catch petty thieves.

Citizens of Harper's Ferry paid no attention to the Old Man as he reconnoitered the scene of his future conquest. Ordinarily, passers-by often stared at him, since he was a gaunt, ceremonious man, with a mixture of Quaker and warrior in his dress, whose walk was the hard, pounding stride of a man climbing an invisible hill. People who had caught a glimpse of him in the streets of Boston were reminded of an Old Testament prophet, but when he was doing his "secret service work," he managed to appear completely harmless and ineffectual. His beard, flowing and patriarchal while raising funds in Boston a few weeks before, was cut close and scraggly. When in enemy territory he cultivated an appearance of intense peacefulness. He wore the clothes of a farmer dressed up for a nervous visit to town, looking a little frightened of the bustle of urban life.

This deceptive air of appealing innocence was maintained with great skill. Crossing over the Potomac Bridge to the Maryland side, he met his agent Cook at a lock keeper's cottage on the Baltimore and Ohio Canal. Cook took Brown, his sons, and Anderson to the craggy heights overlooking the town. There he could see the compact little community, open and defenseless, vulnerable to an attack from the peak itself, as his surveyor's eye told him it was all within range of a Sharps rifle shot.

On the road back, skirting the base of the Maryland heights, he met a genial southerner named Unseld, a slaveholder. Brown told Unseld he was looking for a little farm in a mild climate because the sharp frost of upper New York State had killed off his crops. Unseld told him there was a nice place about five miles up the road. It was for sale by the heirs of a Dr. Kennedy. Brown protested softly that he would not dare buy it outright without renting it first, in his poverty and humility, he was fearful of being "taken advantage of." Unseld grew protective and talked with him for more than an hour. Brown was vague about what he was going to grow but said he might get cattle thereabouts, fatten them up, and drive them on to the North.

Brown's Overview of Harper's Ferry from Maryland

The next time Brown met Mr. Unseld he told him he had rented the Kennedy farm and the two buildings on it. He took pains to show him a receipt for six months' rent. Unseld brushed this aside as none of his business but was greatly impressed by the Old Man's openness and straightforward ways. A week later Unseld came upon Brown in the deep woods on the way to the mountaintop. Brown had his surveyor's compass with him and was figuring the time it would take his guerrillas to get from the Kennedy farm to the arsenal. Brown, with the soft, defensive look of a poor man trying to strike it rich, told Unseld that his compass would tell him if there were any iron deposits there. Unseld was so impressed with Brown that he visited him frequently at the Kennedy farm. He was always asked to come in, but he preferred to sit on his horse and talk.

John Brown now had two houses only five miles away from the arsenal. One was a little farmhouse so solidly built it is still standing today. The other was a very rough little cabin on swampy ground across the road. In this base he had to conceal from twenty to thirty guerrillas, black and white, and all the guns and pikes, all the powder and ball, and all the tools necessary for construction of forts and paths in his mountain hideout.

One false step, the briefest exposure, and his plans of a lifetime would be ruined and he and his men captured or killed. He had to strengthen the illusion that he was a simple farmer, a family man. He wrote to his home in North Elba, New York, for his daughter, Anne and Martha, the wife of his son Oliver, to come do the house-keeping. Anne was sixteen, Martha was seventeen, and they came enthusiastically to join the liberation movement.

The guns were still in Ashtabula, Ohio, the pikes in Connecticut —they had to be smuggled in. His second in command for the operation was a man named John Kagi. Kagi was twenty-four, an intellectual, writer, and printer who had grown up in Maryland and

The Kennedy Farmhouse in Maryland

Virginia. Brown stationed him at Chambersburg, Pennsylvania, the nearest railhead to the farm aside from the Baltimore and Ohio route. Kagi was charged with the responsibility not only of getting in the arms from Ohio and Connecticut but also of assembling men from as far north as Canada. All routes, east and west, led to Harrisburg, Pennsylvania, and a spur branch of the Cumberland Valley railroad led to Chambersburg. The distance from Chambersburg to the farm was fifty miles. Brown brought a covered wagon, a horse, and a mule to express supplies from there. Although his son, Owen, was to handle this trip, Brown himself planned for every contingency along every mile of the route.

Anne Brown was to have absolute command of the "invisibles," as she called the men arriving almost every day. The area of concealment was pitifully small. The ground floor contained a tiny kitchen, a dining room, and a bedroom where she and Martha slept. The men had to spend most of their time in the attic, under a sloping roof. Mostly big men, seven of them over six feet, they were all under thirty and full of boisterous energy. Large and rough as they were, however, under Annie's strict control, they were as mild as happy children. They sang songs, played guessing games, told each other tall stories, and argued for the privilege of putting on an apron and helping the girls clean up the dinner dishes.

Everything was controlled and lighthearted—almost. Deep in them all was a wild, exuberant belief that they were going to make history. There in the hot, stifling attic of the little farmhouse, among the wasps and the undefinable murmurs of closed-in August days, they tried to find ways of passing the time. They assembled the pikes which had been shipped in separately as hoe handles and kitchen tools. They oiled and took apart their Sharps guns. Sometimes a thunderstorm would come and, as the hills reverberated, they would shout and laugh and dance about like wild men. Freed from cautionary silence, they ran out into the wet gloom, dancing and skylarking in the clamorous, shielding rain.

Martha, Oliver's wife, spending all her time in the kitchen, made the house redolent with baking bread. The men loved to sneak down and talk with her, savoring the breath and aura of her young sweetness. She would iron their fancy shirts for them and not allow

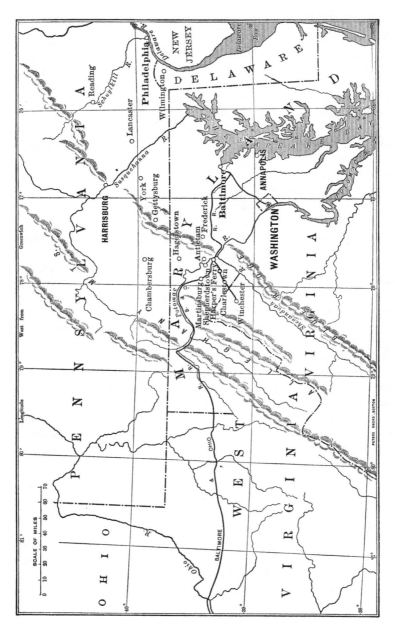

The Harper's Ferry Region

the protesting Annie to lift a hand to anything but keeping watch and washing dishes. In the small compass of the farmhouse the two pretty young girls, serious and with a beautiful, selfless purpose, and the quiet old man, brooding like the father of all the world on the accursed question of man's total emancipation, achieved a curious wholeness and domesticity. The smells, the sights, the sounds were all of family life, of common sharing.

Only Annie felt the fear, watching the road, watching the back of the house, knitting on the porch, holding down the murmur of exploding life. A little fat woman named Huffmaster with a brood of young children had hired a patch of ground from the Kennedys and was raising vegetables there. Her curiosity was insatiable. She came at all hours, supposedly to watch her pumpkins grow. She would sidle up to Annie and try to engage her in gossip, avidly looking and listening. Sometimes she would come when the men were at their dinner. Annie would have to decoy her to the garden while Martha hid whatever she was cooking and the men scurried up to the attic with the food, dishes, tablecloth and all, taking care not to rattle the spoons on the way. Annie had to keep her composure, answer the snooper gently, and keep smiling.

As the hiding place slowly filled with men and guns, packed in like powder in a rifle barrel, critical tensions began to develop. One of the men, Charles Tidd, who had been with Brown all through the Kansas Wars and was a good fighter, had a dark, saturnine nature and was especially quarrelsome. To make matters worse, he began getting letters from friends in Iowa who were ardently anti-slavery but were Quakers and pacifists. In their letters they would softly deplore the violence of the move to come, about which Tidd had indiscreetly told them everything.

Tidd had a habit of starting an argument in the dining room at supper which would quickly accelerate into near-violence. It was generally with his closest crony, Aaron Stevens, who bruised easily and always rose to the bait. One evening when the air was tremulous with distant thunder, Tidd began to wave a letter about, claiming he had just received it from a lady friend. The fact was that both he and Stevens had courted a Quaker girl in Iowa. When Stevens made a grab for the letter, Tidd pushed him off, and the men

Charles Tidd

crowded around and demanded that it be read aloud to all of them.

It was actually an old letter Tidd had received months before, but he was caught up in the game and began to read it. "Dear Charles . . . We feel many misgivings about your situation. The idea of you being in such awful danger makes us all unhappy. We know the great giant with which you contend. I fear it will result in no good to you. You may give the best years of your precious young manhood for something that can never be accomplished by brute force."

The men chuckled at this, but Captain Brown, sitting at his favorite perch, a small stool beside the kitchen stove, straightened up in anger. He was having one of his bad days and trying hard to disguise it. He was often sick with a recurrence of the malaria he had picked up in the swamps and thickets of his guerrilla battle-grounds in Kansas. Sudden fevers would come on him, followed by chills and wearying "shakes." The utterance of the most extreme opinions did not ordinarily disturb him, but it was tactless, to say the least, to talk about the futility of brute force in this particular situation. As a former pacifist, he was oversensitive to any implication that he, or his followers, were bloody-minded men. The next line of the letter brought him to his feet, enraged. "I do not advise anyone to abstain from their duty, but I do not want innocent blood shed for the removal of the great monster, slavery . . . to do so would cause all the efforts for the relief of the bondsmen to come to an end."

The Old Man came stalking to the table, head thrown back, his eyes stabbing Tidd like bayonets. The dialogue stopped. He fixed his gaze on the outspread letter and his voice cut through the heavy air: "I do hope all correspondence except on business of the company will be dropped for the present. If everyone must write some girl or some other extra friend showing our location and tell all about our matters we might as well publish the whole thing in the New York *Herald*."

Tidd started to answer, thought better of it, and lowered his head. Brown went on: "Any person is a stupid fool who expects his friends to keep for him what he cannot keep for himself. All our friends have their special friends and they have theirs and it's not right to lay the burden of keeping a secret on anyone at the end of such a long string."

Without a word the men left the table and went upstairs into the attic. Tidd, in his excitement and shame, left the letter on the table. Annie's eyes filled with tears. It was becoming almost impossible to keep this fragile situation from breaking into bits. She was sorry for the boys, creeping off to bed like whipped puppies. She was sorry about her father's anger; she wanted him to be loved, always. She felt somehow as if she were to blame for the outburst, that it showed a lapse in her watchfulness and security arrangements. Brown looked at her a moment and then asked gently if she were homesick.

"Yes," she said, breaking up, "homesick and sick of living this life, where I have to live a lie . . . going by another name and telling so many lies, or what is the same, *acting* them. I wish you would hurry and get through with me, and let me go home where I can be myself and have my own name."

Her father gave a long sigh of discouragement. Aaron Stevens came back downstairs to rescue Annie from her father's wrath. He said lightly, "Annie, let me give you a piece of advice. Always tell the truth, the whole truth, and nothing but the truth. But if you do have to tell a lie, tell a whopper!" Annie laughed, and the men upstairs joined in. Stevens then told the Captain that no one paid any attention to Tidd; the men enjoyed his sourness and cynicism without being affected by it. Tidd provided a healthy grain of salt for their own runaway optimism. Brown said it was not his sourness that bothered him but the fear that someone could be giving aid and comfort to a Judas.

The matter was dropped, but the Old Man's instincts were right: a kind of benign betrayal was taking place, by precisely those people who were writing these discouraging letters. An Iowa Quaker named Varney had revealed Brown's plans in exact detail to two young men, saying, "Something must be done to save their lives. I cannot betray their confidence in me. Consult your friends. Do something!"

The young men, also with the best intentions, decided that if they wrote anonymously to the Secretary of War, exposing the coming raid, he would increase the guard around the arsenal, and that this would deter Brown, or at least warn him to call off the attempt and lead his men back to safety. The letter, dated August 20, 1859, reached the Secretary of War; it was very explicit:

> I have discovered the existence of a secret association having for its object the liberation of slaves at the South. The leader of the movement is *Old John Brown,* late of Kansas. He has been in Canada during the winter, drilling the Negroes there, and they are only waiting his word to start from the South to assist the slaves. They have one of their leading men (a white man) in an armory in Maryland. . . . They will pass down through Pennsylvania and Maryland and enter Virginia at Harper's Ferry. . . . will arm the Negroes and strike the blow in a few weeks.

The Secretary, John B. Floyd, gave the letter some thought, and later published it, but did not act on it at the time. He was thrown off by the location of the arsenal in Maryland, rather than in Virginia. "Besides," he declared afterward, "I was satisfied that a scheme of such wickedness and outrage could not be entertained by any citizen of the United States."

The Old Man's luck was still holding out. About this time, too, the guns came through from the cache in Ohio and were delivered at the farm, making their complicated passage through the canal down the western border of Pennsylvania to Pittsburgh, from there by railroad to Harrisburg, then transshipped on a spur line to Chambersburg. There was another moment of great elation when Brown received a letter from his son, John, Jr., his northern recruiting agent. It said "Fred'k" with another young man was coming to meet him at Chambersburg. "Fred'k" was Frederick Douglass, the black leader, a titan of a man who had escaped from slavery in 1838, made his way north, and despite the absence of schooling had become a brilliant editor and the outstanding orator and strategist of the abolition movement.

The Old Man and Frederick Douglass had been close friends for many years. Brown had based much of his faith in the ability of the black race to determine its political destiny on Douglass, as the archetype of what the black race could accomplish when its chains were taken off. Now that Douglass was joining the conspiracy, coming to take his place as the head of the provisional government, Brown felt that the plan could not fail.

The letter also said that Douglass would be accompanied "by the woman." The woman was Harriet Tubman, born a slave in Maryland in 1820, and known as the most successful practical liberator in the country. Singlehanded, she had conducted more than three hundred slaves to freedom without losing one to the pursuers and their dogs. The South had put a reward of $10,000, dead or alive, on her head; to John Brown, she was "General Tubman," the wisest person in America, the great black, protecting mother of the new state. A mystic, she told him once of seeing in a dream, in a wilderness place, a noble serpent raising his head above some rock and then becoming the head of an old man with a long white beard who looked at her as if he were going to speak. When she first met John Brown in Canada, she told him he was the head in her dream, and asked him what he wanted to say to her. He said to come with him to Harper's Ferry, and she agreed. But she did not tell him how her

Harriet Tubman

dream ended—she had seen a great crowd of men coming to cut off the heads of two handsome young men, one on either side of him. She thought the two heads, that looked at her wistfully, were those of his sons.

Before starting for the meeting with Douglass and Tubman at Chambersburg, the Old Man called in his agent at the Ferry, John E. Cook, for a final briefing. Law student, schoolteacher, and poet, Cook was a slightly built young man with long blonde hair and innocent blue eyes. There were many things about him that Brown deplored: he talked far too much, sometimes tripping over his own words in his rush to have something to say on every conceivable subject, and the other recruits complained that he was always showing off. With little encouragement Cook would display his gun collection, boast about his Kansas experiences, and hint that he was soon to take part in a daring raid to free the slaves.

On the other hand, he was a trained guerrilla, a superb marksman, and fantastically loyal to the Old Man. He was also very well connected, his brother-in-law being Governor of Indiana. When John Brown first mentioned the attack on Harper's Ferry, Cook had insisted on going there and scouting out the situation to solve the problems. At first Brown did not want him to go because of his loose tongue, but Cook persisted and after he arrived there, his reports became very valuable to the Old Man.

John Brown was quiet and restrained in his speech; Henry Thoreau said he "did not overstate anything." Cook, however, would take some idea of the Captain's and develop it until it was both credible and spectacular. He insisted that the inhabitants at the Ferry were not unsympathetic to antislavery ideas and might be recruited. Although he let it be known that he had fought in the Kansas Wars as a Free State partisan, he got along very well at the Ferry. When Cook first arrived at Harper's Ferry, he got a job as a tender on the lock on the canal which fed water power to the gun shops, and in this way got to know the arsenal and everybody working there. He next took a job as a schoolteacher on the Maryland side and learned about the parents of his students who lived on the farms outside the Ferry. By pretending to be employed by a company that made maps and published accompanying statistics, he

John E. Cook

learned the names, ages, and condition of almost every black person for miles around. As an enthusiastic gun collector, he also wheedled his way into seeing almost every available weapon among the civilian population. He became a "character" around Harper's Ferry, creating such a favorable impression that he courted and married the daughter of one of the most respected families there. It was hard to fault him for such a successful tour of duty, but Brown still had a fear that Cook had blurted out some feature of the plot.

The Old Man had not yet decided which "slave quarter" was to be seized in order to produce the greatest liberating effect. Cook argued that a team should be sent to the plantation of Lewis Washington, the great-grandnephew of General and President Washington. It was situated much farther from the target area than Brown wanted to go, but Cook pointed out what an excellent hostage Washington would be, as a colonel in the Virginia State Militia, and how significant it would be to liberate his slaves, some of whom had descended undoubtedly from George Washington's slaves. When the Old Man told him Frederick Douglass was on his way to join them, Cook pointed out that Lewis Washington had in his possession the ceremonial sword given to the revolutionary commander in chief by Frederick the Great. He entreated the Old Man to let him get this sword and put it into the hands of Frederick Douglass when the latter took command of the slaves who had been freed. It would be the perfect symbol with which to take revolutionary power.

The Old Man reluctantly agreed, but his anxieties were again awakened when Cook declared that Douglass's presence would guarantee at least a hundred volunteers in the Harper's Ferry area alone. Brown sternly reminded Cook that he had given strict orders that the neighboring slaves were not to be told about the plans in advance. Cook softly expostulated that, with one exception, he had not talked to any slaves about it, but that the Old Man had not specifically ruled out recruiting attempts among the discontented white citizens of Virginia. The Old Man stirred uneasily at this but made no comment. He could not deny his high expectation that, as he said later to Governor Wise, a hundred white Virginians would join the conspiracy.

3
Recruiting

When, and only when, the recruit becomes
actual, rather than potential, we can reveal to him the nature of his actual task.
Edward Luttwak
Coup d'État, A Practical Handbook

At Chambersburg the Old Man had gone to earth in an abandoned quarry west of the town. There he could remain in concealment for days, as gray and monolithic as the uncut granite all
around him. Although Douglass was to be his most important recruit, he again followed the rules of the classic coup by not telling
Douglass how far he intended to go until he had agreed to come
along or had given evidence of firm commitment.

The Old Man had known Douglass since late in the 1840s when
the latter visited him while he was living in Springfield, Massachusetts. Douglass had just completed a tour of the West for the
American Anti-Slavery Society, speaking two or three times a day,
and was utterly exhausted by the abuse he had endured. The win-
dowpanes of the hall in which he lectured had been smashed, and
he himself had been pelted with rotten eggs and garbage, struck
by stones and sticks, and insulted with filthy outcries of "Nigger, go
home." While riding on trains or stagecoaches, he was forcibly
ejected from any seat a white man wanted. He was not allowed to
come to the table while any white man sat there and sometimes
went for days without a decent meal while whites feasted sump-
tuously before his eyes.

Through all this, the American Anti-Slavery Society, which employed Douglass, told him to confine his resistance to the truths
that all men are brothers and are enemies only through misunderstanding one another. He was warned that any physical action on
his part might bring about an actual war between the blacks and
whites in which the blacks, a tiny, unarmed minority, would be
slaughtered.

Frederick Douglass Becomes a Militant

Douglass, wondering how much longer he could stand this
physical abuse, went to see some outspoken militants of his own
race, Henry Garnett, J. N. Gloucester, and J. W. Loguen. They insisted that it was not true that all whites would combine against
them if the blacks took up guns. They told him about a group John
Brown had organized in Springfield called the League of Gileadites,
in which this white man had joined with forty-four black people in
an agreement to arm themselves "in case of an attack on any of our
people." The American people, Brown told them, would be more
impressed by the personal bravery of the black man than by the

peaceful recital of his wrongs, however truthful: "Nothing so charms the American people as personal bravery. The trial for life of one bold and to some extent successful man, for defending his rights in good earnest, would arouse more sympathy throughout the nation than the accumulated wrongs and sufferings of more than three millions of our submissive colored population."

Douglass left a description of the Old Man as he first saw him: "He was a lean, strong, and sinewy, built for times of trouble, fitted to grapple with the flintiest hardships. Clad in plain woolens, shod in boots of cowhide, he was straight as a mountain pine. His eyes were gray and were full of light and fire. He moved with a long, springing, racehorse step, neither seeking or shunning conversation."

Since the two men met first at Brown's wool establishment, a prosperous-looking business, Douglass thought Brown was wealthy, but when he went to the Old Man's home he found it a small and simple abode, such as lived in by poor folks. Brown told him money saved by this way of life was to be put into the struggle for black liberation. After a frugal meal, Brown began to talk with Douglass, the pacifist, with a blunt honesty such as the black man had never met with before from any white man. Brown told him he thought the slaves should gain their freedom in any way they could, that the slaveowners had forfeited their right to live, and that neither political action nor nonviolent pleadings and demonstrations could abolish the oppression of the blacks.

Brown told Douglass he had been looking for a long while for black men he could join with in a plan of guerrilla warfare. They would hide themselves in the Allegheny Mountains where they run off to the Deep South. A body of black and white guerrillas, by the use of natural forts, could stand off all attackers and conceal large numbers of liberated slaves until they were trained to carry out wider and wider forays of slave liberation. Brown insisted that he knew these mountains well, as a practical shepherd and a surveyor, and if bodies of guerrillas would swoop down on the slave plantations, it would no longer be possible for the planters to operate with slave labor.

In this way the money value of slavery would be completely wiped out, and the institution along with it. Douglass wanted to know how he would support these fighters, and Brown answered promptly, "We will live off the enemy." He argued that slavery was a state of war and that slaves deserved all their master's property, having earned it through generations of toil. When Douglass suggested the slaveowners might be peacefully converted to freeing their slaves, Brown replied with some heat, "I know their proud hearts; they will never give up until they feel a big stick around their heads."

Douglass was not ready to join the Old Man. "To get this plan in operation, money and men, arms and ammunition, food and clothing were needed," Douglass wrote later, "and these, from the nature of the enterprise, were not easily obtained, and nothing immediately was done. Captain Brown, too, notwithstanding his rigid economy, was poor, and was unable to arm and equip men for the dangerous life he had mapped out. So the work lingered until after the Kansas trouble was over."

However, Douglass's life was profoundly changed by this encounter. The next time he was attacked by a mob, he took a stick and hit back. Shortly after, he broke away from the nonresistant Garrisonians, moved to Rochester, New York, and started a paper known as *The North Star*. In one of its earliest issues he wrote about John Brown, "who, although a white man, is in sympathy a black man, and is deeply interested in our cause as though his own soul had been pierced with the iron of slavery." During the next twelve years they met briefly from time to time, and Douglass had been involved in getting the Old Man out to Kansas, which, as Douglass said, "left him with arms and men, for the men who had been with him in Kansas believed in him, and would follow him in any humane though dangerous enterprise he might undertake."

The Old Man felt that he and Douglass were of the same mind about the Kansas troubles and that a judicious and compelling argument for the attack on Harper's Ferry could be based on them. "I approached the old quarry very cautiously," Douglass later wrote, "for John Brown was generally well armed and regarded strangers with suspicion. As I came near, he regarded me rather suspiciously, but soon recognized me and received me cordially." It was no wonder the Old Man had a light lapse of recognition; instead of

*The Young
Frederick
Douglass*

*Frederick
Douglass at
the Time of
the Event*

the fierce young lion-headed Douglass of the previous decade, he saw a stately and rather portly gentleman of great distinction, moving with the dignity of an ambassador of his race.

Douglass had with him a stalwart young black recruit, Shields Green, who had been attracted to the Old Man when they met in Rochester. The first moment was awkward, however. "Well, Captain," Douglass began, "when I reached Chambersburg a good deal of surprise was expressed, for I was instantly recognized, that I would come there unannounced. I was pressed to make a speech to them, with which invitation I readily complied."

The Old Man had an expression on his worn, anxious face that indicated that public speaking at this juncture was not the best of tactics. "He was then under the ban of the government and heavy rewards were offered for his arrest, for offenses said to have been committed in Kansas," Douglass remembered. "I felt that I was on a dangerous mission and was as little desirous of discovery as himself . . . although no reward was offered for me."

Kagi, on guard high on the rocks in a place of concealment, came down, carrying his Sharps, and the four of them, Douglass, Shields Green, Kagi, and Brown began to discuss plans and possibilities. The conversation lasted the rest of that day and half of the next. The Old Man announced triumphantly that he was at Chambersburg to pick up two hundred new Sharps carbines, two hundred revolvers, and almost a thousand pikes, with which to empower those who would nobly dare to be free. Douglass began to reminisce about the time the Old Man had appeared before the Convention of the Radical Political Abolitionists in June of 1855.

The Convention, a remnant of the defunct Liberty Party, was deep in a discussion of affairs in Kansas.

Kansas was the place where the fault in the American earth—that it was "half-slave, half-free," as Lincoln put it—first broke through at the surface and American citizens confronted one another with arms in their hands and an unbridgeable gulf between them. One hundred and twenty-six thousand square miles of virgin soil, it had been Indian Territory until 1855, and was then opened for settlement. Americans began to confront one another over the question of slavery with guns in their hands and Congress tried to stave off open warfare between these systems with a so-called organic law by which the actual settlers would vote in a plebiscite to make it either a free state or a slave state.

Douglass wrote, "the portentious shadow of a stupendous civil war became more and more visible."

Slaveholders complained bitterly that they were about to be despoiled of their share in a territory won by common warfare, or bought by a common treasure. However, the rapidly growing anti-slavery (but not abolitionist) party in the North insisted that southerners could settle in any part of the Union, along with their "property," so long as "property" was not interpreted to mean men and women. Declaring that the Founding Fathers had not intended the extension or the perpetuity of slavery, they hammered out a slogan for their new Republican Party: Liberty, National; Slavery, Sectional.

The idea of a plebiscite is always politically attractive, and when it was announced, Douglass advocated thousands of free blacks be sent to Kansas to colonize and "stand as a wall of living fire" to keep slavery out. Once the blacks were in Kansas, he argued, "armed with spades and rakes and hoes and other useful implements of defense, they need not be driven out."

At the time of the plebiscite, however, five thousand southerners, armed to the teeth, pushed across the Kansas border on horseback or in wagons, occupied all the polling places, and terrorized the election officials into accepting their ballots, although most of them returned to Missouri the following day. The new government of Kansas became proslavery; the Territorial Legislature passed a law making the advocacy of antislavery a capital crime, punishable by hanging, and both a territorial judiciary (appointed by the pro-slavery National Administration) and the highest officials of the Administration itself gave notice that the new Territorial Legislature was to be backed to the hilt by all the enforcement powers at the government's command.

After the Border Ruffian invasion was sanctioned by the Democratic Administration, Douglass realized that it was almost impossible even for *white* northerners to settle in Kansas. They were damned as "abolitionists" and harassed by roving bands; their cabins were burned and looted, their fences torn down, their crops trampled, and their cattle run off. Finally, as Emerson put it, when "the poor plundered farmer comes into the courts, he finds the ringleader who had robbed him, dismounting from *his* own horse and unbuckling his knife to sit as judge."

Douglass, whose mind had a superb, statesman-like quality, did not agree with other black leaders who felt that the Kansas struggle was irrelevant to them; a white racist struggle between the northern speculators and the slave expansionists. "The important point to me, as one desiring to see the slave power crippled, slavery limited and abolished, was the effect of the Kansas battle upon the moral sentiment of the North, how it made men abolitionists before they themselves became aware of it, and how it rekindled the zeal, stimulated the activity, and strengthened the faith of our old antislavery forces."

He was not surprised to see the Old Man turn up at this 1855 Abolitionist Convention, and to learn from him that five of his sons had gone to Kansas to settle, to help swing the Territory to an antislavery position. The Old Man asked Douglass if he could make an appeal to the Convention for money to buy arms. When this was arranged, Douglass found opposition among many of the members, who had long deplored John Brown's reputation for wanting to solve the question directly with violence and revolution. But when the Old Man got up to speak, his worn face lit from within by long-banked fires, the audience was completely won over and subscribed more than sixty dollars to buy the guns. He read a letter sent him by his son, John, Jr.:

> Dear father . . . I tell you the truth when I say that while the interest of despotism has secured to this cause hundreds and thousands of the meanest and most desperate men, armed to the teeth with revolvers, Bowie knives, rifles, and cannon—while they not only are thoroughly organized, but under pay from slaveholders—the Friends of Freedom are not one fourth of them half armed, and as to Military Organization, among them, it no where exists in the territory. The result of this is that the people here exhibit the most abject and cowardly spirit whenever their

dearest rights are invaded and trampled down by lawless bands.
. . . They boast that they can obtain possession of the polls in
any of our election districts without having to fire a gun. . . . Now
the remedy we propose is that the Anti-slavery portion of the
inhabitants should immediately, thoroughly arm and organize
themselves in military companies. Here are five men of us who
are not only anxious to fully prepare, but are determined to fight.
Now we want you to get for us arms. We need them more than
we do bread.

Sitting there amongst the grim, inhospitable rocks, the Old Man
was heartened by Douglass's recollections of the Convention, since
it seemed to pave the way for the delicate process of recruitment.
His whole plan depended on people's remembering and approving
his deeds in Kansas. He patted Douglass affectionately on the
shoulders and said, "Now it is yourself, Frederick, that we need more
than bread."

The rocks began to grow warm and comfortable about them as
the Old Man began a long, cautious, and roundabout discussion of
affairs in Kansas, laying a firm foundation for their final fusion with
his Harper's Ferry plan. His main point was his ability to raise guns,
money, and men enough to make his move, after his long years of
futile pleading and organizing, years in which Douglass himself had
set up meetings and solicited aid for him with very slight effect. He
knew Douglass approved of what he had done in Kansas in a general way, but he wanted to sound him out in connection with certain
acts there in which he had made himself and his men expendable;
and to find out what Douglass's response would be to an invitation
to be both valuable and expendable, and at the very heart of the
coup.

He took up his story from his departure from the Syracuse Convention and his success in getting a wagonload of arms through to
the embattled farmers of Kansas, driving his team directly through
Missouri at a time when several hundred Sharps rifles of the Free
State National Kansas Committee had been seized on the Missouri
River and were being used by the Border Ruffians against the men
they were intended for.

Brown explained that the Free State Party constantly threatened revolutionary actions without ever performing them. They were always resolving that they would resist the so-called Bogus Laws to the "bloody issue," or that they would organize a Free State Militia to defend the harassed settlers with force and arms, or that, in the last resort, they would set up a revolutionary Free State government and take over the Territory. In fact, their policy was to avoid all confrontations, "to suffer and be strong," and not offend those liberal congressmen who would, in due time, vote Kansas into the Union as a free state.

Consequently, everything the Old Man did in Kansas went against the official Free State position. He first attracted national attention in the so-called Wakarusa War in December of 1855. This began when a Free State man named Dow was murdered by a proslavery partisan. Dow's neighbors threatened reprisals, and one of them, Jake Branson, was arrested on a peace warrant by Sam Jones, the "Bogus" Sheriff of Douglass County. Branson was then rescued by an armed group of Free Staters and taken into Lawrence, the headquarters of the Free State Movement, with the hope that an active resistance would be initiated against the Bogus Laws, the Bogus Sheriff, and the unpunished murders of Free State Settlers.

At a public meeting, however, the rescuers were disavowed and advised to leave town. The leading policy maker for the Party, Dr. Charles Robinson, made it clear that the Lawrence people wanted nothing to do with the rescuers and would not resist a body of men who "pretended to be officers or legislators . . . to do so would refer their rights to the arbitration of violence, which they were not inclined to do." A Committee of Safety was appointed, to save Lawrence from further involvement, but, as so often, such peaceful overtures came too late. Sheriff Jones had informed the Territorial Governor, Wilson Shannon, that an "armed rebellion, centered in Lawrence" had broken out, that armed bands of Free Staters had burnt homes, destroyed personal property, and turned whole families out of doors. He asserted that he had supplied himself with warrants to arrest the rescuers of Jake Branson and demanded a posse of 3,000 men. Notices to this effect were sent to the towns in western Missouri, and men began to come into the territory to wipe out Lawrence, the "abolitionist hell hole," for good.

To arm the swelling Missouri posse, a government arsenal at Liberty, Missouri, was broken into, its custodian forcibly detained, and its total supply of guns, bullets, cannons, and military harness confiscated. As the excitement along the border rose to a pitch, and elements of the huge posse began to camp below Lawrence, four proslavery dignitaries—Judge Cato, who occupied the Federal Bench in the Territory, Judge Wood, a local Bogus judge, Major Clarke, a government Indian agent, and a Colonel Burns, from Westport, Missouri—stopped a party of three Free Staters riding home from Lawrence. Placed under arrest, they turned to make a run for it, and Thomas Barber, totally unarmed, was shot dead by either Major Clarke or Colonel Burns. (They disputed the honor, both having shot from the hip, but Colonel Burns claimed he made the hit because "I saw the fur fly from his old coat.")

When news of the invasion began to get around the Territory, Lawrence began to fill up with Free Staters spoiling for a fight. Soon there were more than five hundred men there. Robinson, and his second-in-command, James Lane, an out-of-office and out-at-elbows politician from Indiana, were hard put to keep things quiet, although they had developed a good technique for confusion. Lane would come on strong with the men in the street, passing resolutions of steadfast defiance, and then Robinson would follow, cooling everyone down, saying they had to go before Congress for their "statehood" with clean hands and a history of obedience to the law. After the killing of Barber, this tactic became more difficult. The Chiefs of the Delaware and Shawnee nations came to offer several hundred braves for the Free State cause, but Robinson sent them away with the declaration that their presence could be a signal for hostilities.

A further exacerbation to the militants was the arrogant entry into town of the titular dignitaries of western Missouri, the colonels and majors, the mayors and sheriffs, who poked around the defenses and counted the defenders of the beleaguered town without interference from the Committee of Safety, giving as conditions for lifting the siege the surrender of the Branson rescuers to be lynched, the confiscation of the Sharps guns sent in by the northern supporters, the destruction of the Free State hotel as the headquarters of the Party, and the demolishing of the Free State newspaper offices.

These outrageous demands usually ended with the reminder that
Governor Shannon was down in their camp ready to give his official
sanction to the coming offensive. After these provocateurs left,
Robinson and Lane would run anxiously about, displaying such a
demeaning caution toward the enemy at their gate that two women
went out to a Free State house on the Sante Fe road, where some
powder and ball had been stored, and brought quantities of it back
concealed under their dresses, to arm and equip, it was rumored, "a
secret company of women, enrolled under women officers, and ready
to defend their homes."

At this point, reported an eyewitness, "when the siege was
pending, John Brown and his four sons arrived in Lawrence.
They looked formidable and were received with great éclat. Having more weapons than he could use, a portion of them were
placed in the hands of those who were more destitute. A small
military company was organized at once and the command given
to Old Brown. From that moment he commenced fomenting
difficulties in camp, disregarding the command of superior officers,
and trying to induce the men to go down to Franklin and make
an attack upon the proslavery forces encamped there."

This account, although hostile, was basically true. When the Old
Man found that Robinson and Lane had gone down to the Ruffian
camp to negotiate a peace, he tried to organize a direct attack.
The Committee of Safety wanted to arrest him, but he had already attracted a large following, and they did not dare. They
succeeded in tying him up in a series of diversionary conferences
until the negotiators arrived back in town, accompanied by Governor Shannon. At that point, the Old Man told Douglass, "the
leading Free State men, finding out his weakness, frailty, and consciousness of the awkward circumstances into which he had really
got himself, took advantage of his cowardice and folly, and by
means of that and the free use of whisky, and some trickery,
succeeded in getting a written agreement much to their liking."

As their conversation continued, Douglass found a thronelike
niche in the granite and sat there in quiet grandeur, his face
impassive and brooding. The Old Man's bent figure gave the
effect of briefly arrested motion, of someone crouching to spring.

From time to time, he would straighten up and kick the muscular weariness and stiffness out of his legs. Douglass asked the Old Man if the widely reported account of his protesting the treaty were true. "Perfectly," said the Old Man, "I told Robinson that all he had done was a farce. In six months Shannon would call out the Bogus militia again, and the same demands would be made upon Lawrence, and he would have no forces to resist them —no one would believe in him. I got up on some loose lumber and proposed an attack on the Ruffian camp. The wind was in a gale. I could tell by the weather that their camp would be demoralized; their tents blowing away, their mules off their tethers, and their bonfires scattering sparks and coals all over them. With a few men armed and carrying lanterns we would surround the camp and shout and fire on the enemy. I do believe the whole lot would have cut and run. I felt that I had a right to urge my own policy, Robinson had his. I had my own guns, as I have now, and they could not disarm me by their own rules of private property."

The Old Man fully understood that it was having his own guns and not his revolutionary rhetoric that gave him his edge in the struggle and gained him the support of the considerable antitreaty faction. The only other weapons available were those supplied by the New England Emigrant Aid Society and kept under lock and key by Robinson, to be used only in the last extremity. Nor did the Old Man, in his long day's work of recruiting, ever let Douglass forget that crucial arms cache had been made possible by the latter's support of his appeal to the Syracuse Convention.

"How did they stop you?" asked Frederick. "I understand the attack never took place."

"Oh, the wind came up worse and the loose lumber began to blow about the street. People were getting hurt so we all broke for cover. But the same condition obtained in the camp below. I was thinking of the General Sertorious, in Plutarch, a writer I insist that all my young men read. Once when he was outnumbered by an enemy in an impregnable position, but to the windward, he had his soldiers build huge piles of loose earth near the enemy camp. The wind came up, the eyes of the enemy were

filled with dust, they could scarcely breathe and could not fight,
and so surrendered to the wind. There was such a wind blowing
then in Lawrence. We could have taken that camp with the wind
at our backs."

The Old Man's conversational style was as deliberate as his
walk: there was no heading him off once he got started on a
planned course. Douglass was beginning to find the rocks getting
harder and harder; the September sun was dropping fast, and a
chill wind seemed to be rising straight up from the dark waters
of the quarry. He was also beginning to feel a little foolish that
he had given a public speech just before meeting a man who had
a price on his head and was fair game for the law at any moment
his simple disguises were penetrated. The Old Man, who wanted
to eliminate in advance certain objections to his plan that had
come up many times before in his recruiting, paused for breath,
and Douglass said, "In Kansas you must have felt that now, after
so many years of waiting, your hour had come."

"It was more than that," the Old Man responded. "When I made
my speech against the treaty there in Lawrence, I began . . . as I
always begin . . . by saying that I am an abolitionist, dyed in the
wool, and that I think it is time to draw a little blood. In spite of
this, I did not see the least sign of cowardice or want of self-
possession exhibited by any volunteer of the Free State companies
that I talked to. I had never expected to see an equal number of
such well-behaved, cool, determined men, fully, I believe, sus-
taining the high character of the revolutionary fathers."

He was trying to convince Douglass—by describing the actions,
rather than presenting arguments—that there were many white
men, since the Kansas Wars, with a consciousness raised to a
revolutionary flash point. One objection raised against Brown's
plan was that he had no organization to discuss and propagandize
the theory of his coup, no body of oath-bound supporters who
would rally to him when he made his move. But the Old Man did
not believe this was necessary. He felt a spontaneous uprising
would take place, that the logic of history would move the North
from the mere defense of free institutions on the far-off plains
of Kansas to "meddling directly with the peculiar institution—

carrying the war into Africa," to keep slavery from occupying the West by attacking it in its lair. He knew that few white Americans would approve, before the fact, the idea of the slaves rising and freeing themselves. Once it had taken place, however, their hearts would rule their heads and they would accept it, and aid it, in the same way they had defied the government by rescuing fugitive slaves, and had raised vast sums of money and supplies to support the Free State side in the Kansas Wars. As a black, Douglass needed the assurance that John Brown could attract a white following, and he went on with a review of his Kansas experience with this purpose in mind.

True to the Old Man's predictions, a little more than six months later another huge Ruffian posse was encamped below Lawrence, ready to sack the town. But this time their action did not have to rest upon the shaky legalism of Sheriff Jones's peace warrant. President Pierce had sent a message to Congress in January, 1856, that the proslavery legislature, however elected, was completely legal and that the Free State Party was subversive, since it was advocating "treasonable insurrection, going to the length of organized resistance by force to the fundamental, or any other Federal law, and to the authority of the general government." In February he issued a proclamation putting the army and the courts on the side of the proslavery forces and against the Free State Party. It was clear that the next step would be, as a Kansas historian put it, "the assumption that the attitude of the Free State men toward the Bogus laws was rebellion and the actors in the movement were guilty of treason. They proposed to have the Free State leaders indicted for high crimes, and either have them arrested or compelled to flee from the Territory." As soon as the muddy Kansas roads became suitable for traveling, proslavery grand juries began handing down secret indictments for treason against the Free State leadership.

Lawrence in particular was a target, and indictments were found against the Free State Hotel, which was claimed to be "a fortress," and two Free State newspapers, *The Herald of Freedom* and *The Kansas Free State.* When the winter had broken up, whole companies of Georgians and South Carolinians came into the Territory to colonize and drive out the abolitionists on one final and federally authorized push. Three more Free State men were killed, and now the score of unavenged and unpunishable murders stood at five.

The Old Man rapidly sketched in the background: "We were called to the relief of Lawrence, May 22, and every man turned out. John was captain of a company to which Jason belonged; the other six were a little company by ourselves." Lawrence had fallen without a shot fired, surrendering all its guns and armaments to the enemy. The Free State Hotel was battered down with a small cannon, the type for the newspapers thrown into the nearby river. All known Free State leaders were arrested and interned. While the North was being informed of this humiliating defeat, Charles Sumner, the Senator from Massachusetts, made a speech on "The Crime Against Kansas" and was attacked in the Senate Chamber and beaten so badly on the head that it was thought that he would not live. When the news reached Boston, Josiah Quincy, eighty-five years old, whose father has established the Revolutionary Committees of Correspondence between the Northern and Southern States, who was himself a former Congressman and a retired president of Harvard, declared: "I can think of nothing and speak of nothing but the outrages of slaveholders at Kansas, and the outrages of slaveholders at Washington . . . outrages, which, if not met in the spirit of our fathers of the Revolution, our liberties are but a name and our Union proves a curse. But alas, I see no principle of vitality in what is called freedom in these times, in the so-called Free States."

"The next day," recounted the Old Man, "our little company left, and we encountered quite a number of proslavery men. We were immediately accused after this of murdering five men at Pottawatomie. . . . I can only say about them that they had a perfect right to be hung." There was no need to spell out details to a man like Douglass. He knew, as did almost every politician in the country, that the Old Man had suggested to some of the more militant Free Staters that a bloody reprisal be carried out to cancel out the shame of the last few days. Brown's son had told Douglass about it: "The general import of our intentions . . . some radical retaliatory measure, some killing, was well understood by the whole

Charles Sumner Beaten in the U.S. Senate Chamber

camp. You never heard such cheering as they gave us when we started out. We went back to the Pottawatomie country which was the headquarters for the proslavery men under Judge Cato, to pick off the designated men prominent in enforcing Border Ruffian laws." In other words, the Old Man had a list including the District Attorney; the most virulent member of the Grand Jury; his son, who was Bailiff of the Court; his other son who was the Bailiff's assistant, and lastly, the man who owned the building in which the Bogus Court was held, a Court, which like all others over the Territory, was indicting Free State men for the capital crime of treason.

And so, in utter silence and darkness, and with the unerring precision of a surveyor, John Brown went down the county line to the three cabins of the enemy. Like Samson, eyeless in Gaza, he did not know how many of his enemies would be holed up in these cabins, or if they would be prepared to resist and kill him. His attack came as a complete surprise, the Bogus men thinking the Free State locals were still tied up at Lawrence. He executed the five of them with some old swords, saying he was from "The Northern Army."

"The story was told, Captain Brown," Douglass suggested, "that these men were not hung, but had their heads chopped off with old swords."

The Old Man shrugged impassively. Although he did not see why a fugitive slave should have qualms over how his enslavers were disposed of, he would neither boast about the Pottawatomie executions, nor defend or explain them. When accused of the deed, he would say, "God is my judge" or "I killed no innocent man," a form of evasion far short of a declaration of innocence. He was thankful that the people who mattered to him all knew about the incident and that he did not have to discuss it with them. Nevertheless, it was important to mark Pottawatomie as a starting point, and to make clear what followed it—rejection by his Free State neighbors, and the capture and imprisonment of his sons John and Jason, during which John went mad.

"My sons John and Jason, who were not present at Pottawatomie, were betrayed at the so-called Free State town of Osawatomie in the hands of the Bogus men and imprisoned for no other crime than opposition to Bogus enactments, and most barbarously treated for a time . . . the cruelty, sufferings, and anxiety he underwent made John a maniac—yes, a maniac. The names of my little company were given to a Bogus jury by these same Free State men. We were named murderers and indicted as such. But the cowardly, mean conduct of Osawatomie did not save them, for the Ruffian posse came down on them, made numerous prisoners of the very men that denounced us, fired their buildings, and robbed them. After burning these houses, this self-same Ruffian posse, some forty in number, set out on the track of my little company, boasting with awful profanity, that they would have our scalps. They, however, passed the place where we hid, and robbed a town some four or five miles beyond our camp in the timber."

The Old Man began talking about the famous victory at Black

Jack, the first counterstroke in the Kansas War; as always, to avoid the danger of bragging, he wanted to give God all the credit.

"We rested there, like David of old, dwelling with the serpents of the rocks and the wild beasts of the wilderness; being obliged to hide away from our friends as well as enemies, destitute of money and almost in a state of starvation. But he who sees not as men see, did lay the guilt of innocent blood to our charge. We were not given to the will of our enemies . . . but he delivered them into our hands.

"On learning this party was in pursuit of us, my little company, now increased to ten in all, started after them. We were all mounted as we travelled. [He did not mention that the horses were stolen from the proslavery men he had executed.] We were out all night but could find nothing of them until about six o'clock the next morning, when we prepared to attack them on foot. We got to within a mile of their camp before being discovered by their scouts, and then moved at a brisk pace. My company had no long shooters. We did not fire a gun until we gained the head of a bank about fifteen or twenty rods to the right of the enemy, where we commenced and soon compelled them to hide in a ravine. After the firing had continued for some two or three hours, the Ruffian posse of twenty-three men, two badly wounded, laid down their arms to nine men (one son was wounded), myself included."

Slowly, and as if it were an afterthought, the Old Man continued, "I ought to say further that a Captain Abbott, being some miles distant with a company, came onward promptly to sustain us, but could not reach us until the fight was over. After the fight numerous Free State men who could not be got out before were on hand . . ."

In fact, the entire situation had changed. Whole companies of mounted Free State guerrillas began to concentrate and move toward the fixed southern settlements. The Ruffian town of Franklin was attacked, with no more justification than that it was a "mischievous camp." Other Free State men threw the timorous restraints of party leaders to the winds and organized, as the St. Louis *Evening News* deplored, "Roving, roystering bands of

guerrillas fighting under the plea that war prevails . . . every man
had been compelled to join one party or another and become active
in its behalf."

The Old Man, with his grim Pottawatomie policy, had overcome
the "suffer and be strong" policy of the Free State leadership.
Most of the men now collecting at the Kennedy farm were among
his band of guerrillas. Aaron Stevens had been captain of his own
band, and in one raid alone, had run off eighty "pro-slavery"
horses.

Douglass, who had followed the Kansas Wars closely for the last
three years—and had written and lectured about them himself—
recalled his pleasure in reading, in the northern press, that Free
State guerrillas had driven out southern colonies at New Georgia,
on the Marais des Cygnes River, and at a marshaling point called
Fort Titus, where more than a hundred men fought a pitched
battle. The southern papers placed the Old Man at the head of
all these raids, and the New York *Times* reporter called him "the
terror of all Missouri" and "the Old Terrifier." This was gross exag-
geration, but there were eyewitness accounts of his band as they
"came swiftly over the brow of the hill, in full view, with Brown
at their head, and, without halting or even slackening their speed,
swung into the line of battle. Only thirty men! Yet they presented a
formidable array. The line was formed two deep and stretched out
to give the men full room for action. Brown sprang his horse
in front of the ranks, waving his long broadsword and on they
came, sweeping down on us with irresistible force."

The hyperbole about the Old Man, fed to a northern people
hungry for news of victory in Kansas, even affected Douglass, who
had written that Brown had "met persecution with persecution,
war with war, strategy with strategy, assassination and house-
burning with terrible and signal retaliation until even the blood-
thirsty propagandists of slavery were compelled to cry for quarter.
The horror wrought by his iron hand cannot be contemplated
without a shudder."

But Douglass gave no sign of this slight revulsion now as he sat
there in the quarry, listening to the Old Man reminisce about
Osawatomie: the battle in which he and thirty of his men had

taken on a Ruffian army of two hundred and fifty mounted men and a six-pound cannon, organized and operated from Missouri for the particular purpose of "taking Old Brown." This battle had begun with the killing of his son Frederick. "Early one morning of the 30th of August the enemy's scouts approached to within one mile of the western boundary of the town of Osawatomie. The scouts, led by a proslavery preacher named Martin White, shot my son dead in the road, while he . . . as it was later ascertained . . . supposed them to be friendly. I had no organized force, but only some twelve or fifteen recruits. I said, men, come on, and they left their preparations for breakfast and followed me into town, as soon as this news was brought to me. I had no means of learning correctly the amount of enemy, so we started in their direction. After going a few rods we could see them approaching the town in line of battle, about half a mile off, upon a hill west of the village. I then gave up all idea of doing more than to annoy, from the timber near the town, into which we all retreated, and which was filled with a thick growth of underbrush. When the left wing of the enemy had approached to within common rifle shot, we commenced firing, and very soon threw the northern branch of the enemy's line into disorder. This continued some fifteen or twenty minutes, which gave us an uncommon opportunity to annoy them. After they rallied, we kept up our fire, until, by the leaving of one and another, we had but six or seven left, the others having been wounded. We then retired across the river, escaping as well as we could. We had one man killed in the fight. The loss of the enemy, as we learn by different statements of our own, as well as *their* people, was some thirty-one or -two killed, and from forty to fifty wounded. After burning the town to ashes and killing a Mr. Williams they had taken, whom neither party claimed, they took hasty leave, carrying their dead and wounded with them. They did not attempt to cross the river, nor to search for us and never again returned to look over their work."

Despite the retreat, Osawatomie was always acclaimed as a great victory for the Free State cause, because of the awful mauling the invaders had taken at the hands of Brown's little force. The national image persisted of the gallant leader with a handful of green young recruits, beating off hordes of southern invaders. For a day or two there was a report that Brown had been killed there. General Reid, the southern commander, had officially reported that, "I moved with 250 men on the Abolition fort and town of Osawatomie, the headquarters of Old Brown, on the night before last, marched about forty miles and attacked the town about sunrise on yesterday. We killed about thirty of them, among the number, *certain,* a son of Old Brown, and almost certain Brown himself." But Reid's army, part of a much larger force of 1,200 men, masking themselves as the Kansas Territorial Militia, withered away on hearing that the Old Man was still alive and his company still intact. In Washington, the Pierce administration, worrying about getting a peace in Kansas before the coming elections in November, appointed a new governor for the Territory, John W. Geary, and gave him orders to use federal troops to intervene and put down guerrillas on both sides.

It was at this point that the Old Man made his separation from the Free State Party full and complete—inwardly, if not visibly. He explained carefully to Douglass that Robinson, the head of the Party, had sent for him and told him that he had just talked with the new Governor and that an amnesty was being arranged for the Free State fighters and that no attempt would be made to arrest the Old Man on the warrants out for him. "Robinson offered me considerable money," the Old Man told Douglass, "or land, or both if I preferred, to act for him 'without commission,' in defending a new town he was setting up for the eastern speculators. Without him having any responsibility for my actions, or culpability for my future crimes, I would be expected to keep the young southerners from harassing the settlers. I supposed he meant for me to kill them off. In short, to obey his orders, keep his secrets, and be his hired assassin. As a down payment he handed me this endorsement." He passed to Douglass a much creased and fondled paper:

Capt. John Brown:
My dear Sir, I take this opportunity to express to you my sincere gratification that the late report that you were among the killed at the battle of Osawatomie is incorrect. Your course, so far as

I have been informed, has been such as to merit the highest praise from every patriot, and I cheerfully accord to you my heartfelt thanks for your prompt, efficient, and timely action against the invaders of our rights and the murderers of our citizens. History will give you a proud place on your pages, and posterity will pay homage to your heroism in the cause of God and humanity.

"But you never did this . . . you never became his hired assassin!" Douglass said.

"Of course," said the Old Man, "But when I thought of all the guns and military supplies under Robinson's control, and how I might acquire them under his service and use them, without commission, for my *greatest* and *principle* object . . . the nature of which I need not go into with you, Frederick, I told Robinson I would give him an answer after a little thought. After I had left him, I was told by someone in the street that Robinson and company, fearing to become entangled in the Fugitive Slave Law, had driven a poor fugitive from town . . . poor, whipped man who had come all the way from a failed insurrection in Tennessee. I sent word to Robinson that if he knew of any job of the sort he had offered me, 'I advise you to do it yourself.' "

Douglass started to give him a word of praise, but the Old Man held up a silencing hand. He had to explain to Douglass how he had been able, in a certain way, to transfer the northern militancy over the defense of Kansas into a direct attack on slavery itself. He went into it, step by step, this vital and amazing transformation. Soon after the battle, he had suffered a severe attack of malaria and dysentery, and had gone to the cabin of a Kansas friend, Augustus Wattles, to recover. "While I was there," Brown went on, "A company of United States Dragoons burst in, asking for me. Emma Wattles said I had departed for the States. A Lieutenant Carr then informed the Wattles that the murder warrant against me had been put into the hands of a new U.S. Marshal and that he had been given a company of U.S. soldiers to arrest me. I was in the attic, and looking down between the roof boards and the top log of the wall, I could see every movement of the soldier, with two loaded Colt revolvers in his hand. He would have made a complete search of the house but for Emma serving him and his men with some of the highly regarded Wattles' melons. This created a distraction and they left, after informing the Wattles that I was being hunted by the army between there and the Nebraska border, and that the Secretary of War, Mr. Jefferson Davis, had requested daily reports on their operations. What had happened was that certain Free State men were trying to ingratiate themselves with the new governor by turning me in. Sam Walker, a Free State captain, with thirty-seven indictments against him by the Bogus courts, had a promise they would all be dropped if he would become a Federal Deputy Marshal and make up a posse of 'law abiding' Free State men, of which there were all too many. After he agreed to this, an orderly came from Governor Geary with a warrant against me, and told Walker to take me dead or alive, and that for this, he would be held personally responsible. Of course, Sam Walker had sent in the Dragoons while he skulked somewhere in the bush as he knew fully well, that Free State or not, if he tried to serve any warrant on me, I would kill him. It is well known that I will never be taken alive, nor am I prepared to die alone."

It was then, the Old Man said, he had left the Kansas scene, "watered with the blood and tears of my family," and made his torturous way to the Nebraska border, lying concealed in the bed of a wagon, eluding troops all the way. On the road from Lawrence to Topeka, he searched the clumps of elder bushes along the way, and suddenly, by the sound of his beating heart, located the fugitive driven by Robinson out of Lawrence. His name was Richard Richardson, and he had joined with other slaves in Missouri in trying to carry out an insurrection with some old scythe blades and sharpened hoes.

Their escape ended in the little town of Tabor, on the southwest border of Iowa, the final marshaling place for the introduction of arms and military supplies into Kansas. Everywhere they looked they saw what the residents called "Kansas furniture," barrels of powder and boxes of brand-new rifles. It seemed that every bed and chair at the house they were stopping at, that of Mr. Jonas Jones, had a weapon thrown carelessly on it, along with cartridge belts and bowie knives in leather sheaths. All this material, lodged there useless and inert, was infuriating, while slaves were fighting and dying with the crudest of weapons. The Old Man asked why he could not have some of these unused arms, and Jones explained that he was bonded for the value of each article and could not give them out unless he received a requisition from a company of settlers going into Kansas, with a roster of men and officers and the endorsement of the National Kansas Committee. He also declared that the National Kansas Committee was seriously divided between a group advocating continued action against the southern aggressors and a much larger group who were ready to give up all military action in Kansas and depend on a heavy influx of settlers, together with an agreement with the new Governor that all armed partisans would be suppressed. This meant the guns already there in Tabor were not available. Jones held out a ray of hope, however, telling Brown that a shipment of arms was still on the way, contributed totally by the Massachusetts Kansas Committee, a group still fully committed to aggressive action in Kansas.

At this point the Old Man began a fascinating exercise in revolutionary duplicity. To get control of the arms of Richardson and his brothers, he decided to go to Boston, submit an elaborate and convincing plan for a defensive force in Kansas, and acquire the last shipment of arms, the two hundred Sharps rifles, as well as other military accouterments. It was all a lie, and a swindle, as he conceded to Douglass without the slightest sense of guilt, but what was to be said of the hypocrisy by which the Kansas Committee would give him the arms at Tabor and those still being shipped there, in order to shoot other white Americans from another section of the country, for the sake of some lands and settlements a thousand miles away from their cities, while shrinking as if from the fires of hell if he had proposed giving the guns to black Americans for insurrection?

He began his proposal with a clear statement of purpose:

For immediate action on my part, I purpose to go immediately to Kansas and when there at once to look up every able-bodied

Free State man, and to get them organized into companies, etc.,
to lead them to the choice of officers best calculated by their
courage, energy, general intelligence, experience, and practical
good common sense, to secure the respect and confidence of
their neighbors, and success to their movements . . .

In his mind, however, for every mention of "able-bodied Free
State men" he substituted "black Americans in bondage," and where
he had written "companies could be brought together under arms,"
he thought "black Americans held under cruel and fraudulent oppression could be brought together, etc." Although his conscience
had been formed in stern Calvinist commandments against telling
lies and embezzling private property, the moral demands of a
just revolution came first.

"Mr. Richardson and myself," he told Douglass, "then and
there decided to acquire all the arms and supplies we could and
work our way back east and to make an attack on the arsenal at
Harper's Ferry and to occupy it for a few hours to give the signal
out that the long-awaited struggle against the sum of all villainies
has begun."

The Old Man, wearied by the long recital of his purposes,
resources, and favorable chances for success in the undertaking
before him, made his last remarks almost in a whisper. Douglass
was shocked. His first response was only a halting comment that
by occupying the Ferry, "he was going into a perfect steel trap, and
that once in, he would never get out alive; that he would be surrounded at once and escape would be impossible."

"No," Brown calmly disagreed, "the Ferry itself is in a defile,
from which a small amount of men can stand off vastly greater
numbers. Furthermore, the arsenal itself is entirely defended by
civilian watchmen; there are no military guards posted there and
the northern operatives who make the guns are simply good
craftsmen and mechanics who do their own work and appear to
have no interest in the politics of either the North of the South."

"But you are in the middle of slave country," Douglass protested.
The whites could raise a posse against you in that position in a matter of two or three hours."

"I expect some of the whites there to join us," said the Old Man. "Governor Wise has lately come out with the astounding assertion that Virginia has no fear of the insurrection of the blacks, but of the poor whites. This statement was made as he was trying to put through his legislature a bill to restrict the slaves from learning the mechanic arts, with the design of restoring their trades to the poor whites. But this is merely a sop; the poor whites have nearly broken away and made a separate state in the mountain regions. . . . They nearly did it during the Nat Turner troubles and could again, with some slight encouragement."

Douglass, recovering from his shock at the revelation of the impending attack at Harper's Ferry, began a powerful and emotional denunciation of the plan. "I at once," he wrote later, "opposed the measure with all the arguments at my command. To me such a measure would be fatal to all engaged in doing so. It would be an attack upon the Federal Government, and would array the whole country against us."

But the Old Man knew all these arguments like a litany. "What country?" he asked. "We have two countries here. Even Mr. Sanborn and the Massachusetts men, conservative as they are, feel the country is split apart beyond redemption . . . and that only an uprising of the slaves and a separation by the poor whites can unite the country again, without the slaveholders. I know you distrust the Republicans, but I have not talked to one yet who would not wink now at any number of escaping slaves making their way north."

"I would not care if the whole Government in Washington winked at them," said Douglass. "Nothing short of an open recognition of the Negro's manhood and of his rights to have a country and to defend that country would move me into such a desperate scheme as this."

"That is exactly what we intend to do. After occupying the arsenal, which will serve as notice to the slaves that their friends have come, and a trumpet to rally us to them, we will move into the mountains and you will have your country, or at least a provisional state. If we can hold a stated area for a month at least, I am sure our northern friends will alter the whole fabric of the present government. This is why I need you, Frederick. You must take power, be the first president of the new provisional government."

The Old Man's position began to make more sense to Douglass. "After the close of his Kansas work, Captain Brown came to my house in Rochester," Douglass later recorded. "He said he desired to stop with me several weeks, 'but,' he added, 'I will not stay unless you allow me to pay board.' Knowing he was no trifler and meant all he said, and desirous of retaining him under my roof, I charged three dollars a week. When he was not writing letters, he was writing and revising a constitution which he meant to put into operation by the men who would go with him into the mountains. He said that, to avoid anarchy and confusion, there should be a regularly constituted government, which each man who came with him should be sworn to honor and support. I have a copy of this constitution in Captain Brown's own handwriting, as prepared by himself at my house. . . . Once in a while he would say he could, with a few resolute men, capture Harper's Ferry and supply himself with arms belonging to the government at that place; but he never announced his intention to do so. It was, however, very evidently passing in his mind as a thing he might do."

But at the moment Douglass was confronted with this plan, he was appalled. He had come down to see the Old Man in good faith, assuming that he was ready to carry out the plan described more than ten years previously, "to take twenty or twenty-five discreet men into the mountains, selecting secure and comfortable retreats where they could defend themselves in case of attack and subsist upon the country thereabout. They were to be well armed but were to avoid battle or violence, unless compelled by pursuit or self-defense."

Douglass argued desperately that this new plan would be absolutely fatal to the purpose of gradually running off slaves from nearby plantations. "Hating slavery as I do, Captain Brown, and making its abolition the object of my life, I am ready to welcome any new mode of attack on the system that has any chance of success. I approved of your old plan. . . . I was ready to join it. But my field of labor for the abolition of slavery has not been extended to an attack upon the United States arsenal . . . nothing as rash and wild as this."

"Rash and wild," the Old Man repeated sadly. "Have you lost confidence in me, Frederick?"

"By no means," protested Douglass. "In Kansas you have shown the greatest military skill . . . at all times you selected your ground so carefully and handled your men so skillfully and attacked your enemies so vigorously that they could neither run nor fight. . . . But what are you going to do in that steel trap? What will you do if both bridges are occupied?"

"I have means for cutting my way out," said the Old Man, confidently, "even if I do become surrounded, which I doubt. I will have a number of the best citizens of the neighborhood as my prisoners at the start, and by holding them as hostages, if worst comes to worst, I can bargain my way out with them."

"I look at you with complete astonishment, Captain," Douglass exclaimed. "How can you rest your hope on such a belief? Virginia would blow you and your hostages sky high before they would allow you to hold Harper's Ferry for an hour!"

This was the bluntest tone in which Douglass had ever addressed the Old Man, and he received no reply. Brown bent painfully in his seat, as if crushed under a falling rock. Douglass tried to soften the blow: "Why don't you forget about this Harper's Ferry attack and resume the policy we have agreed on of gradually and unaccountably drawing off the slaves to the mountains?"

"Because," said the Old Man sadly, "gradually and unaccountably the slaveholders will surround us and slaughter us and the world will know nothing about it until we are dead—as those slaves in rebellion in the other states have been killed first, and their brave deeds described afterward as utter failures. Gradually and unaccountably our friends in the North, who are always talking and giving lip service to a movement among the slaves, will hear of it and give us their sympathy and some support, at least to the survivors, if any. But they will not be part of the movement, they will not be called upon and depended upon to give us their practical support, at the hour and at the time we are carrying out what should be the noblest task an American can perform. They must know about it straightway that it happens, and they must be called upon to join us, they must be called into the battle. And as far as attacking the U.S. arsenal is concerned, there is nothing sacred about it—it is as much ours as it is theirs. They have been using the arms to suppress other Americans; we have the same right to use those guns to free them. I care nothing about it being a federal arsenal, or federal property, other than to show the slaves how to do something as well as their oppressors."

There was no reply, and a long silence came up between the two men. Finally Douglass said he was no match for the Old Man in this argument, and the latter, seeing the darkness closing in, told him to go back to the village and sleep on it and come back the next day. Douglass and Shields Green left, and the Old Man lay down to rest in a quarried-out hollow, while Kagi stayed on guard all night.

The next morning, a Sunday, Douglass and Shields Green appeared as the church bells began to ring in the village. Owen Brown had joined them, having brought up the mule wagon to carry back a load of rifles to the Kennedy farm. The Old Man looked hopefully at Douglass, but the black statesman's expression was infinitely sad. The dialogue resumed. Douglass had one name on his lips—Hugh Forbes. "Captain, I thought you had given up this Harper's Ferry plan. I did not quite believe it when Hugh Forbes told me about it."

Hugh Forbes was an English soldier of fortune, a self-described professional revolutionary, living in New York and eking out a precarious living as a sometime fencing master, contributor to the New York *Tribune,* poet, engineer, and writer of Deist tracts attacking all religions. He had been with Garibaldi in the Italian revolution of 1848 and been entrusted with command of his rear guard! Now in exile, he hung about radical meetings of all persuasions and was known as the main author of an enormous two-volume work on guerrilla warfare. A highly sophisticated man of fifty, a graduate of Oxford who had served out a commission in the Coldstream Guards, he was arrogant and cynical, unlike Brown in every way.

When the Old Man went east in the early days of 1858 on his highly successful attempt to get control of Kansas money and arms for Harper's Ferry, he was advised, while in New York, to get in touch with Forbes as a teacher for his "Kansas Volunteers." He was shown Forbes's work on guerrilla warfare and was highly impressed, as he was with every written word that agreed with his own notions. He approached Forbes and offered him a job training guerrilla fighters, agreeing to pay him one hundred dollars a month.

Forbes completely took the Old Man in. He told Brown that as a professional revolutionary, he was not interested in any struggle designed to protect the land speculations of the northern capitalists. He would only fight "in that kind of a war which, if it succeeds, is called a Revolution, and its soldiers lauded and distinguished as patriots, while, if it fails, due to superior force, or to treachery, it is called Rebellion, and the soldiers are hung like robbers." These sentiments pleased the Old Man enormously and he felt confident that he could tell Forbes that his real plan was not to operate in Kansas but Virginia. They made a deal to meet back in Iowa, where the guns were stored, in a month's time. Forbes talked the Old Man into giving him six months' wages in advance, so he could condense his work of guerrilla warfare into one volume, to be called *Manual of the Patriotic Volunteer.* The Old Man felt it should be required reading for his young recruits.

After many vexing delays, which he blamed on his publishing difficulties, he finally joined the Old Man at Tabor in Iowa. There he found only one recruit on the scene, Jason Brown, and the money running out fast. During the New York interview, the Old Man had been assiduous in dropping some of the names he had hoped would be heavy contributors, governors, senators and Massachusetts millionaires. Forbes now became convinced that Brown was either holding back money or was too stupid to get it out of the numerous philanthropists he had mentioned.

They started to quarrel over who was most fit for command. The Old Man began to realize there was a profound incompatibility between them. He had tried to convince Forbes of the effectiveness of his "well-matured plan" to attack the arsenal, destroy what arms he could not carry off, establish forts and hideouts in the mountains, divide his men into smaller groups, each under two or three or the original band, which would beat up other slave quarters when more men were sent to join him. The U.S. troops, presently in the West fighting Indians and Mormons, would take weeks to get back to Virginia. In the meantime, "his New England partisans would call a northern convention, restore tranquility, and overthrow the pro-slavery administration." What the Old Man meant by "restoring tranquility" was his adherence to the policy of John Quincy Adams, as expressed by him many times in Congressional debates, that in case of a war between any of the states, the government had the power to abolish slavery.

Forbes poured well-bred scorn on the whole idea, insisting that the preliminary attack could trigger an insurrection which would quickly get out of control. As to the intercession from the North, "Brown's friends would not have courage to show themselves, so long as the issue was doubtful." Forbes's plan was to stage a series of tightly controlled slave raids along the North-South borders, a classic guerrilla operation working toward a long and bloody erosion of the social and economic infrastructure of the slave states. The slaves freed in the raids were to be sent with such speed to Canada that pursuit would be hopeless. Brown pretended to accept a combination of both plans that would make it impossible to hold slaves near the borders, and drive the institution deeper and deeper into the South.

About a month later, when he decided the Old Man's money had run out, Forbes left Iowa to make the rounds of all known Brown supporters, while denouncing him as a simple-minded religious bigot and scheming to be hired in his stead as the leader of what he thought was a powerful and well-funded northern revolutionary movement.

Douglass thought that mention of Forbes's betrayal would make the Old Man give up his plan. "Forbes came to me and told me all about this Harper's Ferry plan. I informed you so at the time. I could not believe it, the man was such a scoundrel, and now it appears he was telling the truth. He wore me and my friends out with his endless begging, and when he could get no more money that way, he threatened to expose you and all connected with you. He told everyone that would listen, from Horace Greeley to various government officials, what you were up to. And now you have this plan under way, an adventure betrayed ten times over. You must have known he has been a Judas to you and yet you plan to go on."

The Old Man shrugged and said the only concern he had with Forbes was how to get his money back. "I am not afraid of him. In fact I find his so-called betrayal fortuitous. He has spread the good word far better than I could. Not one of the people he told has given me any trouble, with the exception of Senator Wilson of Massachusetts, and that was merely a temporary setback. One of the greatest encouragements I have yet received was, after hearing that he had informed Senator Seward of my intentions, the Senator made a most remarkable address, predicting an 'Irrepressible Conflict' between the free and the slave states, clearly declaring that they could no longer live in peace together and civil war would break out any day now."

"You don't know exactly *who* he has told or what is the extent of the damage to you," Douglass said. "The government may be lying in wait for you to make your move, spies and agents may be examining your mail, watching your headquarters there in Maryland."

"Tut, tut," responded the Old Man. "If a movement can be destroyed by the revelations of one man, it is of little use anyway. If the Administration is watching us, they will hold off until they can capture everyone involved. As soon as the action takes place, it will be too late. We will be in and out of the Ferry before they can collect enough forces to defeat us. I do not intend to strike on the date given out. I will move before that."

Douglass shook his head, unconvinced. Brown went on: "I have carefully calculated all these possibilities. The most I expect to come up against us would be some poorly armed units of the local militia—drunkards, barkeepers, braggarts, and ne'er-do-wells, out for a spree of drinking and firing off valuable gunpowder at random. My men of the rear guard with the Sharps rifles, which

I will leave in a convenient cache on the Maryland shore, a little schoolhouse there, will be more than a match for them. The effective slaveholders will stay home on their plantations, watching their own slaves, lest they run off in the excitement. You worry too much, Frederick. Our friends are coming in from Canada. My son John is up there now, rounding them up. Richard Richardson, the man I picked up as a fugitive slave on the road from Lawrence to Topeka, will be one of them. Men are coming in from Kansas, from Ohio . . . men who have fought with me in the Kansas Wars."

"How can you be sure they are coming?" Douglass asked. "What if they don't come?"

The Old Man looked painfully at Douglass a moment and shook his head. "Say no more, say no more on that side, Frederick."

He paused, trying to find a way to convince Douglass what a strange new doctrine this act, whether successful or not, would preach to the four million suffering slaves, even if it ended in horror and bloodshed. The slave would know there were love and sympathy for him, even to the death. Instinctively, he fell back on religious language in trying to express his deepest emotions.

"Did not my Master Jesus Christ come down from heaven and sacrifice himself for the race and should I, not worthy to lace his boots, refuse myself? If my bleeding body or my hanged body can tell the slaves that there are white men in this country that love them, let it be."

Douglass recoiled at this. He was not white and he knew that any number of dead black men, free or slaves, would make very little difference.

The Old Man saw him flinch, understood, and said quickly, "Oh, they will come, I know they will. If they are held up in some way, I am sure enough that our Philadelphia friends will be here to keep the bridges open. A hundred riflemen posted across the Potomac can get us out of the Ferry and deep into the Virginia mountains in an hour."

Douglass, out of love for Brown and his family, filled with a great sadness, made one more attempt to discourage him by disclosing some news he had been withholding. The black militants in New York and Philadelphia, on whom the Old Man had been

counting, were not going to come. Forbes had managed to convince them that Brown's white recruits were not men of principle
but were in the expedition for loot, and that Brown himself was the
dupe of eastern capitalists trying to manipulate the price of cotton.
Douglass could not come out and say it, but he was being forced
into a tragic dilemma, being asked to make a choice between the
Old Man and some of the leaders of his own race. The nature of
this conflict was well documented by Richard Hinton, one of
Brown's earliest recruits: "Colonel Forbes must have got into relations with a small coterie of clever colored men, revolving around
a well-known physician of that race, now deceased. They held the
theory that it was the duty of all educated colored men to mold their
people into separate and violent resistance. They wanted no help
from white men." (W. E. B. DuBois also supports this interpreta-
tion: "Forbes was at this time in the confidence of McCune Smith
and the able Negro group who had developed a not unnatural distrust of whites, and a desire to foster race pride.")

The Old Man's response to this crippling blow was simple and
direct. Throwing his arms around Douglass, he cried out, "Then
you must come with me, Douglass. I will defend you with my life.
When I strike, the bees will swarm, and I shall want you to hive
them."

Douglass shook his head in painful rejection. The encounter
seemed over, but there was yet a sequel. As Douglass reported later,
"When about to leave, I asked Shields Green what he had decided
to do, and was surprised by his coolly saying, in his broken way,
'I believe I'll go wid de old man.' "

The four men sat silently on the rocks watching Douglass make
his stately and careful way down through the half-hewn granite to
the rutted road back to the village. Kagi glanced from time to time
at the Old Man's face; how often had he been told that Douglass
would be an excellent head of state for the Provisional Government.
Brown had written the Constitution at Douglass's house in Rochester. Douglass knew every word of it and had made suggestions
and corrections of immense value, coming from the consciousness
of a black man and an ex-slave. Finally Kagi broke the silence.
"We'll get him yet, Captain. I know just how to do it."

The Old Man looked away and ordered Owen to take Shields

Green back to the farm on foot, to escape detection. He then went back to Kagi's boardinghouse, where Kagi drafted a very ingenious letter to Frederick Douglass, which he said he would have signed by all the militant blacks of Philadelphia:

> F.D. Esq.
> Dear Sir:
>
> The undersigned feel it to be of the utmost importance that our class be properly represented in a convention to come off right away near Chambersburg in this state. We think you are the man of all others to represent us, and we severally pledge ourselves that in case you come right on we will see your family well provided for during your absence or until your safe return to them. Answer to us or to John Henrie, Esq., Chambersburg, Penn., at once. We have now collected quite a number of good, but not very intelligent, representatives. Some of our members are ready to go with you.

It was a forlorn hope, but Brown had the indomitable faith of the revolutionary. Money, too, was a problem; ever since he had begun, his men had either put up with the cheapest possible living conditions or had gone to work to support themselves and the others. It had cost well over a hundred dollars for freight rates on the guns and supplies. Hundreds had been spent on railroad fares to bring in his men, and the two girls to keep house. Every dollar he got had to be begged from his white liberal supporters in the North who pretended not to know what he was doing but often complained that he was not doing it fast enough.

On their way back, Owen and Shields Green had to travel at night; in Maryland slave country it was unthinkable for a white man and a black man to walk together in a normal way. Early one morning, just as they had got past Hagerstown, they crept into a cornfield for some roasting ears. A man driving by caught sight of Shield's shirt and went into the cornfield to investigate. Owen had to fire several revolver shots over his head to fend him off. The man, taking Shields Green for a fugitive, ran off for reinforcements.

Owen and Shields ran for the bush of the South Mountains. When they came, breathlessly, to the river at Antietam, Owen

Shields Green

learned that Shields could not swim a stroke. He managed to swim across the river with Shields on his back. With the hoofbeats of the returning pursuers in their ears, they scrambled at last to the cover of the mountain slopes. For hours and miles afterward they could hear the hunters crashing through the bush behind them and the fervid shouts of men hot on the trail of their prey. "Oh, what a poor fool I am," Green moaned. "I had got all the way from South Carolina out of slavery and here I got back into the eagle's claw again."

When Owen got back to the farm after this harrowing experience, he began to be plagued with the most agonizing doubts about his father's plan. He was the most skeptical of all Brown's sons, and the only one who dared meet his father head-on in an argument. When he told the other men about Shields Green's narrow escape, they shook their heads in anxious doubt. Charles Tidd spoke directly of the whole idea as hopeless. Owen told the men frankly about Fred-

Owen Brown

erick Douglass's refusal to come with them and was saddened to find most of the men agreed, in principle, with the latter's objections. Suddenly, he felt responsible for telling his father about these doubts, knowing no one else would dare to.

Owen decided to waste no time, and at the risk of being recognized, he made his way back to Chambersburg on foot. His father should be warned of a possible mass defection. But the Old Man received the news without anger, conceding that he, too, was discouraged about the lack of recruits and the absence of some who had promised to be there. Sometimes he felt like giving up the whole thing. Hearing this, Owen, who had expected a vigorous argument that would set his own fears at rest, began to defend the plan, saying that they couldn't give it up after having gone this far. Kagi, who was also present, said it was ridiculous to stop at this stage of the operation and spoke with great buoyancy and trust about the way things were going. Captain Brown asked Kagi to come back with him to have it out with the men and decide, once and for all, whether they were going to attack the Ferry or break up.

When they arrived at dawn the next day, there was an ominous silence at the farm. Early in the morning before the travelers got on the front road, the house would usually throb with singing. Two of the men, Tidd and Aaron Stevens, loved to harmonize on the most sentimental songs of the day. One in particular, "Faded Flowers," they sang over and over. Stevens, who had been an army bugler, had a fine, resonant bass—like the low notes of a horn. The Old Man loved to listen to them, and they made a practice of singing a greeting to him when they saw his wagon rattle up the lane. This morning, however, he heard nothing as he approached the farmhouse.

Without stopping for breakfast, he called the men together and told them he was aware of their dissatisfaction with his plans. He assured them that he was not so strenuous about carrying out his particular project if to do so would do an injury to the cause for which they were all struggling. If they were all opposed to attacking the arsenal, he would resign. They could choose another leader, and he would faithfully serve him, reserving for himself, however, "the privilege of giving counsel and advice when he thought a better course could be adopted." He said he would leave the room so the question could be discussed without prejudice.

Annie Brown

Just before he left, Aaron Stevens asked him what his own thoughts were in the matter, after the disagreement of Frederick Douglass. He declined to answer this. Tidd then asked, rather belligerently, what he would do if all decided against it. The Old Man, taken by surprise, quickly said, "If no one else goes, I will do it by myself. We have but one life to live and once to die. And if we lose our lives in this cause, it will perhaps do more for the cause than our lives would be worth in any other way." Then he walked out, his feet dragging and looking every year of his age and hard life.

Annie asked her father to come sit with her on the porch. She knew the situation that was developing but said nothing. She had heard of this plan since she was a little girl; indeed, once when she was at school at North Elba, she refused to answer questions about the state of Virginia, in fear that she would somehow reveal her father's intentions. This plan had been nourished for so long in her mind—and that of her mother and brothers and sisters—that she could not think of its being wiped out without a trial. She tried to tell the Captain she was ready to volunteer herself, but his attention seemed to be totally diverted by two little wrens that kept flying up to him and twittering in a kind of human anguish and anxiety. He told Annie the birds wanted something of him, were asking for help. He went off the porch to look for their nest and found a snake about to devour some little fledglings. He killed the snake with a stick and came back smiling. The birds sat still and sang. The Old Man saw this little incident as a sign, a confirmation of the rightness of his plan. His doubts seemed to go away, and he looked up at the blue shadows of the mountain beyond in perfect peace of mind.

Shortly after, he heard the men break into song. It was an air that Scottish clansmen were supposed to sing to their leader before going into battle, "Hail to the Chief Who in Triumph Advances." Brown knew then he had won them all back. Owen came out and handed him this note:

> We have all agreed to sustain your decision until you have proved yourself incompetent. Many of us will adhere to your decision so long as you will. Your friend, Owen.

It was good news, but the Captain knew by reading the last sentence that his sons would have gone with him, even if no one else had agreed, saying, as they had in the discussion just past, "We will not let our father die alone."

He asked Owen how Tidd had taken the verdict. "He was wrathy," Owen said. "He's going to stay with Cook at Harper's Ferry for a few days and cool off."

And then he asked about Shields Green. Owen said, "The same as before. He believes he's going to stay with the Old Man."

4

In John Brown's House

There was no milk and water sentimentality—no offensive contempt for the Negro, while working for his cause. In John Brown's cause and in John Brown's presence . . . no ghost of a distinction found space to enter.

Osborn Anderson
A Voice from Harper's Ferry

The great hurt and discouragement over Douglass' decision was eased for the Old Man by Shields Green and by the coming of another black man, Osborn Anderson. He had made his way down from Canada and carried the promise of several more recruits soon to be on their way. Anderson was a printer and a reporter, working for a black press in Canada. He sensed at once that if there had been any secret racism, any condescension among Brown's other recruits, the coming of Shields Green and himself to live with them in that crowded little attic, under the strains of discovery and a sacrificial future, would have brought it to the surface.

People have tried to discover a distinction in the fact that John Brown gave captain's commissions to the white men in the group. Anderson anticipated and disposed of this slur: "John Brown did offer the captaincy to colored men equally with others, but holding a civil position, I declined a captain's commission. . . . The same must be said of other colored men." The *civil position* that Anderson mentions was as a member of the congress for the new, revolutionary state in the mountains. Shields Green was also made an officer of this ruling body. Although Shields Green was illiterate and Anderson highly intellectual, both understood with the utmost clarity what John Brown meant to the movement. "He regarded slavery as a state of perpetual war against the slave and was fully impressed with the ideas that himself and his friends had the right

Osborn Anderson

to take liberty and to use arms in defending the same." Anderson continues, "Slavery was to him the corrupt tree, and the duty of every Christian man was to strike down slavery and to commit its fragments to the flames." Whatever the fears of John Brown's men, political or religious guilt was not one of them.

Things tightened during the three weeks of Osborn Anderson's residence at the Kennedy farm. His favorite character among the guerrillas was John Kagi, Brown's agent at Chambersburg. He had met him in Canada and regarded him as second in leadership to Brown himself. Kagi was young, only twenty-four, born of Virginia stock, with relatives still living about the Ferry. In appearance, like many of Brown's men, he was bearded, tall, and handsome, very careless in dress—"one leg of his pantaloons properly adjusted, and the other partly tucked into his high boot top; unbrushed, unshaven, and in utter disregard of the latest style."

On the other hand, he wrote and talked with a surpassing eloquence. He had fought daringly as a guerrilla in Kansas and, through his newsletters in the New York *Tribune,* gained thousands of sympathizers for the cause. He was also a schoolteacher and had taught mathematics, English, and Latin successfully. Better than most of Brown's men, he could put into words his monumental hatred of human slavery: "I am opposed to theft, robbery, and murder—for slavery is all of these. It steals babes in the cradle; I might say in the mother's womb. It robs women of their chastity and men of their wives. It kills, with sorrow, uncheered labor and the various forms of cruelty, more slowly, surely, but more in number than the sword."

Brown made him his second-in-command because he knew that Kagi, like himself, regarded whites simply on a one-to-one basis with all blacks. As Anderson put it, Brown and his men "saw in the most degraded slave a man and a brother, whose appeal for his

John Henri Kagi
During Kansas Days

Dangerfield Newby

God-given rights no one should disregard; in the toddling slave child a captive whose release is as imperative, and whose prerogative is as weighty as the most famous in the land.

It was this feeling that drew to the farm, and then to the Ferry, Dangerfield Newby, free himself, but with a wife and seven children doomed forever to chattel slavery. Newby was tall and strong, well over six feet, and an excellent farmer. He hired himself out to toil in other men's fields, feeling that somehow, perhaps, he could earn enough money to buy his own wife and children from their white Virginia owner. But he was already forty-eight years old. The price of a black on the flesh market—whether man, woman, or child —averaged five hundred dollars. He would have to live strong and work hard for a great many years before he could accumulate four thousand dollars.

He used to slip wraithlike into the farmhouse whenever he could get away from his work on the Pennsylvania border. It was the only

hopeful place he had ever known. He liked to turn a certain page in
the Provisional Constitution which would govern the new state in
the mountains. It was Article XLII: "The marriage relation shall
be at all times respected and families kept together, as far as possible; and broken families encouraged to unite and intelligence
offices established for that purpose."

Getting his freedom had broken up Dangerfield's family. He and
his wife, Harriet, had lived on adjoining farms in Fauquier County,
Virginia. When his white father had died, and freed him in his will,
Dangerfield had been forced to leave Virginia; by law, freed slaves
were not allowed to live there. In addition, according to the law, the
children of a black family had their mother's condition, and his wife
Harriet, although an intelligent and talented woman, remained a
slave. Hoping that Dangerfield could carry out his promise to buy
his family, she wrote him:

> Dear Dangerfield,
> I am well. I know this is of the greatest importance to you. I
> have no news to write only that the children are all well. I want
> to see you very much . . . looking forward to the promised time
> of your coming. Oh, dear Dangerfield, come this fall without
> fail . . . money or no money, I want to see you so much, that is
> the one bright hope I have before me.

Dangerfield carried this letter with him. When he first came to
see John Brown, he showed him the letter to prove how urgent and
desperate his desire was to join the movement. He was strengthened
by his meeting with the quiet old revolutionary and believed,
without question, that Brown was going to succeed. He would often
study the Old Man's maps of the operation. The Provisional Government was to be established between the mountain gaps of
Harper's Ferry and the Manassas Gap some thirty miles south. As
one came down from the mountains to the Gap, it was not far to
the town of Warrington, where Harriet and the children were enslaved. He could see himself and the other liberators dashing to the
plantation of Harriet's owner, Jesse Jennings, gathering up Harriet
and the children, and bringing them back to the new black state.
There they could carry out the rest of Article XLII: "Schools and

churches to be established, as soon as may be, for the purpose of religious and other instructions of the young and ignorant." Harriet could read and write, but in slavery the children would never be allowed to go to school.

Dangerfield was the most restless of the liberators, the most anxious to go and get it over with. He got another letter from Harriet which he showed the other men, helping to build their urgency:

> Dear Dangerfield,
> I want you to buy me as soon as possible, for if you do not get me somebody else will. It is said Master is in want of money. . . . If so, I know not what time he may sell me and then all my bright hopes to cheer me in all my troubles will fade. If I thought I should never see you, this earth would have no charms for me. Do all you can for me which I have no doubt you will. The baby cannot walk yet. It can step around anything by holding on. I must bring my letter to close as I have no news to write. You must write me soon and say when you think you can come.

"When can I answer her?" Newby used to ask. Brown could only say, "Soon, soon, Dangerfield." And when the question came up about calling off the whole thing, the Old Man told Newby as he told the others, he would go anyway. Newby also heard John Brown's three sons, during the dispute about carrying out the plan, say they would follow their father no matter how hopeless it seemed.

Watson Brown was particularly sensitive to Dangerfield's anguish of spirit. His one child had been born, like Dangerfield's last baby, after he had left home. Of course, unlike Dangerfield, he had voluntarily left his wife, who lived with the Brown family in North Elba in the Adirondacks of New York. Her two brothers, William and Dauphin Thompson, had come down to the farm with Watson to join the movement, and she approved fully of what John Brown was doing. But it was sad for Watson, nevertheless, and talking with Dangerfield made him think of Belle and his new little baby. He used to write her whenever he had a chance to be alone.

Watson, aged twenty-four, had the same compulsion as John

Watson Brown

Brown's other sons to live out the Golden Rule and to die to en-
force it. They all argued with their father about religion. None was
orthodox, as he was. Some were even rationalists and agnostics.
But when Watson sat down to comfort his wife and ease his own
loneliness and fears, he expressed very simply the ethic his father
had somehow fed into the blood of his children: "I sometimes feel
as though I could not make the sacrifice; but what would I want
others to do, were I in their place?" Watson knew what Dangerfield Newby wanted the others to do. Difficult as it was, he could
put himself in Newby's place, and the place of all other enslaved
men and women and children.

We have only two black men with us now; one of these has
a wife and seven children in slavery. Oh, Belle, I do want to see
you and the little fellow very much. He is not quite a reality to
me yet. But I must wait. There was a slave near here whose wife
was sold off South the other day, and he was found in his master's

orchard, dead, the next morning. Cannot come home so long as such things are done here. I sometimes think perhaps we shall not meet again. If we should not, you have an object to live for . . . to be a mother to our little Fred.

(Even the newborn child had this terrible compulsion put on him: he was named for Watson's brother, Frederick, who had been shot down unarmed in Kansas by a proslavery preacher.)

Statements such as this may be read by some as easy sentimentality, but these men were not at all sentimental. Consider Aaron Stevens, for example, a rough and passionate man, six-feet-two and strong as a bull. He would spend hours arguing with Brown from a well-thumbed copy of Thomas Paine's *Age of Reason,* the most devastating attack on organized religion ever written. His letters are again instructive:

> The Christian religion never looked consistent to me and, therefore, I had to look elsewhere for religion and found it in the

Aaron Stevens

great Bible of Nature. Christians think that a person who believes as I do never has the feeling that comes over a person when they *experience* religion, but that is not so. That feeling will come upon everyone who will put away the *great self,* and try to do unto others as they would have others do unto them; then they will feel happy and be ready to die at any time.

Here we see how deeply John Brown was able to organize his men around the Golden Rule and make it revolutionary. That, perhaps, was his real fanaticism and the common element that drew men to him. But, of course, it is harder to get people to accept this than the mysticism of prayer and so-called holy living. Stevens's life was far from holy. Only fifteen, he had been a soldier in the Mexican War. After being honorably discharged, he went back to his home in Connecticut, but life was dull and he reenlisted in the army as a bugler. While serving in the West, as the commanding officer's orderly, however, he began to rebel at the small, daily tyrannies of regular army life. He saw a soldier, disobeying some petty order, inhumanly beaten by the Major in command. Stevens lost his temper and fell on the Major, beating him over the head with his bugle until it was a shapeless clump of brass. The officer came close to dying. Stevens was court-martialed and sentenced to death at Fort Leavenworth, after being marched through Indian Territory with a ball and chain attached to him.

His striking appearance, his courage, his grace in speech, and his beautiful baritone voice developed sympathy for him among the other officers at the Fort. His sentence was reduced to hard labor and the ball and chain for three years. He broke away one night and went to live among the Delaware Indians, who successfully concealed him until the spring of 1856. Then came the Free State uprising in Kansas. As a fully trained fighting man he was invited to join and soon became Colonel of the Free State Mounted Militia. It was not too long before he was given a brigadier general's commission. Then he met John Brown and became a private again. The U.S. Army could not contain him, nor could the promise of rich Kansas farmlands as a Free State partisan. Only John Brown could keep him in line and, with a word or two, put down his violent fits

Oliver Brown and His Wife, Martha

of temper. John Brown took all the hatred Stevens had for a hypo-
critical society and turned it against slavery. "You know nothing
of slavery," Stevens would say. "I know a great deal. It is the crime
of the century. I hate it more and more, the longer I live. I hear
everywhere, the crying of slave children torn from their parents."

Having Aaron Stevens shut up in that tiny house was like living
with a caged lion. His temper was often just under the boiling point,
and the habitual mockeries of Charles Tidd brought on many an
explosion. Only the icy authority of John Brown made the situation bearable, or when he was away, driving back and forth to
Chambersburg, the softness and spunk of young Annie Brown
kept Stevens under control. She would let him sing, along with
Tidd, for hours on end while she sat and knitted on the porch, her
hands trembling with the fear that they would be heard by someone
passing by on the road.

Brown allowed his men to vent their pent-up energies in argument. He made a point of reading a chapter from the Bible every morning, knowing that Stevens, with his copy of *Age of Reason,* would spend the rest of the day tearing it apart. Finally, he would give a prayer and ask God for the liberation of the oppressed all over the world; he knew Stevens would give no argument there.

Other stabilizing forces were Oliver Brown and his wife, Martha. She at sixteen, and Oliver just turned twenty, were called Mother and Father by Tidd. William Thompson, Watson's brother-in-law, was the clown of the company, blond and burly, with an enormous appetite. He spent the hours before dinner every day describing meals that they hadn't the remotest chance of getting. He was a superb mimic, and he had Brown's walk and voice down to perfection. Many times, when the boys were cutting up, he would leave the attic and, by his footfalls on the floor below, startle the revelers into thinking their stern captain had returned. They would

William Thompson

break off their skylarking and nervously snatch up their guns or the reading matter the Old Man had provided for them. Seeing the silly, beaming face of William, ringed around with an aura of bright red hair, poking up from the stairway, they would fall on him and pummel him with boisterous laughter.

At the opposite pole from William was young Stewart Taylor, a white Canadian recruit. Taylor was a practicing spiritualist and convinced that a better life awaited him after death. He was twenty-two but still a beardless boy in appearance. His strange, almost happy acceptance of an imminent and violent death did not depress the men. Over and over again he would say that he would be the first to fall, even describing the exact manner in which he would meet his end, but there did not seem to be anything gloomy or morbid about it. The men knew he had tried harder than anyone else to join the group. He was out of touch with Brown for some time: "I kept waiting day after day for word, and at last gave it up. I felt as if I was deprived of my chief object in life. I could imagine no other cause than want of ability or confidence." Then came news of the gathering at the farm, and he came joyously, paying his own passage, and telling Kagi, "I believe fate has decreed me for this undertaking. I had given up being wanted, but all came right when I found I was necessary." Sitting on the porch at night, watching the stars fall, he used to talk of other worlds to Annie, making her flesh creep. One night he described taking the long walk to the Ferry, enveloped in mist, finding the town absolutely deserted, and walking triumphantly through the factories, among the piles of stacked arms, and suddenly it all blew up without his seeing the face of a single enemy. One day he sat down and wrote out his will. The other boys were somewhat disturbed because he did not think it realistic to leave *them* anything; no one could convince him that they were not all going to their certain deaths.

Obviously, not all of John Brown's men were this strange or colorful. There were two Quaker farm boys from Iowa, Barclay and Edwin Coppoc, who had never in their lives handled a gun or fired a shot in anger. In a way, their being drawn into this violent confrontation with slavery was among the oddest things in the whole episode. They were fatherless boys whose gentleness and decency

Stewart Taylor   *Edwin Coppoc*   *Barclay Coppoc*

were the pride of their widowed mother's heart. Barclay was twenty-one and Edwin twenty-four; simple and innocent, they were deeply aroused by the seeming unending agony of the slaves. John Brown had passed through their village the winter before, bringing rescued slaves out of Missouri, and they quickly and fully gave him their loyalty. Their mother, resisting, made every argument possible against shedding human blood for any cause. A strong abolitionist, she had brought up her boys to believe slavery was the greatest of human sins, but she had not reckoned with their meeting John Brown and being caught in the compelling force of his hypnotic eyes. When the fatal letters arrived from Chambersburg, summoning them to action, Edwin told his mother that they had to go to Ohio. "Ohio," she answered sadly, "I believe you are going with Old Brown. When you get halters around your neck, will you think of me?" "Mother," he said, "when John Brown fixes his eye on you and says you have to come . . . you have to come."

In contrast to the Quaker boys were Will Leeman and Albert Hazlett. Hazlett was twenty-three and from Pennsylvania, tall, strong, and very open and genial in his ways. Far from pious, he was sometimes overheard, by Captain Brown, using profanity. Annie Brown said he was not trying awfully hard "to climb the golden stairs." His particular crony was Will Leeman, aged twenty, who was the only one of Brown's men to admit that he smoked and drank. Leeman was a wild, reckless lad who had joined Brown in Kansas at the age of seventeen, and the Old Man thought the world of him. He had worked in a shoe factory in Haverhill, Massachusetts, and could make good boots and knew leather. Two weeks before the attack, he wrote his mother, "I am warring with slavery, the greatest curse that ever infested America." When John Brown learned he had sent out such a dangerous clue this close to the day of decision, he gave him a dressing down. Leeman, who was less afraid of Brown's rage than anyone else, said it was "in explanation of my absence from my mother for too long a time."

"What in heaven's name did you tell her?" asked the Old Man.

"That for three years I have engaged in a secret association of as gallant fellows as ever pulled a trigger, with the sole purpose of the Extermination of Slavery!"

Brown shook his head in defeat.

Annie found Hazlett and Leeman the hardest of her "invisibles" to keep under control. They took off every night just after dark, roaming, they said, through the woods to mark trails and routes, but she would overhear them telling the others of adventures down at Harper's Ferry, visits to Cook's house, and encounters with railroad men. They used to bring her gifts of wild grapes and pawpaws, and smother her objections with armfuls of wild flowers for her. Two of the other boys, Barclay Coppoc and Dauphin Thompson, the brother of William Thompson, used to want to go with them. Leeman always put them down. Dauphin Thompson was a quiet, blond, curly-haired young man, just turned twenty-one, the youngest child in a family of eighteen. Leeman used to tell him and Barclay they were too much like good girls to make soldiers, and they should have gone to Kansas and got toughened up before they joined Brown's guerrillas.

There was no single "radical type" among Brown's men. Some were hard, some soft, but they were all intelligent and hated slavery. Above all, they knew what they were doing. If there was one among them who best suited Brown's idea of the guerrilla, it was Jeremiah Anderson. Brown liked him because he was unusually closemouthed, although when required, he could use the stirring revolutionary rhetoric that the Old Man found, next to his Bible, his favorite form of discourse.

Albert   *Will*   *Dauphin*
Hazlett   *Leeman*   *Thompson*

Anderson was very dark. People looked twice at him, some taking him for a mulatto. He was twenty-seven years old and dignified. He had been arrested several times in the Kansas Wars and fought stoutly on the side of the Free State guerrillas. His finest hour, in Brown's eyes, was when he and some other irregulars attacked a company of regular United States Cavalry and gave them such a drubbing that their Captain was discharged from the Army for cowardice. He was inflexibly opposed to anyone defending slavery, regardless of uniforms or flags. As to attacking by force: "Millions of human beings require it of us . . . their cries for help go out to the universe every day. There are a few who dare to answer this call in a way that will make this land of 'liberty and equality' shake to the center."

This, then, was the full roster of Brown's men as the day of decision drew close. His own three sons, the two Thompsons, the two Coppocs, Aaron Stevens, Charles Tidd, Albert Hazlett, John E. Cook, Stewart Taylor, John Kagi, Will Leeman, Jerry Anderson . . . and only three blacks, Osborn Anderson, Dangerfield Newby, and Shields Green . . . against the State of Virginia. The faces of these men have grown dim with time—a few scraps of yellowed letters, a criminal record, bloody deaths, and neglected graves are all that is left of them. And yet, they were among the bravest of our heroes, certainly among the most selfless of all who have ever gone forth to battle. The only one who has written of them at length and taken care to preserve their histories was their old comrade, Richard Hinton, who believed the reason that they were ignored "is due most directly to the strange fact that their lives were given for the Negro; that they fought for those who were then the poorest and most wretched of all Americans. That in itself is an hostility to the canons of good taste and an offense against a spirit which worships success even in altruism."

But it was still September, the rifles and the pikes had just arrived. Brown thought perhaps he had a few more days, even weeks, to hold on and recruit. Then one Saturday night, as had been their habit, he and Annie went to a church meeting nearby. This is deserving of attention because, although a very religious man, he had found during his long life very few churches he could regularly attend. He would not set foot in one that maintained segregated seating for

Jeremiah Anderson

blacks, as most of them did and would not tolerate any preacher who spoke as if God were the implacable defender and upholder of the Republic and the status quo, as most of them did. "My Captain of Liberty," the God who would break every yoke and set the oppressed forever free, was the one he wanted to commune with.

This little Dunker Church just up the road from the farmhouse suited him perfectly. The Dunkers were an old German sect, much like the Quakers, who would neither take oaths nor fight, nor go to the law, nor take interest in money. They had no regular minister, and every brother with something to say was allowed to preach. John Brown preached there several times a week and made the congregation antislavery, if they were not so before. He could not get them to act, to use force, but he loved them just the same and was often going about the neighborhood doctoring their animals, for he was a good veterinarian; once he even lanced a boil on a woman's neck with the precision of a surgeon. It was risky, however, to become too well known, and it was important to be accepted as a peaceful, rustic old gentleman seeking a comfortable place to spend his old age.

When John Brown and Annie came back from meeting that night, they found that Mrs. Huffmaster, with no lookout replacing Annie at her regular post, had penetrated to the farm dining room and seen Will Leeman, Barclay Coppoc, and, worst of all, Shields Green, cleaning off the table. She had straightway accused the two white men of using the farm and the neighborhood to keep "run-off niggers." Annie was dispatched at once to see Mrs. Huffmaster and try to bribe her into silence with a few gifts and reassurances. Brown had to make immediate plans to ship Annie and Martha back to North Elba.

He decided to go to Philadelphia to see if there had been any response to the letter Kagi had drafted in a final effort to recruit Frederick Douglass. He had to borrow forty dollars from Barclay Coppoc; he was going to allow Oliver, regardless of the cost, to escort Annie and his wife as far as Troy, New York. The situation of Oliver and Martha held an extra pathos, since she was pregnant and completely aware of the risks her husband would face in a matter of days. She was never known to have complained about this, but the Old Man could not begrudge the couple this good-by journey together.

With his passion for precise timing, and his belief that he could estimate the exact time potential supporters needed to make the trip from Philadelphia, he told Oliver, Annie, and Martha that he would be on the depot platform at Harrisburg on the way back from Philadelphia at the same time the young people would be taking the train for New York. His passion for order, his ability to bring things off on schedule—this is why everybody believed, deep in their hearts, that John Brown could not fail.

The leading modern expert in guerrilla warfare says that a guerrilla chief must be like a fisherman casting a net. He must be able to spread it out, as well as draw it in. When a fisherman spreads out his net, he must know everything about where it will fall. He must know the depth of the water, the speed of the current, and the presence or absence of obstructions to drawing it in. Brown's net for men reached from Philadelphia to Boston, to Canada, to Ohio. He was trying to draw it in now, to get the men he so desperately wanted.

Exactly on schedule, he met Oliver, Martha, and Annie on the train platform in Harrisburg. The parting was sad, and Annie had to tell him of another deeply troubling experience. "While we were on the road to Chambersburg, driving along the great pike to Hagerstown, a man rode rapidly toward us from another road, as if he had been waiting for the wagon to appear . . . at least we thought so, and that he might be a patroller. He passed by and then, wheeling around, came up with Watson, who was then riding behind us."

The man rode alongside Watson for some distance, watching him closely. Finally he asked, "What are you carrying in there?" and before Watson could stop him, he rode quickly to the tailgate of the wagon and threw open the back flap of the canvas cover. "I have two girls in there now," Watson said. The Deputy, or Sheriff, was embarrassed and made a polite bow of the head. "Excuse me, ladies," he said to Annie and Martha, "I didn't know you were in there."

Oliver, driving the mule between the shafts, kept a steady pace and a steady hand on the reins. The Deputy dropped back for another word with Watson. "What is it you carry in that wagon? You drive by here so often we are all curious. Is it wool?"

"Yes," Watson answered, close-lipped and cool. After another awkward few minutes in which the Deputy studied Watson closely for any signs of nervousness or guilt, he turned off on another road. They thought they would be arrested or picked up farther down the road, but nothing further happened. They left Watson and the wagon in Chambersburg and went on to Harrisburg.

The Old Man was disturbed by Annie's story. "They are closing in on us," he told Kagi. "We have got to move fast." He said goodby to Annie, and she began to cry. "Let's all be cheerful," her father urged kindly. "Take the next train back from Troy," he told Oliver. "We do not know but what we may have to make our move before you return."

When he got back to the farm, he told the other men that his journey to Philadelphia had not been successful—there was no word from Douglass. It was another tense and doubtful moment for the recruits. As Osborn Anderson wrote later, "Brown and Kagi went to Philadelphia on business of great importance. How important, men there and elsewhere now know. How affecting the main features of the enterprise, we at the farm knew full well, after their return, as the old Captain, in the fullness of his overflowing, saddened heart, detailed point after point of interest."

Warnings and alarms came thick and fast. Dangerfield Newby was adept in picking up rumors throughout the countryside around the Pennsylvania border. He reported to Kagi that there would be an attempt to search the buildings at the Kennedy farm to satisfy suspicious neighbors who said the little wagon seen so often coming away from there was either running stolen guns out of the arsenal or fugitives from the deep South. Kagi wrote to the Kansas men, "We hear that a warrant will be issued to search our house here, so we have got to make the strike eight days earlier than the date fixed in our previous notice to you. Start at once. Study map. We will try to hold out until you meet us."

Brown hoped the men coming in after the middle of the month

would have sense enough to hang back at Chambersburg or Harrisburg until the attack began. This was stated cryptically in the urgent letters to distant places, the outermost edges of the fisherman's net.

Brown wrote his final instructions to John, Jr.: "Any person or thing that reaches this place on Thursday, the 6th of October, will find the road open, but beyond that day we cannot at all be certain. . . . From Harrisburg by railroad, remember."

He appealed to him to set up some other actions to divert the enemy elsewhere. "Associations to hinder, delay, and prevent our adversaries, might possibly effect much. Our active enemies should be spotted to a man, and some shrewd person should be on the border to look after that matter somewhat extensively."

To his family in North Elba he wrote an assurance that "We shall do all in our power to provide for the wants of the whole as one family [meaning the Browns and the Thompsons], until we return." But he warned them that they would have to read about Oliver, Watson, Owen, and himself from then on in the New York *Tribune;* personal communication would be cut off. "Read the *Tribune* carefully. It may not always be certainly true, however."

Kagi wrote his last letter to the West. After October 10, no more men were to come through without further instructions. Communications would be resumed after the strike, if possible. The right time to move had come. The crops had been harvested and housed and in the best condition for capturing. The slaves, resting from the harvest, and bitter that the earth's rich bounty that they had raised and reaped was denied them, would be at the peak of their discontent. A religious revival was taking place, and under its influence even some of the most hardened slaveholders were testifying that, indeed, slavery was a great sin against God's mercy and they were, personally, great sinners who must seek salvation.

Brown, coming back to the farm, found the men in an unusually serious mood. The fooling and talking so prevalent when the young girls were around had stopped. Cook was with them now. He had sent his wife away from the Ferry and into the care of Kagi at Chambersburg. The men faithfully studied their Provisional Constitution and the tract that Brown had commissioned from Hugh

Forbes, *Manual of the Patriotic Volunteer.* Cook, in charge of in-
doctrinating the men in its teaching, made them underline, and
memorize, certain precepts:

> To form an army it is not sufficient to collect men and put
> arms in their hands. Principle should be given precedence over
> every other consideration.
>
> Under slavery, self and privilege, the noble qualities of men,
> have been suppressed. Therefore, revolution has become a neces-
> sity, and what is more, a duty.
>
> The war of insurrection must lean for support upon the popu-
> lar element, or it will fail.
>
> Nothing short of a total deficiency of ammunition, food or
> water can justify a surrender. To deter it with every form of
> procrastination must be practiced.
>
> Let it be remembered that although the pen may prepare men's
> minds for a change . . . it is the sword which will ultimately
> decide between slavery and liberty.

The Old Man's spirits were rising again, but he now faced another problem: The Sharps carbines, which he considered his most
important defensive weapon, were without caps. Somewhat like the
caps in a child's toy pistol, they were fired off by little tablets which,
when struck by the hammer of the gun, ignited the powder and ball
in the gun's magazine. Brown felt that he needed 40,000 of them,
which would cost close to a hundred dollars, and he had nowhere
near that in the treasury.

While he was thinking desperately about whom to approach for
a contribution to cover this, an event in Boston provided an almost
miraculous solution. Brown had sent one of his last-minute recruiting letters to a man named Lewis Hayden, a fugitive slave from
Kentucky and the leader of Boston's black community. Employed at
the State House in Boston, as messenger for the Secretary of State,
Hayden was fully devoted to John Brown's mission and would have
gone with him if he had not been past the right age for intensive
guerrilla warfare. He had six recruits ready to go, and was trying
to raise money to pay their train fares from the poor blacks in his
community.

EXTRACTS

FROM THE

MANUAL FOR THE

PATRIOTIC VOLUNTEER

ON ACTIVE SERVICE

IN REGULAR AND IRREGULAR WAR,

BEING THE ART AND SCIENCE OF OBTAINING AND MAINTAINING

LIBERTY AND INDEPENDENCE.

BY

HUGH FORBES.

" To form an army, it is not sufficient to collect men and put arms in their hands." DUFOUR

———◆———

NEW YORK:
W. H. TINSON, PRINTER AND STEREOTYPER,
43 AND 45 CENTRE STREET.
1857.

The Book on Guerrilla Warfare Used by Brown's Men

One morning, crossing Boston Common on his way to the post office, he ran into Francis Meriam, a young man who had just turned twenty-one and inherited a small sum of money. Raised from infancy in an abolitionist atmosphere, he had let it be known

Francis Meriam

that his inheritance would be totally devoted to antislavery purposes. When Hayden saw him, he addressed him boldly, "I want five hundred dollars and must have it." Meriam was momentarily startled, but knowing Hayden, said manfully, "If you have a good cause, I could get it for you."

Lewis Hayden told him about John Brown's immediate needs, and Meriam answered without hesitation. "If you will tell me where John Brown is, you can have my money and me along with it." It turned out that he, along with hundreds of others, knew all about Brown's plan to free the slaves by force, and he had been trying to get in touch with him for weeks. Meriam had only one eye and was physically weak, but he had the devotion and self-sacrifice that the situation required.

He went directly to the bank and drew out the money for the fares, outfitted for Hayden's black recruits, and set out himself for Chambersburg. There he got in touch with Kagi, offering him all he had. On hearing of the desperate nature of the mission, he went to a local lawyer and drew up his will, leaving all he had for antislavery purposes. Kagi told him about the pressing need for caps

*Lewis
Leary*

*John
Copeland*

for the guns. Meriam then went to Philadelphia and to Baltimore to acquire, as quietly as possible, these very necessary materials; he had to wire Boston for six hundred dollars in gold, and it came by express to Baltimore two days later.

The Old Man felt that one hurdle after another was being successfully overcome. He made another trip to Philadelphia to join Meriam and to make a final try at some news from Frederick Douglass. There was nothing concrete, but he learned from a telegrapher named John Hurn, an admirer of Douglass and very active in the movement, that his hoped-for Head of State was to be in Philadelphia on October 17, to give a lecture at the National Hall on "Self-made Men." Brown took this as a very good sign, perhaps a commitment.

When he returned to the farm he found two excellent recruits who had come on from Cleveland, Ohio. Their names were Lewis Leary and John Copeland, their ages twenty-four and twenty-five. Leary was an excellent leatherworker and saddler. Copeland had been a student at Oberlin College. They had both been involved in a famous slave-rescue case in which thirty-seven Americans were put on trial for seizing a black man near Oberlin from marshal's deputies who had kidnaped him and were attempting to send him back to perpetual bondage. Clearly, these were men who agreed with the Old Man that the liberty of a man supersedes all enactments binding him in slavery. Best of all, both of them were black.

On Sunday morning, October 16, John Brown read the Bible to his men, as usual; the text referred to those in bondage and the duty of others to free them. Osborn Anderson tells us that the reading was "impressive beyond expression. Every man there assembled seemed to respond from the depths of his soul." After the service, Anderson was made a chairman of the meeting of the Revolutionary Council and posted a sentinel, Owen Brown, outside the door.

John Brown told the men that they were to move into battle that night. He wanted them to talk over the action. The newest recruits he remarked, had not read the Provisional Constitution; it was important that they know it.

Brown told his men they were to move against Harper's Ferry that night. He suggested that the newest recruits be sworn in under the Provisional Constitution. Osborn Anderson asked Aaron Stevens, the most military in bearing and experience of all the men, to read it. The men were silent, but they were not really listening. Everything in it had already permeated the farmhouse so completely that it could be imbibed without listening. It was a Declaration of Independence from the United States they knew: from the tolerance of slavery as a sectional problem, from the political power of the slaveocracy, from the Dred Scott decision that the blacks had no rights that white men needed to respect, and from all the built-in inequities and compromises that had encrusted and befouled the old promises. It took away from them all consciousness of guilt. They were striking out against slavery's "perpetual imprisonment and hopeless servitude or absolute extermination in utter disregard of those eternal and self-evident truths set forth in our Declaration of Independence."

The Old Man broke into reading only once to stress article 32. "No prisoner will be treated with any cruelty, insult, or needless severity, but it will be the duty of all persons, male or female, connected herewith to treat all prisoners with every degree of kindness and respect."

After all the men had sworn . . . and the Quaker boys *affirmed* . . . their support of the Constitution, the Old Man went off to preach to the little congregation of Dunkers. In the afternoon, he called the men together again and issued a whole series of written orders, covering their positions and actions after taking over the ferry. The men tried to sleep, to write letters of farewell and hope, to steel themselves by talking out all the expectations and possible accidents in the job ahead. When it got dark, about eight o'clock, John Brown roused them. "Men, get on your arms. We will proceed to the Ferry."

Gone was the quiet old man, trying to keep out of the way, soothing his chills in the morning on his stool by the fire. Gone was the weary bookkeeper, ceaselessly counting every penny and its apportionment. The pious and sincere churchgoer, the Bible reader, the father worrying and carping over the behavior of his extended family, was now transformed. Doubts and fears had fallen away, and he stood erect and free, glowing with purpose and faith.

Trying to visualize John Brown as he prepared for battle, one recalls the words of young Frank Sanborn, his principal money-raiser in Massachusetts: "His eyes were those of an eagle, piercing blue gray in color and were alternately flashing with energy or drooping and hooded, his frame angular, his voice deep and metallic, his walk positive and intrepid, though commonly slow. His figure was tall, wiry and commanding, his bearing military." Or Bronson Alcott, who saw him in Concord, and wrote: "Nature obviously was deeply intent in the making of him. He is of imposing appearance, tall, with square shoulders and standing . . . couchant, as if ready to spring at the least rustling, set lips, his voice suppressed yet metallic, suggesting deep reserves, the countenance and frame charged with power without. Though sixty years old, he is agile and alert and ready for any audacity, in any crisis. . . . I think him just about the manliest man I have ever seen."

Thoreau described him as "a New England farmer, a man of great common sense, deliberate and practical as that class is and tenfold more so, like the best of those who stood at Concord Bridge once, on Lexington Common and Bunker Hill."

The Old Man gave his men their last instruction before setting out on the road to the Ferry. "And now, gentlemen, let me impress this one thing on your minds. You all know how dear life is to you, and how dear your life is to your friends. And in remembering that, consider that the lives of others are as dear to them as yours are to you. Do not, therefore, take the life of anyone, if you can possibly avoid it; but if it is necessary to take life in order to save your own, then make sure work of it."

And so all the brave young men went forth to dubious battle, bound by their Captain's promise to the men of principle who had supplied them not to shed blood except in self-defense and not to promote vengeful insurrection among the slaves.

The Schoolhouse near the Potomac Bridge Where the Weapons Were Cached

5

A New Declaration

Whereas Slavery, throughout its entire existence in the United States, is none other than a most barbarous, unprovoked and unjustifiable War of one portion of its citizens upon another portion; in utter disregard and violation of those eternal and self-evident truths set forth in our Declaration of Independence . . . We, Citizens of the United States, and the Oppressed People, together with all other people degraded by the laws thereof, Do, for the time being ordain and establish for ourselves, the following *Provisional Constitution.* . . .

John Brown
Preamble to Provisional Constitution

There were nineteen men going down that road to Harper's Ferry in the thick damp and mizzling dusk of an October night, nineteen men ready to take on the slavery and tyranny of the state of Virginia. Their aim was to confront the slaveholding South in such a way that either it went down, or they did. Three men were left behind to guard the arms and meet unknown supporters; Owen Brown, who had a withered arm; Francis Meriam, who had a missing eye; and Barclay Coppoc, so young and untried it seemed as if his mother should be giving him orders instead of John Brown.

They all knew what they had to do, at the moment and in the larger plan of the new state with its Provisional Constitution. Later, people would say that it was all unclear, but the men most concerned understood very well.

The Old Man was driving the wagon, wearing his "Kansas cap," a peaked cap with earlaps hanging down given him by an Ottawa Indian leader. It symbolized for him the continuity of his struggle. In the wagon were twenty pikes, a crowbar, a sledge hammer, and some pine fagots and bundles of tow for incendiary purposes. It was five miles to the Maryland end of the Potomac Bridge; Brown's company walked two by two down the rutted dirt road. It was chilly, and they wore gray shawls which were folded over their Sharps carbines. Cook and Charles Tidd went first; they were to cut the telegraph wires to Washington and Baltimore on poles just outside the bridge.

Before they entered the long, dark cavern of the covered bridge, Brown ordered them to fasten their cartridge boxes outside their shawls and to cock their carbines. John Kagi and Aaron Stevens moved in a half trot to the Virginia end of the bridge as the others paused at the entrance. A watchman came toward them with a lantern in his hand, alarmed by their bustling motion. They held him, and told him that he was their prisoner but that no harm was intended to him. Stevens took the watchman's lantern and waved it in a wide arc to tell Brown and the others it was safe to enter. The watchman, unperturbed, stood quietly until Cook and Watson Brown came along, cradling their Sharps guns in their arms. He began to laugh when he saw the blond, long-haired Cook trying to look threatening. Even with his Sharps gun, two revolvers in his belt, and the swagger of a pirate on his quarter-deck, he was unconvincing.

As the wagon entered the dark cavern of the bridge, the hoofbeats of the little horse echoed with a slow and steady timber, like drumbeats for marching men not now on parade. Sitting above the steady, even clop, clop, clop, clop, the Old Man tried to fix himself into a pace of thought and action that would be as even and deliberate. He must not hurry, make snap judgments, or show panic in any way. The action should be done with revolutionary decorum, with a decent respect for the opinions of mankind. He made another little prayer. "Please God, our Father, make it so there will be very little blood."

His head ached and his hands, trembling slightly on the reins, reminded him of the irreversible ills that years had accumulated. It was now or never; the twenty-four hours ahead would be the climax of his life. Everything he had ever read about revolution, about the classic coup, had to be remembered now.

The slow plod through the pitch-black darkness of the bridge was oppressive. But at last he could see ahead the arcing glint of a lantern, signaling all's well. There were no shots, no outcries of hurt and death. So far the passage to the trial by fire was favoring him.

The watchman at the bridge was laughing until he saw the Old Man come up. Then he stopped. Coming out of the bridge, the men trotted, almost frolicking, after long days penned up in the farm-house attic. The bridge head emptied people and trains into a kind of public square. To the right as the travelers came out was, first, the train depot joined to a hotel called the Wager House. On the left was a shoddy saloon known as the Galt House. Straight ahead was an impressive three-story building where the completed guns were stored. To the right again, just beyond the hotel, was John Brown's target area, the Government Armory. This was the setting for the impending drama—all within a scale of sixty paces.

The first act of violence against the United States took place at the Armory Gate. It was locked shut. Tidd and Aaron Stevens tried to force it open. Daniel Whelan, a watchman in the United States service, was in the watchhouse, which was in the third bay of a brick building known as the Engine House because two of the bays held the arsenal fire-fighting equipment. Brown wanted to use this stout building as headquarters. Whelan, hearing the wagon rattling over the cobblestones of the square, and then stop, came out of the watchhouse, shouting: "Hold on!" He walked over to the gate, and he saw the men, wrapped in gray shawls and carrying deadly weapons; some of them were already leaping over the fence, filled with the alertness and energy that a dangerous mission releases in trained fighters.

Whelan had to tell his story many times, officially and otherwise. It never changed, and has the ring of truth: "I told them I would not open the gate and one of them jumped on the pier of the gate over my head and another fellow ran and put his hand on me and caught me by the coat and held me. I was inside and they were outside and the fellow standing was over my head upon the pier. And then when I still would not open the gate for them, five or six ran in from the wagon, clapped their guns against my breast and told me I should deliver the key. I told them I could not and another fellow said they had no time to be waiting for a key, to go to the wagon and bring out the crowbar and large hammer. They went to the little wagon and brought a large crowbar out of it. There is a large chain around two sides of the wagon-gate going in. They twisted the crowbar in the chain and they opened it. And in they ran. One fellow took me. They all gathered about me and looked in my face; I was nearly scared to death with so many guns about me. I did not know the minute or hour that I would drop. They told me to be very quiet and make no noise, else they would put me into eternity. The wagon was marched in. Brown dispatched all the men out of the yard, but he left a man at each side of the gate, along with himself. He, himself, had me and Bill Williams [the other guard] and then he said, "I came here from Kansas, and this is a slave state. I want to free all the Negroes in this state. I have possession of the United States Armory now and if the citizens interfere with me, I must only burn the town and have blood."

The battle stations to which the men were dispatched had been carefully planned. Two were to be at each bridge. Three were to occupy the arsenal standing outside the grounds, but near enough for protective cover in a fire fight; and another company, under the command of Kagi, was to take over Hall's Rifle Works, about a half-mile up the river on Shenandoah Street. This move was a very chancy one; it separated effective fighters from the main force and tied up Kagi, who was second in command to Brown and the best thinker among the liberators.

But the Old Man's overriding compulsion was to prevent bloodshed. He felt that keeping the thousands of guns at Hall's out of the hands of the counterattackers was worth the very great risk of extending his men so far from the center of control. The men there would be fighting not to expand the area of battle, but to contain it.

After Kagi, Copeland, and some others were sent off, the streets of the lower town began to resound to the footfalls of grimly marching men. The Old Man stayed just outside the Engine House, his command post. He began to question closely the captive watchman about the personnel of the Government Works—who was Superintendent, the next in command, and so on. He learned they would all be reporting for work at daybreak and planned to take them

Gateway to Arsenal with Corner of Engine House at Right

into custody. After a while, the men came back with the watchman from the rifle works and he and Mr. Whelan were politely told to retire to the watchhouse.

Almost precisely at twelve o'clock, a fatal accident took place which would open up the cleft through which carefully laid plans would disappear into hopeless ruin. Another bridge watchman, Patrick Higgins, came to his post to work his twelve-hour shift. He noticed that the lights supposed to be burning at each end of the bridge were out. First conscientiously pulling the indicator recording his arrival at work, he started down the length of the dark bridge, calling, "Bill, Bill," the name of the missing watchman. About a third of the way down, he ran into Oliver Brown and William Thompson. The guards at the bridge had orders to detain people, using pikes, if they had to, but not to shoot. Oliver seized Higgins by the arm and told him to come along, intending to put him into the watchhouse at the arsenal with the other watchman.

Higgins walked along quietly until his lantern struck a glint of steel from some pikes and rifles leaning against the bridge rail. Balking at this like a frightened horse, he was able to wrench his arm from Oliver's grasp. Oliver lunged at him, but Higgins swung his hot lantern against Oliver's face and Oliver fell backward against the side of the bridge. William Thompson picked up a rifle and fired, putting a bullet through Higgins's hat and grazing his scalp. This was a violation of one of the Old Man's orders: the men occupying blocking positions on the bridges were to "stand on opposite sides, a rod apart, and if any one entered the bridge, they were to let him get in between them. Pikes were to be used, not Sharps rifles."

It was this random and disobedient shot that sent Higgins racing to the home of the other watchman to investigate what was happening to him. It woke a man named Starry who was to organize, in a few hours, the total opposing forces. It woke the night clerk at the Wager House, dozing on a couch in the lobby. Starry had no idea what the shooting was about, but the night clerk, named Throgmorton, recalled seeing a wagon coming over the bridge two hours before. He now remembered it vividly because a young black man, a slave employed in the kitchen, had suddenly appeared and gone to the door in great excitement.

"What is it?" he asked the slave. "Just some gypsies," the slave answered quickly, but his obvious excitement had disturbed the hotel clerk and he had ordered the slave downstairs to bed.

Throgmorton went out on to the hotel porch from where he could see Oliver and William guarding the bridge. His anxiety grew, but he decided not to get involved. There had been rumors that the men at the arsenal were going on strike for higher wages and he thought that might be the explanation for the excitement. He could not see that people walking down the street, and crossing the bridges, were quietly being taken into custody.

At 1:30, the train from Wheeling to Baltimore came in. It was a mail train, it was on time and paused only long enough to pick up one passenger before starting out of the Ferry. When it stopped at a branch of a Y construction at the end of the bridge, the train's impatient chuffing and squeaking, and the metallic clang of its

Harper's Ferry

stroking pistons were amplified by the wooden walls about it. Throgmorton decided to say nothing and let it go through. The last thing the hotel would want was trouble with the trains; strike or no strike, they must go through. Nor did the Old Man want the train stopped until he had thoroughly consolidated his position. But as the iron monster, grinding and groaning, started to roll away, Higgins ran into the train shed and shouted at the engineer to stop. The brakes squealed. Higgins yelled that the bridge was in the possession of some crazy people who had put out the lights, were taking people prisoner, and had done God knows what to the rails and roadbed. The engineer quickly put the train in reverse, moving it back to the loading platform. The conductor came swinging off the car steps, his lantern glaring in alarm.

Two or three passengers followed him. Mr. Throgmorton from the hotel came up, and the engineer climbed nervously down from his cab. Higgins told his story of being shot at, showed the wound on his scalp, and predicted dire consequences if the train moved out. Phelps, the conductor, said he doubted anyone would dare to stop the U.S. mail from going through, but that they ought to take a look. They were joined by the porter at the depot, a black man named Shephard Hayward. Hayward was free, but since he wanted to stay in Virginia, he allowed himself to be legally registered as the stationmaster's slave. He was a huge, bulky, hulking man, very gentle, and well-liked by all the whites, whom he served with great courtesy and a proper humility.

As the group of men moved down the shed where the Y joined with the length of the bridge, they saw dimly ahead four men with rifles pointed at them. Oliver, thinking it was Higgins back with reinforcements, cried, "Halt!" The men started to retreat. William Thompson fired a shot over their heads, and Shephard Hayward began moving his formidable shambling form in their direction. "Damn you, halt!" Thompson shouted and fired his Sharps gun at Hayward. Hayward broke and ran, but without thinking, Thompson threw in another cartridge and fired at the back of the retreating man. It was the second casualty of the raid; the ball entered Hayward's body, coming out just above his left nipple. He began to stagger and flung his arm around Pat Higgins, who dragged him to cover in the depot office. Deep tragedy had begun to stain the seemingly pure success of the coup; none of the guards on the bridge even knew that Hayward was black.

John Brown did not know that Hayward had been shot, but he was not pleased to hear the train's snuffling presence just across the Armory yard. A panic began to seize its passengers. Someone put out the train's lights. The women were brought into the Wager House and given smelling salts. Men passengers clutched dolefully at their money belts, fearing the worst. But the Old Man ignored the whole scene at the train, hoping the shock effect would immobilize this sector of the battlefield.

In a coup of this sort, there can be a certain advantage in keeping purposes vague. John Brown did not want to fight the train's passengers or even have them know what was happening. But when, after an hour or so, he saw the train still standing there, he made an attempt to get it out of the way. At three o'clock he sent an elderly

The Bridge over the Potomac from the Harper's Ferry Side

man named Grist, who had been picked up on the Shenandoah
Bridge, to tell the train conductor it could go on. When Grist got
to the door of the hotel, it was locked, the lights were out, and he
could not force his way in. When he got to the depot, Phelps, the
conductor, asked angrily, "What the hell was this all about?"

Mr. Grist answered him softly, as courteous as the Old Man himself: "The parties who have arrested me allowed me to come out on
condition that I would tell you you might cross the bridge with
your train."

"Damn it," said Phelps. "I won't take this train through that
bridge until it is daylight and I can see that it is safe."

Mr. Grist, arrested while coming back from a revival meeting,
had become slightly partial to the Old Man, who had told him he
was merely trying to make everybody equal as the "Good Book
says." He said solemnly, "I was told that if we would all be peace-
able, no one would be hurt." But the conductor imperiously waved
him away, and Grist could do nothing but report back to Brown.

"Thank you very much," said the Old Man. "You may go home now, Mr. Grist." Grist did not go home, however, but went back to the hotel; he was afraid that Brown's men might pick him up again, yet he liked being around the action.

The strange behavior of Mr. Grist, allowed to walk away, unaccompanied by any guard, to carry a message; and then walking directly back into the trap, happened with other prisoners. Every captive taken was given personal consideration by the Old Man. Some were asked if their families would be worried by their absence. If they said yes, Brown sent them under guard to their homes to report that they were unavoidably detained on business and would return safe and sound in good time.

In his desire to keep the action bloodless, the Old Man incorrectly calculated that men not in arms against them were not their enemies. Dr. Starry went boldly to the arsenal gate and demanded to know what was going on. He was told that unless he was a slaveholder it did not concern him. He went into the depot, talked to the wounded black, Shephard Hayward, and became increasingly hostile to the invaders. He walked, unmolested, while others were being arrested, to the end of the bridge and up through the town, waking people up, telling them they were invaded, asking them to arm themselves and resist. He found, as Cook had promised the Old Man, "that all the guns that they knew of were inside the arsenal and in possession of these men." Instead of resisting, the citizens began to put out the lights all over town and to evacuate their homes, rushing through back yards and across fields into the countryside not even daring to take to the road.

Dr. Starry had the bells rung in the Lutheran Church, but this only compounded the panic. As daybreak started to come, he got out his horse and rode up to Hall's Rifle Works, only to find that source of defense in the hands of the invaders. He went on, seething with anger to the home of Mr. Kitzmiller, the Superintendent of the whole Government Works, and told him that armed strangers had it in their possession. Mr. Kitzmiller got dressed to go and investigate. Dr. Starry went to the second-in-command, the Master Machinist, Armstead Ball, and a third official, Mr. Brua; they all did precisely what the Old Man wanted them to—they walked down to the gate of the Armory to be taken captive.

Brown told them imperturbably that he was not making war on the people, but on slavery, and that their persons and property would be safe. However, he had captured the town and it was now within his power to strike a blow against slavery and he meant to do it at all costs.

Armstead Ball reported, "He then gave me permission to return to my family, to assure them of my safety and get my breakfast. I was accompanied by two armed men who stopped at the door. Breakfast was not ready. I went back and was allowed to return home again at a later hour."

The righteous Dr. Starry, seeing the most prominent citizens moving about the town under armed escort but without argument or resistance, whipped up his horse in disgust. He started the long run into Charlestown, the county seat, a counterrevolutionary Paul Revere.

Meanwhile, a citizen of the Ferry, having seen his lady friend off on the canal boat to Washington City, was coming back over the bridge where the Old Man was observing Oliver and William Thompson, whose scuffles with the watchman and Shephard Hayward deeply disturbed him. Seeing Brown's stern figure stalking in his direction, the citizen thought he was a great detective sent by the government to investigate some robbery at the arsenal. When the Old Man ordered him to halt, he tried to brush by him, saying, "Let me go, I know nothing about your robberies." The Old Man taking this as an inference that *he* was a robber, angrily ordered the unoffending citizen to be taken into custody with the other prisoners.

A similar, almost fatal misunderstanding came as the arsenal bell ringer came down to the gate to ring the workers to their morning toil. Seeing a black man standing there bearing arms, he hit him angrily with his lantern, saying "Drop that gun, you God-damned uppity nigger." Shields Green, in an instantaneous response, put the muzzle of his Sharps against the bell ringer's head. Watson Brown, standing by, knocked the gun aside with a laugh, saving the bell ringer's life.

The heart of the Old Man's strategy was to keep certain highly significant hostages. Officials of the arsenal were to be seized as they reported for work; their presence would fend off the fire of those few local people with good guns. To thwart the neighboring slaveholders, several of *them* would be rounded up and put on display. Brown felt that the life of no prominent white man would be traded for the life of a fleeing slave or his white comrade-in-arms.

The first and most important seizure was put in motion shortly after midnight. Aaron Stevens was put in command of a party of three blacks and three whites to go up High Street and then go west for about five miles to the plantation of Lewis Washington. The blacks chosen were Osborn Anderson, Shields, and Lewis Leary; the whites were John Cook and Tidd, both boon companions of Stevens. At about 1:30 they stood at Lewis Washington's door with flaming torches in their hands. "Colonel Washington," Stevens greeted the alarmed slaveholder, "you are our prisoner."

"For God's sake, put down that torch," Washington said, "you will burn down my house. Come inside so I can light the candles." Washington was a colonel on the staff of Governor Wise and the most prominent local dignitary. He was flabbergasted at the intrusion and even more astonished to see peeping from under Stevens' herculean arm, the neat, bland face of John E. Cook. He recognized Cook instantly as someone he had met at Harper's Ferry, invited out to the plantation, and shown all its treasures. Cook knew that Colonel Washington had two rare pistols, given the First President by Lafayette. He had handled every prized gun in the Colonel's collection and profusely admired a great National Relic, the sword presented by Frederick the Great to General Washington, which the latter had used during the last years of the Revolution as his dress sword. Following orders, Stevens demanded this sword from Colonel Washington, telling him to place it in the hands of Osborn Anderson. This was the Old Man's way of informing the southern gentry that black revolutionaries were of the same order of nobility as the noblest of whites.

Washington rushed about in his dressing gown, greatly excited. When Cook told him they were after his slaves, he could only mutter, "Take them, take them, and please go." Tidd, with his rough tongue, told Washington he had to come along as well. When he recoiled at this, Stevens explained in a kindly way that he had to come along; they had come to Virginia to abolish slavery, but no one would be hurt who did not resist. Washington got out the

Bourbon and offered everyone a drink. It was refused. Cook ran through the house picking out prizes he had already scouted, accumulating a fine double-barreled shotgun, a small rifle, two horse pistols, and another sword that was believed to have been used by General Washington.

Mindful of clause thirty-six in the Provisional Constitution, "The entire personal and real property of all persons known to be acting directly or indirectly with or for the enemy, or found in arms with them, or found willfully holding slaves, shall be confiscated and taken whenever and wherever it may be found in either free or slave states . . . ," Stevens asked the Colonel if he had a watch.

"I have," said he.

"Where is it?" asked Stevens. "On my person," the Colonel replied.

"I want it," Stevens said.

"You shall not have it," the Colonel insisted.

"Take care, sir," Stevens warned.

"I am going to speak very plainly," said the Colonel. "You told me your purpose was philanthropic, but you did not mention that at the same time it was robbery and rascality. I do not choose to surrender my watch. Now there are four of you with arms in your hands and you have the advantage of me, but . . ."

"We will not press the matter," Stevens said, turning away and striding about the room. He noticed in a china cabinet a silver dinner service of rare and beautiful workmanship. "I do not know but what we shall want that," he said to Colonel Washington.

"But that is a family heirloom," said Washington, outraged. "It belonged to General Arista in the Mexican War. It is already willed to my daughter."

"How did you get it?" questioned Stevens sharply. "Spoils of war, I presume? Then what is wrong with us taking it for the same reason? We feel you have been making war on poor black people for hundreds of years. You have spoiled them—and now they are going to spoil you!"

Stevens reached in, took out one of the elaborately chased dishes, and weighed it in his hand. "I don't know but this is plated ware, not silver that can be melted down." He put it back in the cabinet. "I don't think my Captain would care for any such geegaws as that."

He turned abruptly on the Colonel, who was downing another stiff Bourbon. "I presume you have heard of Osawatomie Brown?"

"No, I have not," said the Colonel.

"Then you have paid very little attention to Kansas affairs." The Colonel sniffed haughtily and finished off his glass. "I have become disgusted with Kansas and everything connected with it. Whenever I see a column in the paper with Kansas at the head of it, I turn it over and I do not read it."

"Well," Stevens responded with a little smile, "you will see him this morning and you may regret you didn't pay a little more mind to Kansas affairs."

After a time the slaves were brought from their quarters, a huge four-horse wagon was hitched up, Washington's fancy private carriage was brought round to the door, and all were loaded in for the ride to the Ferry. Washington's slaves came willingly, if not joyfully. The little cortege stopped next a piece down the road at another slaveowner's named Allstadt, where they wrenched a rail out of his fence and used it as a battering ram against his door. Allstadt's daughters thrust their heads out of the window and cried murder and confusion.

Stevens, Tidd, and Cook stepped through the shattered door and told Allstadt to dress and get ready to go. He asked them why. Stevens told him they were ridding Virginia of slavery, and he was to go with them to Harper's Ferry as a hostage. His eighteen-year-old son came down the stairs and was taken, too. When Allstadt was ready and going through the door, he was thunderstruck to see six of his slaves waiting to be put in the wagon and carried off. He was placed in the wagon with his servants and three of Washington's, much to his expressed distaste. Matters were made worse when, after the wagon had started up, an overlooked slave of Washington's ran down the road to join the liberation. Washington explained this delicately later: "He heard something was wrong and got into the wagon at Allstadt's."

It was Osborn Anderson's testimony that

On the road we met some colored men to whom we made known our purpose when they agreed to join us. They said they had been long waiting for an opportunity of the kind. Stevens asked them to go around the colored people and circulate the news, when each started off in a different direction. The result was that many colored men gathered to the scene of action. One old colored lady, at whose house we stopped, had a good time over the message we brought her. This liberating the slaves was the very thing she had longed for, prayed for, and dreamed about, time and time again, and her heart was full of rejoicing over the fulfillment of a prophecy which had been her faith for long years.

The coming of the two vehicles from the Washington plantation was the great moment of triumph for the Old Man. As they rattled into the Armory Yard just as the day started to lighten, they were still veiled and almost mythical in outline. The captured U.S. Armory executives, who were already standing in the yard, stared in wonderment as the calvacade of Washington in his fancy carriage and the big four-horse wagon came to a halt in front of the Engine House. The slaves were standing erect in the wagon, freed. In front sat Osborn Anderson with the sword of the Revolution across his knees. The Old Man stepped forward with a slight but confident smile.

Colonel Washington climbed stiffly out of his carriage, silent and morose. The Old Man looked condescendingly at him for a moment. Here was the living blood of the great General Washington; although Brown despised Washington as a slaveholder, he grudgingly admired him as a practical and successful revolutionary. Brown addressed his captive with great dignity: "Sir, I presume you are Mr. Washington. It is too dark to write at this time, but when it shall have cleared off a little and becomes lighter, I will furnish you with pen and paper. I shall require you to write to some of your friends to send a stout, able-bodied Negro. I think, after a while, I shall be able to release you, but only on the condition of getting your friends to send a Negro man as a ransom."

Washington began to shiver in the cold. It was still damp and drizzly. Brown motioned toward the watchhouse. "You will find a fire in there, sir. It is rather cold this morning."

As Washington began to move toward the watchhouse door, the

Old Man added, quizzically, "I shall be very attentive to you, sir, for I may get the worst of it in my first encounter, and if so, your life is worth as much as mine. My particular reason for taking you first was that, as aide to the Governor of Virginia, I know you would try to perform your duty and perhaps you would be a troublesome customer to me. Apart from that, I wanted you for the moral effect it would give our cause, having one of your name as prisoner."

The freed blacks were also brought in to be warmed by the fire. Washington avoided looking at them. Brown sent two men to his little wagon to fetch out the twenty pikes. They were brought to the street in front of the Armory gate, the most public place in Harper's Ferry. The rising sun appeared through scudding clouds as the Old Man got ready to perform another symbolic act.

The freed slaves were called out to stand by the gate while Osborn Anderson handed them pikes with which to guard their masters. Down Shenandoah Street, astonished eyes were watching this arming of blacks; it seemed to be the beginning of what the country had been dreading ever since it was founded. A man named Thomas Boerly, the keeper of a small grocery store and local strongman and brawler, felt called upon to act. Snatching up his gun, he ran to the nearest corner to the gate, dropped to one knee, and fired into the ranks of the black men with the pikes. Shields Green, standing by, fired back, killing him instantly. There were no further shots.

When the Old Man was told of this, he shrugged, and told all to take cover if they could. He still held many of the hostages, more than forty men, in a group between the Armory gate and the Engine House. He wanted his men and the freed slaves to stand among them so that anyone firing at them would risk striking a neighbor and a friend. He had sent some hostages home for their breakfast; one, the barkeep of the hotel, was sent over to the hotel with a note, in Brown's clear and uncompromising script that needed no signature, "You will furnish forty-seven men with a good breakfast."

Mr. Throgmorton from the hotel was drawn, like the others, to find out what was happening. He noticed many hostages; armed blacks were going in and out of the watchhouse to get warm, and the Old Man's courtly manner was completely disarming.

Seeing the hotel clerk go into the lion's mouth and remain unscathed, the train conductor also ventured into the Armory enclosure.

Edwin Coppoc was the guard at the gate. "What does it all mean?" asked the conductor. "What do you want of my train?"

Coppoc looked at him in surprise. "We don't want to injure you or detain your train. You could have gone at three o'clock. You'd better speak to our Captain."

Conductor Phelps went manfully up to the Old Man and asked, "Can I cross the bridge?"

"No," Brown answered peremptorily. "Your man just said you meant no harm to my train." The Old Man's expression changed. "Oh, are you the conductor on that train? Why, I sent word at three o'clock that you could pass. I thought you were out of here long ago."

The conductor was silent, taken aback by Brown's reproving tone. Mr. Throgmorton approached the Old Man deferentially, an anxious waiter trying to please a temperamental customer. "I came about the breakfasts," he said. "I don't know how you want it served." The Old Man smiled bleakly. "We will offer no difficulty. You may pass back and forth at will . . . but don't cross me, or I'll take over the hotel." Mr. Throgmorton bowed and trotted back to the kitchen.

The Old Man turned back to Conductor Phelps. "I have a great many men to worry about here." "How many?" the conductor asked quickly. "Oh, hundreds!" the Old Man answered blandly, "black as well as white." He called to Osborn Anderson, in command of the freed slaves, and introduced him to the conductor. He added confidentially, "The sword Mr. Anderson is carrying is the one used by the late General Washington of Virginia." After hesitating a moment about letting the train go through at this late hour, Brown had decided to make it the instrument of a grand national communiqué, informing the world that a band of black and white revolutionaries had seized and were successfully holding a United States Government arsenal. He prayed it would mobilize the many doubters who thought he would never get around to acting.

He took the conductor by the arm and began walking in the

direction of the bridge. The conductor said, apologetically, "After being stopped by armed men on the bridge, I would not pass with my train." The Old Man said he was very sorry, it was not his intention that any blood would be spilled, but there had been bad judgment used by the men in charge of the bridge. The conductor then asked what security he would have that the train could pass through safely. "My head for it, you will not be hurt," the Old Man replied, and said he would walk over the bridge ahead of the train with him. Brown motioned for Stevens to join him; they were both carrying rifles. When they got to the hotel porch, another man, a passenger who happened to be a great secret admirer of Osawatomie Brown, wanted to accompany them. Brown gruffly ordered him to get on the train or he would take them all prisoners in five minutes.

As they walked across the bridge, the train started up with all its groaning and puffing. The Old Man strode down the middle of the track, never once looking back at the monster at his heels, while the conductor and Stevens walked rather gingerly at the side of the rails. "You doubtless wonder," Brown said to the conductor, "what a man of my age should be doing here with a band of armed men, but if you knew of my past history you would not wonder at it so much."

By then, the train was through the bridge. The Old Man shook hands with the conductor and asked him to return the favor by not mentioning what was going on at the Ferry. The conductor said yes and jumped on his train as it steamed past. The engineer waved, and a head stuck out of every window on the long line of cars.

Shortly after the Old Man and Stevens got back to the Engine House, Mr. Throgmorton came across the yard with the breakfasts. The food was in a handcart pushed by a young black, the same one who had appeared to be anticipating the attack on the Ferry. On the way over, Mr. Throgmorton remembered that he had seen this slave in earnest conversation with Cook the previous Saturday morning. Nevertheless, he made a genial and hospitable ceremony out of the serving of the good Virginia breakfast of ham, hot cakes, potatoes, eggs, and coffee. Both Mr. Washington and Mr. Allstadt refused to eat, saying they were afraid that a sleeping potion or some form of mild poison might have been put into the food, to make it easier to keep them captives.

The Old Man also refused breakfast; it was all far too rich for his abstemious ways. Mr. Throgmorton said afterward, "I had intended to prepare a special breakfast for him, he treated me so gentlemanly, but I forgot." As the men devoured the steamy meal, they laughed and joked. When it was over, Mr. Throgmorton looked for the boy to pack up the dirty plates. He found him talking excitedly with one of the armed blacks and ordered him to pack up and get back to the kitchen. The Old Man laughed as the boy answered saucily that he would when he got ready, that he was as much boss as Throgmorton. The hotelman later reported, "I told him I had no nigger blood in me."

Time was running out fast. Brown sent Osborn Anderson and Shields Green to back up the men in the arsenal buildings, and Lewis Leary and three freed slaves down to Hall's Works to reinforce Kagi. He sent William Thompson over the bridge to tell Cook and company to hurry the rifles onward. Every move showed his deep concern that weapons of death would fall into the enemy's hands.

At about daybreak when everything could be clearly seen, the big four-horse wagon had been sent across the bridge into Maryland. Riding it were John E. Cook, Tidd, Will Leeman, and four of the liberated slaves. The hostages, standing in the arsenal yard, got the impression that the wagon had been loaded with government rifles which were being taken to Brown's men, waiting in the Maryland woods to be armed and brought into the attack. None of the hostages, especially Colonel Washington, believed that such a daring attack would have been attempted without hundreds, or even a thousand men, concealed and ready to move as the inevitable opposition grew. It was civil war.

Their worst fears were realized when they saw, at the last minute, a stout young black man carrying Lewis Washington's fine English shotgun jump on the tailgate of the moving wagon. Cradling the gun across his chest, he stared at the hostages, who shuddered at his arrogance and power. The black man with the shotgun—to this day he stands unidentified; it is not even clear whose slave he was supposed to be—was a significant presence among the soldiers of the rear guard, destroying the historical fiction that none of the liberated slaves really wanted to fight alongside John Brown.

John E. Cook was in charge of the wagon. Before leaving, he shook hands ceremoniously with the Old Man and hinted that when he returned it would be with a rifle company and at least one hundred fifty fighting slaves. Brown said fervently that he hoped so. "Move fast," he added curtly.

His orders were that Cook, Tidd, and Will Leeman were to ride the wagon as far as the plantation of Terence Byrne, a Maryland slaveholder. They were to stop there, take Byrne as hostage, and liberate his slaves. The three were to wait until the wagon continued up to the Kennedy farm, and transport the guns which were there down to the schoolhouse. The Old Man's orders were clear, but they were complicated and always involved several acts which had to mesh with one another.

Terence Byrne related that he had ridden some distance down the road from his house when he saw Cook in the big wagon. Cook got down and came to the side of his horse. "Mr. Byrne, I am sorry to inform you that you are my prisoner," he said, politely. Byrne thought he was joking, recognizing him as a familiar face around the Ferry. Then he saw the rifle held under Cook's coat, protected from the drizzle. Tidd came up and said roughly, "No parley here, or I will put a ball in you. You must go back with us to your place . . . we want your Negroes."

They went to Byrne's house. Byrne met his brother on the porch and whispered, "Civil war" to him. As Byrne nervously paced the floor of his parlor, Tidd, Leeman, and Cook seated themselves. Cook began to talk about the right of the slaves to revolution. Byrne says, "My mind was busy with the future and I paid very little attention to what he said."

Byrne's cousin, an excitable southern lady, came indignantly into the room, and said, "Cowhide these scoundrels out of the house." Byrne paid no attention to her, his mind still trying to comprehend the enormity of the upheaval he was now facing.

Cook began to try out one of the propositions of the new Constitution, telling Byrne that if he would give up his slaves voluntarily,

they would enter into an agreement with him to protect his person
and property. Byrne said he would never do this; that the state of
Maryland and the U.S. Government would do this for him. Tidd
said, "We will take them anyway."

Byrne said, "You will have to find them; my men have gone off,
and only the women and children are left." Tidd then took the
wagon on up to the Kennedy farm, where Owen Brown had been
left in charge. Owen had not slept since his father had driven off to
the Ferry in the drizzle and the dark. Tidd merely told him, "Everything is going all right." The men at the farm loaded the big wagon
with boxes of Sharps rifles, with powder and everything valuable
to hand. Owen fed them all breakfast. It was a slow process, uncon-
scionably slow, and it was almost three hours later before the wagon
got off to the place of deposit at the schoolhouse. Tidd seemed to be
listless and uninterested.

When the wagon got back to Terence Byrne's, he was told he
must be taken down to the Ferry as a hostage. He went without
argument. Cook had informed him that their company had possession of the Armory, railroad bridges, and the telegraph, and that
Colonel Washington was a prisoner. As Byrne came out to the
wagon, he saw the black man with the shotgun sitting on the tailgate and recognized the weapon as Washington's much-prized fowl-
ing piece.

The wagon halted at the schoolhouse, where Tidd, Cook, and the
slaves were left to unload the arms, while Byrne and Leeman set out
for the Ferry on foot. A drenching shower came up; they ran together under a tree, and Byrne offered Leeman room under his
umbrella. William Thompson came along with the news that the
Ferry was completely under the control of the liberators. He shook
hands with Byrne and went on to report to Cook that the Old Man
wanted the rear guard to hurry—he was anxious to see the big
wagon coming back over the bridge. Brown had calculated to a matter of minutes just how long it would take to move the guns.

Again the dignity of the event and its amazingly nonaggressive
quality had its effect. Byrne, remembering those moments when he
was being taken to become a hostage in a bitter confrontation, said,
"I was disposed to assume a character that I did not have at the

time, that of cheerfulness. My mind was busy with the future. I was fearful of a bloody civil war. I was under the impression that, unless they were in great numbers, they would not be foolish enough to make an attack on the borders of two slaveholding states."

Leeman and Byrne crossed the bridge. Two guards saluted them, and one of them, Oliver Brown, shook hands with Byrne. He showed no hostility. Leeman's gun remained under his shawl. He had never pointed it at his prisoner. Put among the other hostages, Byrne greeted them with feigned cheerfulness, "Good morning, gentlemen. I hope I am in good company." It was between nine and ten o'clock.

6

Wheeling and Dealing

After breakfast, a strange euphoria persisted around the Engine House. Some of the hostages went into the warm watchhouse and took naps. The Old Man walked about briskly, checking the bridge, the arsenal, and the men around the Engine House. Osborn Anderson, watching him from the window of the arsenal, said, "I could not help thinking that at times he appeared somewhat puzzled." It was true: the Old Man *was* puzzled—things were much too quiet, and the total submission by the townspeople was rather unnatural, despite his guarantees of no unnecessary violence. Brown wanted to negotiate, to pick up a few more slaves and move out into the Virginia Mountains. He knew that Fontaine Beckham, a man his own age and the railroad agent at Harper's Ferry, was the mayor. He had anticipated that Beckham would get in touch with him and make a deal for the evacuation of the intruders. But Beckham was lying low, peeking out of the back windows of the Wager House at him, aware that time was on the side of the townspeople, and massive help from outside would not be long in coming. The Old Man sent Jere Anderson to see Kagi at the rifle works, and Anderson brought back an urgent message that Kagi thought they should move out, right away. Brown sent a reply for Kagi to hang on a little longer; he did not want to leave the men and the Sharps guns abandoned on the Maryland side. Kagi stayed, against his better judgment.

The train, rocking and whistling down the track to Baltimore, stopped at about seven o'clock at Monocacy Station to telegraph the fearful news. Conductor Phelps's first dispatch was fervent:

AN INSURRECTION HAS BROKEN OUT AT HARPER'S FERRY, WHERE AN ARMED BAND OF ABOLITIONISTS HAVE FULL POSSESSION OF THE GOVERNMENT ARSENAL AND THE TOWN. THE INSURRECTIONISTS NUMBER 250 WHITES AND ARE AIDED BY A GANG OF NEGROES. THE BRIDGE ACROSS THE POTOMAC IS FILLED WITH INSURGENTS, ALL ARMED. EVERY LIGHT IN THE TOWN WAS EXTINGUISHED AND THE HOTEL CLOSED. ALL STREETS ARE IN POSSESSION OF THE MOB AND EVERY ROAD AND LANE LEADING THEREIN BARRICADED AND GUARDED. THE PARTY IS COMMANDED, OR LED BY A MAN NAMED ANDERSON, AND NUMBERS OVER 200 BLACKS AND WHITES. A WAGON HAS BEEN LOADED WITH ARMS FROM THE ARSENAL AND DISPATCHED INTO MARYLAND FOR THE REINFORCEMENTS. THE INSURRECTIONISTS SAY THEY HAVE COME TO FREE THE SLAVES AND INTEND TO DO IT AT ALL HAZARDS. THE LEADER OF THOSE MEN REQUESTED ME TO SAY TO YOU THAT THIS IS THE LAST TRAIN THAT SHALL PASS THE BRIDGE EITHER EAST OR WEST. IF IT IS ATTEMPTED, IT WILL BE AT THE PERIL OF THE LIVES OF THOSE HAVING THEM IN CHARGE. IT HAS BEEN SUGGESTED THAT THE SECRETARY OF WAR BE NOTIFIED AT ONCE. THE TELEGRAPH WIRES ARE CUT EAST AND WEST AND THIS IS THE FIRST STATION I COULD SEND A DISPATCH FROM.

Thus, Conductor Phelps carried out for the Old Man the first requirement of the coup communiqué, conveying its reality and strength instead of trying to justify it. Meanwhile, passengers tossed notes out of the window as they chuffed through the Maryland countryside. Such a process created the most exaggerated rumors, since some put the number of the invaders at over a thousand and announced that townspeople were in a state of absolute terror, several having been killed and the town about to be burned.

Awakened by the terrible news of a slave and abolitionist insurrection, President Buchanan was so disturbed that he begged everyone concerned not to spread the news. He was afraid of a similar uprising in the city of Washington, where at the time no enlisted army men were stationed. This fact is confirmed in some lines from a letter sent by J. E. B. Stuart to his mother: "Colonel Robert E. Lee was sent to command the forces at Harper's Ferry. I had no command whatever. The United States Marines sent are a branch of the naval forces—there was not an enlisted man of the Army at hand . . ."

But it was absurd for the President to think he could suppress such news. After reading the morning papers and the alarming dispatches that kept coming in, he had to organize a civilian militia to guard the two arsenals at Washington City. He called in Lee and told him he was sending to the Ferry a company of ninety marines, the only troops available, by special train, in command of a Lieutenant Green. He wanted Lee to take over total command of all forces at the Ferry and put down rebellion against the United States of America.

The Ferry itself, however, was as calm as the eye of a tornado. The Old Man held several very frustrating conversations with the hostages, trying to dicker with them. He asked Armstead Ball, the master machinist at the works, if he would accept a proposition to deliver into his possession all the munitions of war belonging to the government in exchange for his freedom. Ball answered ironically, "They are already in your possession, as we are." Brown could not understand why, since this was true, the Mayor or some town official was not waiting there, hat in hand, to bargain for the hostages' release. There was nothing more for him to do at the Ferry. He had discussed the possibility of laying powder trains and explosives to blow up the factories, but he really could not bear to destroy that much property, although the balls of tow for igniting the powder were already in the little wagon.

Everything had ground down to an uneasy stalemate. There was

a moment's encouragement when William Thompson came back
from across the river and told him the rear guard was almost ready
to move. He wanted to ask him how many new recruits had arrived
but could not bear to hear the truth. Surely, some—to think otherwise was to make the whole attempt mass suicide. He felt in his
pocket for a letter he had received Saturday:

> Captain Brown,
> I have been disappointed in not seeing you here ere this to take
> charge of your freight. They have been here two weeks now,
> and I have had to superintend the providing for them. It has
> imposed upon me no small task, besides if they are not taken
> off, some of them will go back to Missouri. I wish to know
> definitely what you propose doing. They cannot be kept here
> much longer without risk to themselves and if some of them con-
> clude to go back to the state, it will be a bad termination to your
> enterprise.

These were men being kept at an underground railroad station
on the Pennsylvania Line. As his finger touched the creased paper
in his pocket, he thought his correspondent must know by now what
he "proposed doing." Sadly, this man was begrudging his volunteers a little bread and milk while they were willing to give their
flesh and blood for the same cause the reluctant provider professed
to honor so much. Doubtless they would come on, and Cook, as he
promised, would have a smart little rifle company to escort the
Maryland arms across the bridge.

Just about noon, he picked up the faint echo of a body of men
moving down the road to the bridge on the Maryland side. "They
are coming," he announced to Aaron Stevens. They both listened
for the tramp of marching feet coming their way on the bridge and
went out to the gate to offer a welcome. Then they heard some
heavy firing and saw Oliver, Stewart Taylor, and Dangerfield Newby
come running out from the bridge, then turning to fire at men
behind them. It was foe and not friend that they had heard, and in
formidable numbers.

Alerted by the gunfire, Osborn Anderson, Albert Hazlett, and
Shields Green ran out of the arsenal, while Watson Brown came

over from the other bridge. Osborn Anderson says, "The troops soon came out of the bridge and up the street facing us, we occupying an irregular position. Capt. Brown said, 'Let go on them!' which we did, when several of them fell. Again and again the dose was repeated. There was now consternation among the troops. From marching in scattered columns, they became scattered. Some hastened to seize upon and bear up the wounded. They seemed not to realize at first that we would fire on them, but evidently expected that we would be driven out by them without firing. The consequences of their unexpected reception was, after leaving several wounded on the field, they beat a confused retreat into the bridge, and there stayed under cover until reinforcements came to the Ferry."

The Old Man had driven back the first enemy onslaught, but, in scattering, some found their way into deserted houses at the edge of the action. Dangerfield Newby stood for a moment in the deserted street to look longingly at the Virginia mountains to the south that would carry him safely down to his Harriet and his children. Suddenly he was shot down, and a black became the first of John Brown's men to fall, the first black to die. The gun had been loaded with a spike which tore into his neck, and the blood gushed out from the severed jugular vein. Shields Green, standing beside him, looking up on High Street, thinking the shot had come from there, saw a man on horseback pointing a gun. He shot at once, killing him. Osborn Anderson took him by the arm, telling him they had to take cover or suffer the fate of Newby. Anderson urged him to come back to his post in the arsenal building, but Shields, seeing John Brown under fire, going back into the Armory yard, shook him off and said, "I'm going to go now with the Old Man."

The killing of the man on horseback pointing a gun epitomized the humane limitations of Brown's plan of action. Beside him stood another man, unarmed and therefore unshot at, John C. Rosengarten, to whom we owe one of the most sensitive and understanding eyewitness accounts of the events that day. He was a northerner on his way back from Chicago on the Baltimore train. It had stopped at a small station some miles to the west, held there by the

Will Leeman Shot Trying to Get Across the Potomac River

rumor that there was trouble at Harper's Ferry caused by a strike of the workmen at the arsenal. Rosengarten had gotten off the train and taken the long walk to the Ferry. He finally reached the long hill called High Street, plunging down from Boliver Heights to the arsenal yard. At the crest of the hill he was joined by a man riding up beside him on a well-lathered horse, carrying an army musket. He was a West Point graduate, a retired officer who said his name was Turner, and a slaveholder. He told Rosengarten excitedly that the trouble at Harper's Ferry was that "a band of men were gathered together to set the slaves free." Rosengarten then noticed that he and Turner were the only two people standing in the street, exposed to fire. "Below, not a soul was visible in the streets of Harper's Ferry, and only a few persons could be seen moving about in the arsenal enclosure." Mr. Turner, hearing the shot that felled Dangerfield Newby, raised his musket to his shoulder "when a sudden flash and a sharp report, and a bullet stopped his story and his life." Some townspeople, holding a white flag, darted out of a doorway and carried off the body of Turner, "with hardly a question or a word of explanation."

Mr. Rosengarten, bewildered by what he had just seen, violent death by firearms at the hands of concealed and unknown men, started bravely down High Street, "with some vague notions of being a peacemaker." He was picked up by a group of men from another doorway and taken laboriously down through backyards and over fences to a tavern, the Galt House, to be turned over to militia officers as a suspicious person. Several militia captains were there, drinking immoderately. They seemed "filled with the dread of something yet to come," wrote Rosengarten, "with which the people were manifestly possessed . . . something that only those can know who have lived in a slave state."

Rosengarten protested that he was only an ordinary traveler from a stalled train and offered his ticket as proof of his innocence. It only convinced the captains of his guilty intent. "How could they believe any man from a northern city was innocent of the plot now burning about their ears? If I was set at liberty, would it not only be too easy for me to communicate between the little host already beleaguered in the Engine House and the mythical great host that was gathered in the North and ready to pour itself over the South?" This conviction that the Old Man was the advance party of a full-scale abolitionist revolution was, Rosengarten says, "the staple of their discussion." Rosengarten protested over and over again that he was far from an abolitionist and could be vouched for as a personal friend by Governor Wise of Virginia.

They believed him no more than they did the angry protests of another traveler held with him, "a huge, swaggering, piratical fellow who announced himself as a Border Ruffian of Virginia stock who had fought with the Southern Rights party in the Kansas Wars. He said when he heard of the raid he knew who was at the top and bottom of it, and he described in a truthful sort of way, Osawatomie Brown, Old John Brown. To prove his claim to be a true son of the South, he offered to sally forth with a body of men and fight the Old Man, hand to hand: "Just as they did in Missouri . . . straight on."

His vivid descriptions of Captain Brown's deeds in Kansas only fortified the decision of the Militia Captains not to meet the invaders in battle, but to continue sniping at the Engine House until the federal troops arrived. It was then decided that, for their own safety, both strangers would be taken back to Charlestown and locked up in the county jail.

When the Old Man got back to the Engine House, he found that all the hostages had run for cover in that section of it known as the "watch house." This was not the safest area. The Engine House had three bays, two fitted with big swinging doors for the use of fire engines. The third bay, for the partitioned-off watchhouse, had a door and two windows cut into its front.

The forty-odd frightened men in the watchhouse crowded around Brown as if he were defending instead of imprisoning, them. He announced that he was picking out the ten most prominent men to take into the watchhouse with him; they would get good treatment because if he got the worst of it in a fight, their being in his hands would be of service in procuring good terms. He laid his hand first on Colonel Washington, "You, sir, come along. I know that if you were out and in your position as aide to the Governor, you would be a most dangerous foe." He went to the others, pointing to them and simply saying, "I want you, I want you . . ."

As this group of preferred hostages began to go, one of those left said bitterly, "I suppose you are going to leave the rest of us here to be shot down at random." "No, sir," said Brown. "I am going to defend you as well as the others. I gave you my pledge that you would come out of this unharmed and sent home to your families, and I will keep it." The man gave him a firm handclasp, saying that when the Virginia militia from out back got lickered up, they would shoot everything that moved in their gunsights. "No, no," the Old Man said fervently. "I will protect you."

Here, and not in the facing of the militia on the bridge, Captain Brown had come, at last, to the fatal part of his enterprise. As he walked the chosen ten into the Engine House proper, a group of militia stationed up on the trestlework of the railroad, which ran on the north boundary of the Armory enclosure, opened fire. "They will kill us," moaned one of the hostages. "They will shoot us down with no more compunction than if we were the niggers themselves. They will be so riled up over this that all they will think of is kill, kill, kill."

Brown was shocked into an awareness that there was very little chance anymore of working out a rational settlement. Seeing armed black slaves guarding white men, and knowing other blacks were in the vicinity, carrying guns and firing them, would make the militia trigger-happy, careless even about the lives of their neighbors. Ferocity at the thought of a slave rebellion was already out of hand; someone had come out of one of the houses on Shenandoah Street and sliced the ears off Dangerfield Newby as souvenirs. The Old Man felt compelled to assure the hostages that he would not kill them in any act of retaliation nor use them as living shields behind whom to walk his people out. "Why not?" demanded Stevens, losing his temper. "Isn't that what we have them for?" "Watch your temper, Aaron," the Old Man said. Stevens got angrier. "Let's get out of here," he exploded. "We're already surrounded. You don't know how many men have come into this town by now, they've had all morning to get here!"

Brown glanced around at the hostages. "What about our rear guard? We can't leave now—they may be just about to join us from the other side."

"Then's let's go that way," said Stevens. "Use these people for shields. Three of them are arrant slaveholders and ought to be hung as it is."

"Then what will become of the people in the Hall's Works—Kagi and the others?" the Old Man said.

He went to the door and looked out. Several men on the trestlework were banging away at the Engine House. "Their guns are no good," said Brown. "They're falling short." Stevens went out and began firing his Sharps at them, loading four shots a minute. The snipers fell flat and inched their way over to a square water tower beside the trestlework. "Let's go!" said Stevens, "One way or another. We're fish in a barrel here."

"Tut, tut," said the Old Man, "I have my own plans here."

Mr. Kitzmiller, the Works superintendent, intervened. "Gentlemen, this is getting to be hot work. If you will allow me a suggestion, I can possibly accommodate matters. There are some of us here that are not unsympathetic. Mr. Brua here has been completely won over to your cause. We are not your enemies."

A man, most aptly named Reason Cross, joined the conversation. He suggested that a paper be drawn up and signed by all the hostages and Brown himself that there would be a cease-fire in exchange for the release of the hostages and Brown's retention of the arsenal and the slaves, this question to be settled later by the U.S. Government. This was agreed to all around. William Thompson was selected to escort Mr. Cross over the yard to the hotel. Mr. Cross assured everyone that Mayor Beckham was a fair man and a gentleman and would listen to reason.

As they left, some sniper fire began to come from men concealed behind the water tower. It began to break the window glass in the watchhouse. The Old Man came to the door and shouted after them, "Tell the mayor to get those sharpshooters away from that water tower. They will kill his own citizens."

Thompson had a white handkerchief tied to his gun, but when he got out of range of the Engine House, some men seized him and tied him up. When Reason Cross protested, saying that Brown's treatment of his hostages was kind and respectful, they threatened to tie him up as well. Thompson was taken over to the hotel and put in a room there.

At the Engine House, another crisis erupted. There was the sound now of new and powerful weapon fire coming from the militia. Colonel Baylor, the militia commander, had officially reported that "I do not think we have a hundred muskets in the county of Jefferson." But it was now obvious that this deficiency had been corrected. Some excellent new guns, hidden from the regular stores in the common anticipation of a sectional conflict, were now in the hands of the Virginia Militia and were being shot into the Engine House with murderous accuracy.

Mr. Brua now asked permission for parole, on condition he would straightway return. Impressed by his honest and candid eyes, and with no sign of Thompson coming back with Mr. Cross, the Old Man gave his consent. Mr. Brua walked confidently across the yard, disappeared for some fifteen minutes, and then came back, even more confidently. According to Colonel Washington, he had "brought in a promise that our people would not fire while negotiations were pending."

Mr. Kitzmiller now made a strong plea to the Old Man that he be allowed to carry out the negotiations for the release of the hostages. Here the Old Man made his most serious mistake. He had confidence in Mr. Brua. In addition, noting that no opposing fire had been coming from the bridge head for some time, he figured that by now his rear guard had got there and was holding it. He agreed to let Kitzmiller do the negotiating. "Take Stevens and Watson along," he said. "There is a company of my riflemen on the bridge." Kitzmiller put his white handkerchief on his walking stick and the three started out. When they got to the bridge, Kitzmiller recognized some local people and began to run toward them. Stevens called him back.

In the Galt House nearby, its owner, George Chambers, who was also the town clerk, drew a bead on Aaron Stevens and shot him. Stevens, thrashing like a Samson in his agony and rage, began to pump shots from his Sharps gun into the bridge opening, clearing it of all the militia men. But then another good shot from Chambers, who was firing a new Hall's rifle from the window sill of the second floor of his saloon, brought Stevens down. A parting shot from the bridge hit Watson Brown, penetrating deep within his chest.

Watson crawled painfully back to the Engine House, carefully carrying the rifle along with him. The Old Man lost his temper completely. "What kind of men are they, shooting down my men, butchering them wholesale under a flag of truce?" He tried to stanch Watson's wound, blanching at the sight of the huge hole opened up. The hostages stood by trembling, fearful that their lives would be taken in retaliation, but Brown regained his self-control and assured them again no harm would come to them from him.

Mr. Brua, the only one of the hostages who had become completely won over by the Old Man, said he would go out again to see if he could do something for Stevens and try to make a peace, if he could. "At your own risk," Brown said. "I am sending out no more escorts."

As Mr. Brua was leaving, Will Leeman suggested he go in back of him, using him for cover, and then break for the river

and try to get the rear guard to come in. The Old Man agreed.
But his obsession with weapons of death had become so fixed
that he asked Leeman to try to rescue Stevens's Sharps rifle so
that it would not be used against them. Leeman agreed. He
walked successfully in Brua's cover, then darted quickly to Stevens's
side, snatched his gun, and ran into the hotel. He accidentally
dropped the gun going in the door but kept running through the
hotel hall and out the back door. He made his way down through
a culvert that was nearby and opened onto the river and got into
the shallow water. Holding his own gun high above his head,
he made his way in water breast-high to a rock in the stream and
pulled himself onto it, immobilized with exhaustion. Unfortunately,
the Militia, who rushed out of the barroom after his sudden foray,
began shooting at him from the railroad trestle. With lead raining
around him, Leeman raised his hands in surrender. A Virginia
Militiaman waded out to the rock, placed an enormous horse
pistol against Leeman's head, and fired, blowing most of it off.
Waving jocosely to his friends on the trestlework, he drew a
huge bowie knife and cut off Leeman's coattail for a trophy. Then
he set up the body in a grotesque sitting position, and the
Militiamen, in various stages of drunkenness, used the body for
target practice for the rest of the afternoon.

When Mr. Brua got to Stevens's side, he thought the young
man was already dead. Covered with blood, pale and inert with
shock, his huge form, naturally protuberant with muscle and
contour, seemed to be dissolving into the earth. Brua tried to lift
him, but could not do it alone. Mr. Throgmorton came gallantly
to his assistance, and the two of them dragged Stevens into the
hotel and put him into a chamber. Brua put his head on Stevens's
bloody chest but could not hear a heartbeat, but on lifting his
head, he saw Stevens looking at him with calm, steady eyes.

"What can I do for you, Stevens?" Brua asked.

"Take my body from this land of chains," came the answer,
faintly.

"Have you no family . . . anyone that is dear to you?"

"Everybody that is good is dear to me." The response came
in a boy's simple voice, and Stevens lapsed into unconsciousness.
Brua could hear the Militia in the bar down the hall, shouting,

The First Attack on Brown and His Men from the Potomac River Bridge

breaking glasses, and singing in high glee. He folded Stevens's arms across his chest in the attitude of the quiet dead and ran back to the Engine House and the Old Man.

Fontaine Beckham, the Mayor, seeing this act performed so strangely by one of the Old Man's hostages, finally decided to see what was happening to them, and why they were complaining about the shots from the water tower. He made his way down the trestlework to the water tower, and began peeking around it to see where the shots fired from that angle were hitting.

Back in the Engine Room, with the big door slightly ajar, Edwin Coppoc saw him. One of the hostages, Mr. Allstadt, who was standing next to Coppoc, described the latter's excitement. "If he keeps on peeking, I'm going to shoot," said Coppoc. "Don't fire, man, for God's sake," the prisoners shouted, "they'll shoot in here and kill us all." But Coppoc's shot was already on its way, and Beckham fell to the ground, dead.

The news only increased the bloodlust among the militia.

Without the slightest hesitation, George Chambers and Henry
Hunter ran to the room in which Stevens and William Thompson
were being kept. Hunter leveled his gun at Thompson, whose
hands were tied behind his back. A young lady threw herself between Thompson and the guns, begging them not to kill him
there before her eyes. She said later that she did not want blood-
stains on the rug, being the sister of the hotel owner's wife.
Chambers and Hunter took Thompson by the throat and dragged
him into the trestlework. Standing only three or four feet away,
they fired into his body again and again; then, flinging Thompson
off the bridge, they fired at him with revolvers as he dropped the
forty feet to the river. Thompson's will to live was so powerful
that he managed to climb on a rock for a minute before further
shooting finished him off.

Men at the Water Tower and the Railway Bridge Firing at
the Engine House

William Thompson
Shot and Thrown
Off the Bridge

Hearing about the men of Brown's party at Hall's Works, Hunter and Chambers started up there, hoping for new victims. Kagi, disheartened and demoralized by his lonely hours of separation from the main struggle, was getting ready to abandon the post with his three comrades and some freed slaves. He had sent repeated messages to the Old Man for orders, but only one reply had come through, telling him to hang on. Looking out the window of the rifle factory, he saw himself hemmed in by hundreds of men. Since it was useless simply to spill more blood, they left the factory by the back way, without firing a shot, and

went into the shallow waters of the Shenandoah. Leary, Kagi, and
John Copeland made for a flat rock in the water, hoping to get out
of gunshot range. Kagi was hit and died before he got to the
rock, and another river ran red with the blood of liberators. Leary
was fatally shot climbing onto the rock, but Copeland was unhit.
He said, "The fire of fifty men was then turned on Leary and me.
He got up on some stones and turned his back to the Virginia
side, and was hit. I got behind some stones and floated down river.
I thought they would consider us all killed, but someone coming
out to see Leary saw me. He was pulling me out with the intention of putting a parting shot into me, but someone prevented
it."

Another Virginia Militiaman had waded out to do in Copeland, as Will Leeman had been killed. But his gun was wet and
would not go off. Dr. Starry, still on his horse, who had succeeded in bringing the men down to the Ferry, intervened. While
the other men were knotting together their handkerchiefs to
lynch Copeland, Starry rode between them and Copeland with
his horse and succeeded in staving off the murder. Leary was
brought in from the river and died the next night.

Brown, knowing nothing of the killings in either of the rivers,
was still hoping that the rear guard was coming. About four
o'clock, a company of railroad workers under the command of a
Captain Alburtis, decided they could do what the Virginia
Militia could not—take the Old Man in his lair. His active forces
were now reduced to seven men in the Engine House, including
his son Watson, who was slowly dying. Osborn Anderson and
Albert Hazlett, still occupying the Armory, were as yet undis-
covered.

Captain Alburtis's company marched down the Armory Yard
from the west just as some of Brown's men had come out of the
Engine House, looking for a possible escape route. Again the
assailants were no match for a much smaller force of men with
Sharps guns, and eight of Alburtis's men went down with serious
wounds. During the fight, however, as Alburtis reported, the company was able to get to the back of the watchhouse section of
Brown's headquarters: "We found in the room adjoining the

Captain Alburtis's Company Attack the Engine House and Are Driven Off

Engine House some thirty or forty prisoners who had been captured and confined by the outlaws. The windows were broken open by our party and these men escaped. The whole of the outlaws were now driven into the Engine House, and owing to the great number of wounded requiring our care and not being supported by other companies as we expected, we were obliged to return."

In other words they were beaten. Watson Brown, bleeding internally, had lain on the Engine Room floor firing repeatedly. He fainted after the battle, and it was obvious that now because of this exertion, he was soon to die. The firing stopped again, aside from some sporadic sharpshooting, but the air became hideous with drunken cries, laughter, and revelry. The two barrooms did a record business, and the only truly sober men in Harper's Ferry were the outlaws in the Engine House.

This might have been a moment when the Old Man could have shot his way out of the trap. The enemy was demoralized, drunken, wounded, and sick. The superior firepower represented by seven well-trained men with rapid-loading, highly accurate guns, as opposed to muzzle-loaders in the hands of drunken men, might have overcome the hundreds hemming them in. But the hostages did not want him to go. The sky was heavy with thick, turbulent, scudding clouds, which, almost at predictable intervals, would collide and send sheets of icy rain down on the battleground. The Virginia Militiamen, who lurked in cover behind the water tank and at the corner of the hotel, pouring lead into the Engine House, would then scuttle back to the two bars for the warmth of pot-bellied stoves and free and unlimited liquor. When the rain would ease, they would come merrily out again, to bang away at outlaws who were fair game because they "must have had nigger blood in them, else why would they do this?"

The hostages warned Brown that the men were now drunk enough to come at them head-on, firing recklessly up to the doors of the Engine House. As Washington put it, "If the place be stormed, friend and foe would have to share alike." To placate them, Oliver or Edwin Coppoc would go to the door and fire a few shots, keeping the yard clear from any enemy advance. After this, the firing on the other side would diminish and die away, as the Militia would realize the defenses of the Engine House were being well-manned.

During one of these flurries, Oliver stepped to the door and opened it a foot or so, to fire the warning shots. In the steel-gray air of the afternoon, this doorway was like a vertical marker of black, its deep shadow as definite as the hair on a gun sight. Some Militiaman saw this, took aim, and fired just below the middle of the black line. Oliver fell to the floor dying. It was now out of the question for the Old Man to shoot his way out, but he grimly held control over the hostages, hoping somehow that he could save his wounded sons.

When the hostages saw Brown's second son fall bleeding to the floor, they braced themselves, expecting the worst. As John Daingerfield, one of the hostages, said, "Almost any other man similarly situated would at least have exacted life for life." The Old Man, sensing this, again reassured his captives. As one of the hostages related later, "His intentions were to shoot nobody unless they were carrying arms. He was endeavoring to protect his hostages and constantly said that he wished to make terms more for their safety than his own." His contempt for the Militia, however, could not be hidden: "Your citizens are barbarous. I could have massacred everyone in this town."

Shortly after Oliver was hit, an elderly citizen with a handkerchief tied to his umbrella gingerly approached the Engine House door. "You may as well surrender," he told the Old Man. "Please come in," Brown said, hoping he was a doctor. But the man gave his name stiffly as *Mr.* Samuel Strider and announced in a trembling voice that he had been sent to demand an unconditional surrender. The Old Man scribbled out a note and handed it to him: "In consideration of all my men, whether living or dead, being soon safely in and delivered up to me at this point with all their arms and ammunition, we will then take our prisoners and cross the Potomac Bridge, a little beyond which we will set them at liberty; after which we can negotiate about the Government property as may be best. Also we require the delivery of our horses and harnesses at the hotel. John Brown."

Little old Mr. Strider ran back to the Militia, returning in a short while with a reply:

"Sir, the terms you proposed I cannot accept. Under no consideration will I consent to a removal of our citizens across the river. Robert W. Baylor, Col. Commandant, 3rd Regiment Cavalry."

The Old Man handed it back. "You tell the Colonel that I will never surrender but on my own stated terms. I am expecting reinforcements. . . . I have other companies posted in positions . . ." His voice trailed off; he was very, very weary, having neither slept or eaten for thirty-six hours. As Strider went out the big door, he added quietly, "I would appreciate it greatly if a doctor would come and look at my boys."

7

The Rear Guard

The Patriots left in a town should never be abandoned by their friends —*never*. They must at all hazards be succored, that *all* may feel satisfied that in similar cases they likewise will be thought of. While the Volunteers inside the town defending themselves, a body of Guerrillas must, from without, harass the invaders in their rear and flanks, exerting themselves in every possible manner to prevent the place from being completely surrounded.

Hugh Forbes
Manual of the Patriotic Volunteer

Cook and the rear guard, alone at the schoolhouse, had heard the firing but knew nothing of the fight at the bridge. Tidd and the liberated slaves had gone back to the farm for another load. The reinforcements Cook had so confidently predicted were nowhere visible, and the day had worn away with an agonizing emptiness. When he had first arrived to take possession of the school where he had once taught, he had wanted the students to carry on as if nothing had happened. He wanted to lecture them on antislavery and on the history that was being made before their eyes.

Mr. Currie, the schoolmaster, said this was impossible; the boys were too alarmed to engage in their usual duties. Cook tried to pacify them and tell them stories of liberation, but one little boy went into a fit, and Cook allowed them all to go home. Mr. Currie said he wanted to take the hysterical boy to his father's house. Cook said that he would allow this if Currie would promise to return. In the meantime, the slaves unloading the wagon told Cook that Currie was a slaveholder and lived only a mile up the road from Colonel Washington. As Currie said, "I noticed some change in his manner after I came back; he was rather cooler; but after I was there some time, he became rather more communicative and spoke of a great many things."

Indeed, Cook talked constantly, obsessively, to the schoolmaster all afternoon. They both could hear the firing at the Ferry, rising now and then to a crescendo, and Currie would ask "What does it mean?" Cook would reply, knowingly, "It simply means this; that those people down there are resisting our men and we are shooting them down."

Cook made it sound very simple and remote to Mr. Currie, but he himself was paralyzed by the realization that no reinforcements were coming. While he sat there talking, Dangerfield Newby, William Thompson, Will Leeman, John Kagi, and Lewis Leary had all been killed. It seemed very strange to Mr. Currie, after a sharp volley would drift on the wind from the Ferry, that Cook just sat there. Cook felt obliged to defend his position and said, over and over again, that Captain Brown had ordered him to stay there and guard the arms and that he could not get away. At one point, Currie said, "For God's sake, how many men have you got down there?" Cook said he didn't know; there could be one thousand, or ten thousand, for all he knew. "We are a little band," Cook said another time, "and we may perish in this attempt but there are thousands ready to step into the breach." Since the fight was going on so long, Currie thought they must certainly be already doing this. Finally, getting up his courage, he asked Cook if he could go home. The answer was yes, if he promised not to reveal what had gone on at the schoolhouse.

When Tidd, who had been gone on this second trip for more than three hours, finally came up with the load, Cook snatched up a special long-range sharpshooting gun and began to run down the road to the Ferry. Behind him the black man followed with the shotgun. At the canal lockkeeper's house just above the bridge, a woman told Cook that his friends were hemmed in at the Ferry and several of them had been shot. Cook shouted that he had to go and save his comrades, but the black man with the shotgun demanded that they both go back, take the men they had, and try to blast their way over the bridge in order to set up a covering fire for the Old Man and their comrades in the arsenal and the Engine House. "You go get Tidd," Cook commanded, and began to scramble wildly up the rugged cliff of the Maryland Heights.

There he could see a body of men on High Street, just above the Engine House, pouring fire into the Armory enclosure. He climbed into a tree, got the men in the sights of his long-distance rifle, and fired. No one fell, but the shot kicked up some earth in front of the men, and they turned their guns to the fire from across the river. Even at that distance, a bullet cut away a branch he was holding on to, and he fell about fifteen feet to the sharply sloping rock of the mountain, bruising himself badly.

After this, he staggered painfully down the mountains, and came out by a small, familiar store near the canal. Seeing several heads looking out at him from behind the door, he cocked his gun in their direction and motioned for someone to come out. A man emerged who knew Cook and acted friendly; he said that John Brown was dead, and all his company were killed or taken prisoner.

"John Brown was shot at four o'clock," the man repeated, without any particular satisfaction. He saw the whiteness and desperation of Cook's face and got him a cup of coffee from the store. Cook began hobbling up the road to the schoolhouse, sobbing and stumbling; he had twisted an ankle in his fall on the mountain. The excruciating pain was a kind of cruel narcotic for the shock of hearing of his Captain's death. As he ran, however, he thought he heard firing directly in back of him, but who was being shot at if the liberators themselves were all wiped out? He thought the shots were being fired in hot pursuit of him, illogical as it was that men should be chasing an enemy at such a distance.

When the black man with the shotgun got to Tidd and the little company of blacks at the schoolhouse, he told him breathlessly that the liberators were hemmed in across the bridge and action must be taken to help them get away. "It's hopeless, hopeless," said Tidd, angrily. "It always was. I knew it, I knew." While Tidd walked behind the schoolhouse to sulk, the black man unharnessed one of the horses on the big wagon, rode at a gallop back to the Kennedy farm, and told Owen and the others they must leave at once to join the fight at the Ferry.

Owen tried to put things in order. There were papers and maps to be destroyed. But what was to be done with the implements of warfare still in the farmhouse and the log cabin? Hating waste as much as his father, he took the time to run to a neighboring house to tell the occupants they could help themselves to the provisions left unused. Finally, sensing that the black man with the shotgun akimbo was watching him with eyes of lightly veiled rebuke, he gave the word to abandon the farm. Barclay Coppoc, Meriam, and Owen loaded up all the guns they could carry and started down the road. The black man, still mounted on Washington's horse, seemed to be herding them like cattle to the slaughterhouse.

Marching in the rain, after a disappointing day of waiting, these men were well aware that they were John Brown's last forlorn hope. The rain-filled air began to fuse with the coming dusk. In the half-dark ahead, they saw an armed man. When Owen ordered him to halt, the man raised a Sharps gun quickly to his shoulder. Then Owen saw who it was and called out "Tidd!"

Tidd ran to them, breathless and in panic. "The fact is, boys, we are all used up. The best thing we can do is get away from here as quick as we can."

"We cannot leave my father and our friends," Owen said. He ordered them to go on to the schoolhouse, get the slaves left there, and cross a ravine just back of it which led up through the forest to the rocky cliff from which Cook had fired into the town. Tidd kept saying it was hopeless, but he too became conscious of the black man with the shotgun and reluctantly went along with the others.

Just before they got to the schoolhouse, another armed man came at them, out of the dusk. Owen called on him to halt. He answered, "You halt, yourself, I've got you covered." It was John E. Cook, who broke down into tears while telling Owen the news: "Your father was killed at four o'clock this afternoon. They are all killed, or else they are captured. We have nothing to do but escape ourselves." After the initial shock, however, Owen kept saying he had to be sure, he could still hear a shot or two from the direction of the Ferry.

"They are drunk down there," Cook insisted. "They are firing on each other." He did not tell them of his fear that rifle companies would be coming across the bridge to follow up the pathetic little battle he had started. For some time they stood arguing in the drenching rain: Cook suggested that the schoolhouse might already be occupied by the Virginia Militia, but Owen insisted that they drive on if only to see what had happened to the liberated slaves.

Owen ordered the others to conceal themselves in a thicket, and he and Tidd approached the schoolhouse. Owen whistled a signal to the slaves posted around it; there was no answer. Tidd insisted it was an ambush laid out by the Virginia Militia, and he refused to go farther. But when Owen said he would go alone, Tidd followed him into the schoolhouse, revolver in hand. They pushed back the rickety door, swinging slack-jawed on strips of old leather. It was empty. Battered schoolbooks were flung about, cast aside by the frightened children. In a corner Owen saw a gunnysack full of sweet biscuit which he had made himself. There was a sack of sugar, marked "J.B."; it was one the Old Man had saved and brought all the way from Kansas. These were the only provisions they had for their escape.

After Owen and Tidd came out, they waited with the others in the chilling rain for over an hour, from time to time calling out for the liberated slaves. "The only answer that came to us out of the rain and darkness," Owen reported, "was the firing at Harper's Ferry, only a mile away."

In this way the rear guard turned and ignominiously left the scene of the struggle after firing only a single shot. Owen felt intensely guilty about this and said afterward, "We might have shown our good will by killing one or two of the enemy; still it would surely have cost our lives." Owen was by no means a religious man, but he felt his father would "have wanted" him to save the young lives that were left, rather than going forth to useless self-slaughter.

The black man with the shotgun did not want to leave, but Tidd convinced him that they needed the horse to carry the bags of sugar and biscuit. They went back to the farm, the black man still grumbling, and picked up rubber blankets and some small supplies. Owen, trying not to think of the tragedy at the Ferry, bent his will to the planning and execution of an escape for Cook, Tidd, Meriam, Barclay Coppoc, whose lives he now felt responsible for. He was very conscious of the dour animosity of Charles Tidd, who had predicted the tragedy and tried to break away from it but had been held by the power of the Old Man's presence. Later, Owen wrote, "I had some experience as an engineer on the Underground Railroad, and I had been a woodsman almost all my life. I told the boys if they stuck by me I felt pretty sure I could get them safely through to the North and to Canada, if necessary." It was a task he infinitely preferred to combat in the bloody streets across the river.

He was disturbed by the despondency and resistance that emanated from the black man with the shotgun. Owen wanted to keep him with them as a kind of validation of the whole attack. If at least they could show they had freed one man, and that he had been freed while carrying arms in his hands, everything would not seem such a failure. When they started up the mountain, Owen asked the black man to turn loose the horse, but the latter resisted, saying the animal was worth more than a hundred and fifty dollars and he did not want to part with it. "I had hard work convincing him that his life was worth more than the horse," Owen recalled.

Deep in the laurel bushes on the mountain slopes, Owen told the fugitives that his plan was to take the northwesterly direction of the mountain range, traveling only at night at the edges of clearings, making no fires, buying or stealing no food, not even speaking to one another aloud until they had got beyond Chambersburg. The black, complaining of rheumatism said he couldn't keep up with the march. Finally the others lay down despondently on their rubber blankets, and Owen, who had not slept for two nights, begged the black man to go to sleep and let himself be taken on to freedom. The black man lay down grudgingly, then got

The Old Man

up and began to limp about, groaning that he could not make it, he could not run these mountains. After fighting off his drowsiness, Owen dropped off into a deep slumber; when he woke up, not long after, the black man with the shotgun was gone.

Owen woke the others. Tidd, typically, complained that the black man knew all their escape plans and might betray them. He insisted they start at once, in a different direction than had been planned. They had to cross a valley to more westerly mountains before dawn. There they buried some of their guns. Owen ended up carrying fifty pounds of provisions, while the others, still determined to be warriors, carried two Sharps apiece, two revolvers, and heavy cartridge boxes. It was almost impossible to climb with these heavy loads through clumps of bush and loose rock outcrops, and they finally flung themselves down in utter exhaustion. But what was most disturbing was the sound of gun-fire still coming from the Ferry. It seemed too persistent to be simply the random celebrations of drunken militiamen. They were haunted by the idea that the Old Man could be still fighting for his life down there.

And of course, he was. He even welcomed the darkness, feeling that it would make it that much easier for his rear guard, and the recruits who must have come by now, to get into the Ferry, start an effective fire fight, and get them all safely out of there. As for the black man with the shotgun, whom Tidd had maligned, he had left Owen and the fugitives in order to find the other slaves and see if anything could be done to help the men in the Engine House.

8

Holding Out

No place should be abandoned if it be capable of making a successful resistance. Nothing short of a total deficiency of ammunition, food or water, can justify a surrender—to defer which catastrophe, every species of procrastination must be practiced.

It requires a blockading force *very* superior to that surrounded, to prevent the escape of the latter, when the sortie is aided by an attack upon the besiegers from the rear, especially if it be attempted by night, and at the point of the bayonet, without the party making the sortie firing a shot: such firing wastes powder and attracts the enemy.

Hugh Forbes
Manual of the Patriotic Volunteer

As darkness closed in, the hostages looked carefully at the Old Man for signs of weakness and capitulation. They were more fearful than ever that the Militia would try to take the Engine House by storm, and night would make it impossible to distinguish between friend and foe. But Brown remained calm as he cheerfully asked one of the freed slaves, "You are a pretty stout-looking fellow. Can't you knock a hole through there for me?" He pointed to the brickwork next to the door and handed a hammer and chisel to Big Phil, a stout man rescued from slaveholder Allstadt, and the latter soon knocked out a loophole at eye level from which to fire into the yard. Clearly the Old Man was determined to hold out as long as possible and believed that his reinforcements had been waiting for night before making their move.

Now that it was dark, whole squads of Militiamen could stand up on the trestlework near the water tower and send clusters of lead against the Engine House without being picked off by Brown's men. This advantage was first discovered while Phil was making the loophole, and a freak shot came into the hole and knocked the hammer out of his hand. Motioning him away, Brown made three more loopholes himself, impressing the hostages with his coolness and strength.

From time to time, the Old Man would check on the pulsebeat of his wounded sons, and the hostages would turn their eyes nervously to Shields Green, who had now become the most active defender in the Engine House. If there was to be any retaliation killing, they thought, it would come from him. They were extremely conscious of Green's presence, not threatening but keeping up a cool and methodical return fire out of the loopholes.

Colonel Washington was particularly upset with Green: "I saw him order some gentleman to shut a window, with a rifle raised at them. He said, 'Shut that window, damn you; shut it instantly.' He did it in a very impudent manner." There was no question of the hostages trying to rush Brown, seize weapons, and escape while Shields Green stalked among them and the freed slaves stood by with their pikes in hand.

Sorrowfully, the Old Man began to realize that Oliver's pulse was getting weaker and weaker. From time to time, when the firing died off, he would go to the door and open the fatal hairline sight to enemy fire, looking to see if a doctor was coming. It was almost fully dark, the reinforcements should be coming now if at all. He saw a man carrying a rifle, striding along purposefully, come through the Armory gate. Brown pushed the heavy door open a foot or so and motioned the stranger to come in.

The man entered boldly and introduced himself as Captain Sinn, commander of a volunteer company from Frederick, Maryland. Now the Engine House had to be held against two states' militias. Brown introduced him to the hostages, demonstrating that they were in good shape and fearful only of getting killed by their own militia. Sinn was impressed by the order and discipline existing in the beleaguered Engine House, in contrast to the chaos outside.

The Old Man told Sinn he had a proposition: if he were allowed to take his wagon, his wounded, and his party over the bridge to the edge of the mountain, "then they may take me if they can." Captain Sinn announced that a large contingent of U.S.

Marines and several regular Army officers had just arrived from
Washington, D.C. The Old Man was not particularly alarmed
at this, saying, "I have fought Uncle Sam before and I would do
it again. I know just what I am doing here. I will face all the
consequences."

"But that is treason," said Sinn, appalled. Brown reviewed the
classic abolitionist argument that any attempt of the Federal
Government to use federal troops to defend slavery was a violation
of its legitimate and constitutional powers. He calmly explained
that if the Army attacked them, they would be acting more
illegally than he was. The Constitutional obligation to defend the
states against invasion had nothing to do with slavery. It was
actually unpatriotic and morally wrong for the slaves themselves
to remain in slavery one more hour, if there was any chance for
them to escape.

Captain Sinn replied tartly it was no longer a question of
slavery, that Brown and his men had ruthlessly killed citizens of
the town. "We shot at no unarmed men," said the Old Man.
Sinn reminded him of Shephard Hayward and Fontaine Beckham,
both unarmed and now lying dead, causing the Old Man to lose
his composure. "If the porter had taken care of himself he would
be alive," he cried. "As for the Mayor, how could we tell he was
unarmed, given the position he was in and the suspicious antics
he was carrying on up there? I fight only those who choose to
fight me. I have protected these hostages. My two sons are dying—
one was shot under a flag of truce."

"They must expect to be shot down like dogs if they take up
arms in this way," Sinn replied hotly. The firing from outside
began again, and Brown pulled the big door shut. Looking again at
the dying boys, Sinn said he considered Brown a brave man, and
that it was a pity some honorable end could not be worked out to
these troubles. "Then take back my proposition," Brown insisted.

Captain Sinn shook his head, telling the Old Man the men
outside were completely out of control. There was no hope of
negotiations until the liquor ran out. He told him how Will
Leeman died, and how his body was being used. "I saw your man
Stevens dying in a hotel room, and shamed some young men

trying to shoot him while lying there in his deathbed. I told them if that man could stand on his feet with a pistol in his hand, they would all jump out the window."

Colonel Washington interrupted to say how well-liked Shephard Hayward was: "He was always remarkably civil. He was very trustworthy." The Colonel declared that it was disgraceful that the first blood shed by the great moralists and liberators of slaves was an inoffensive black man with a family. This stung the Old Man to an angry denial. The first man to die, he informed the Colonel, was a black man, Dangerfield Newby, fighting for his family, who were enslaved not forty miles away. How could Newby be condemned for attempting to do for his family with the slaveholders what George Washington had done to the soldiers of his King? Was it not true that George Washington caused thousands of inoffensive family men, civil and trustworthy, to be killed because they wore the uniform of their country and their Sovereign?

Sinn did not see how such an argument applied in this case; he had no sympathy for Brown's acts and was there to bring him to punishment. On the other hand, he declared, he had no sympathy for those southerners who had defiled Newby's body. He said he knew this was true and had been told of it by the reporter from his hometown paper.

Up to this time Brown had been wearing George Washington's sword, perhaps thinking it would provide a basis for better terms in negotiations; now he took it off with a gesture of contempt and laid it on the seat of the fire engine. Taking his gun, he cocked it, and said to Sinn, "We have no choice but to fight to the death, come what may. I can see that is the only honorable, and quite necessary end. Please send a doctor to look at my boys, if you can."

He pushed open the door and let Captain Sinn out. A few minutes later a doctor came, the surgeon attached to Sinn's company, who tried to make Brown's sons comfortable and said he would return at daylight. The hostages and the freed slaves tried to make themselves comfortable on the brick floor, but Brown and his men stayed erect and awake. There were now only four of them left, Edwin Coppoc, Jere Anderson, Dauphin Thompson, and Shields

*Interior of the Engine House: John Brown and His Men;
the Hostages at the Left*

Green. With the exception of Jere Anderson, they were the youngest, the babies of the group. From time to time Brown would
shout, "Men, are you still awake?"

"In the quiet of the night," one of the hostages remembered,
"young Oliver died. He had begged again and again to be shot,
in the agony of his wound, but his father replied to him, 'You
will get over it' and 'If you must die, die like a man.' Now John
Brown talked, from time to time, with my father and Colonel
Washington, but I did not hear what was said. Oliver Brown lay
quietly over in a corner. His father called to him, after a time.
No answer. 'I guess he is dead,' said Brown."

In the darkness of the Armory Yard, the United States Marines
were taking their position for a final assault. Robert E. Lee began
to line up his forces to take four boys and a tired old man. He had
offered the honor to the Virginia Militia, but their Colonel declined, somewhat indignantly. He said he had come only to protect the people of Harper's Ferry; the Marines were being paid
for this kind of work. He could not expose citizens to such a risk
while there were mercenaries present to do the job. The Governor

of Virginia said afterward that Robert E. Lee had "tendered the assault, in State pride, to the Virginia volunteers . . . his gallantry was mortified . . . he felt the regular army and his native State were alike, dishonored." The Governor would have "given my arm to its shoulder for that feat to have been performed by the Volunteers of Virginia before the Marines arrived there." Later the Militia Colonel said he called for twenty volunteers to storm the Engine House "but could not get a single man, from all the brave and bold from Martinsburg, Harper's Ferry, and Charlestown."

When the first gleams of light came to the morning sky, Shields Green, standing on guard at one of the firing loops, saw a man standing on a little elevation, intently studying the Engine House doors. Robert E. Lee was well within firing range as Green drew back the hammer of his Sharps gun. One shot and the future Commander-in Chief of the Confederate Armies would have gone down, but John Brown, at another embrasure, saw that this strange man was unarmed, and told Green not to shoot.

The Old Man, looking further about the Armory Yard, saw U.S. Marines, muskets at the ready, in every deep shadow, every corner and angle of the adjoining buildings. Brown immediately made preparations for resisting them. He pushed the little hand tub fire engine against the door and began to secure the doors with heavy ropes. He tied them a little loosely, so that the door would not have the rigidity of an immovable object but would give way at the stroke of a battering ram and then spring back. "Load your weapons," he ordered, and his men prepared their extra guns, laying them on handy resting places on the fire engine.

Brown saw the unarmed stranger in civilian dress move to a protected position behind one of the stone piers of the Armory fence and begin giving hand signals to the Marines. It was an elaborate plan of attack, in which Lee's principle agent was another man soon to be a Confederate General, J. E. B. Stuart. Lee provided a dubious sop to the pride of the Virginia Militia by having then "form around on the outside of the government property and clear the streets of all citizens and spectators, to prevent them from firing random shots, to the great danger of our Marines."

With a wave of his hand, Robert E. Lee sent Jeb Stuart marching with a flag of truce up to the door of the Engine House. "Hold your fire until orders," said the Old Man. He opened the door, placing his body so that it completely filled the crack. "He had a cocked carbine in his hand," Stuart recalled later, "hence his remark after his capture that he could have wiped me out like a mosquito. The parley was a long one. He presented his propositions in every possible shape, and with admirable tact, but all amounted to this: that the only condition upon which he would surrender was that he and his party be allowed to escape."

Stuart said that was out of the question; all he could do was to surrender and trust to the clemency of the U.S. Government. The Old Man replied he knew what that meant—"a rope for my men and myself. I prefer to die just here."

Stuart stepped quickly back from the door, took off his feathered hat, and waved it at Lee. The attack began, Twelve Marines ran swiftly to the Engine House door. Three had sledge hammers and began dealing powerful strokes at it. The door would spring back but, thanks to the Old Man's clever tying, would not let go. The men inside held their fire. Even Lewis Washington was compelled to admiration: the Old Man, he said, was "the coolest and firmest man I ever saw in defying danger and death. With one son dead at his side, and another shot through, he felt the pulse of his dying son with one hand and held his rifle with the other, and commanded his men with the utmost composure, encouraging them to be firm and sell their lives as dearly as they could." Brown's advice to his men was that affirmation of total resistance he had worked out long ago: "Stand by one another and your friends while a drop of blood remains. Be hanged if you must, but tell no tales out of school."

The hostages, to their surprise, were not used as human barricades but were told to take whatever cover they could. The officer actually leading the attack was a Lieutenant Green, also to become a high-ranking leader of the Confederate Armies. At first he was baffled at the door's resistance to the sledge hammers; then Lee sent up some men with a ladder which had been standing against one of the Armory buildings. At the second stroke from the

The Onslaught on the Men in the Engine House

ladder, the lower corner of the door broke off raggedly, and one of the hostages managed to roll back the wagon. Lieutenant Green, a small but exceedingly agile man, dashed through the low ragged hole in the door and jumped like a wildcat on the fire engine. "There is Osawatomie Brown," Colonel Washington shouted. "Now men, fire!" shouted the Old Man, and the two sides fired, muzzle to muzzle.

Brown was on his knees, still holding his thumb on Watson's failing pulse. Leaping about twelve feet from the fire engine, Lieutenant Green tried to bury his sword deep into Brown, hoping to kill him instantly and end the story then and there. The Old Man began to scramble to his feet, in excruciating pain; the Lieutenant's sword had been partially deflected by Brown's cartridge belt and was now bent out of shape. Lieutenant Green seized his sword at the middle of the blade and began, with an unnatural fury, to strike Brown over the head. The Old Man fell across Watson's body in a last embrace.

As the Marines, bayonets at the ready, followed their leader through the rathole in the door, Shields Green fired the last shot, killing Private Luke Quin instantly. He threw down his gun, stripped off his cartridge box, and went to stand by the slaves. The Marines bayoneted Dauphin Thompson under the fire engine, and one of them drove his weapon into Jere Anderson's body with such force that the blade stuck into the wall, leaving him impaled there, like a specimen butterfly. Swinging around in his death throes, his feet were higher than his head. A Marine made two short, vicious bayonet jabs in the Old Man's side, just below the rib cage, as he lay unconscious, apparently dead, over the body of his son.

The dead and wounded were carried out and laid on the bruised grass of the Armory Yard. The Virginia Militia and the spectators ran shrieking into the enclosure, while the Marines made a hollow square around the dead and dying liberators. Everyone was looking for Captain Brown, dead or alive. Before them was the wizened ancient figure of a man, his body drawn up in the fetal position of someone in massive pain. His thick hair was matted with blood, and his face, grimy and wet with the smoke from black powder, made him look like a half-squashed bug. The crowd, its hatred unsatisfied, wanted to rush forward and stomp

*John Brown Commanding the Resistance While Feeling the
Pulse of His Dying Son*

him to death. They began to move forward against the Marines, shouting, "Kill them, lynch them." The thin line of uniformed men swayed ominously. Then the hostages came out and a great cheer went up, echoing through the mountains.

There was a babble of voices as the crowd of over a thousand, filling the railroad trestle, then the square outside the Armory, began to press closer with irresistible energy. The brave young liberators were brought out and laid on the sorrowing grass at Brown's side. Oliver, dead; Watson, almost dead. Dauphin Thompson, dead, Jere Anderson, breathing his last. Stewart Taylor, dead, and Aaron Stevens, brought dying from the hotel. When they brought out the body of the young Marine, and his hat came off, and a shock of bright blond hair fell to the ground, there was a low groan and the lynch cry began again. Three of the hostages, seeing what was happening, began to walk to the crowd's now turbulent edges. John Daingerfield saw the leader of the lynch mob looking around for a way to break the hollow square of

*The Final Resistance of Shields Green After the Taking of
the Engine House*

Marines. "Old Brown should be killed here and now," the man said. "Look what he has done, to his own as well as ours."

"Leave him to heaven," said Daingerfield, placing a restraining hand on the man's arm. "He is dying. He won't last another hour!"

"Heaven will not have that buzzard," answered the man. "It will spew him forth. Let him live then, and we can see him hung, drawn, and quartered, and all the traitors that sent him here— Seward, Greeley, and all the black Republicans . . . and the nigger Douglass hung the highest of them all. We will let one of you hostages put the noose on Old Brown."

"I would not go to see him hanged," Daingerfield answered, bravely. "He made me a prisoner but he spared my life and that of the other gentlemen. When his sons were shot down beside him, almost any other man would have taken a life for a life. I look on him as a prisoner of war who has fought fairly."

9

The Carpetbag

When I transmitted to Captain Brown copies of all my correspondence with his friends, I never dreamed that the most terrible engine of destruction which he would carry with him in his campaign would be a carpetbag loaded with four hundred letters, to be turned against his friends, of whom the journals assert that more than forty-seven are already compromised.

Colonel Hugh Forbes
New York *Herald*

In the bright morning glare of October 18, John Brown's wounded body lay inert with exhaustion and shock on the Armory grass. Beyond the protective hollow square formed by the Marines, the citizens of Virginia waited in silence for the death rattle that would mean his expected end. But suddenly there was a stir of life as the Old Man stretched himself, straightened out his legs, and put his trembling hands behind his head.

Reporters dashed forward, notebooks in hand, from the New York *Times, Herald,* and *Tribune,* the Associated Press, the Baltimore and Richmond papers, and the Washington, D.C., papers. There were also artist-journalists from the big picture periodicals, *Leslie's Weekly* and *Harper's Weekly,* the *Life* and *Look* of their day. But the first man to reach the Old Man's side was John Rosengarten, a friend of Governor Wise, whose vivid impressions found their way later into the *Atlantic Monthly.* The Old Man's first words were, "Where is my son?—is he still alive?" Rosengarten told Brown Watson was still living and was being cared for, and was thanked in a gentle voice.

Rosengarten's account has a quality of exaltation:

> If his being likened to anything in history could have made the scene more solemn, it would have been to a roundhead Puri-

tan dying for his faith and silently glorying in the sacrifice not only of life, but of all that made life dearest to him. His wounded men showed in their patient endurance the influence of his example, while the vulgar herd of lookers-on, fair examples of the cowardly militiamen who had waited for the little force of regulars to achieve the capture of the engine house and its garrison, were ready to prove their further cowardice by maltreating the prisoners. The Marines, who alone had sacrificed life in the attack, were sturdily bent on guarding them from harsh handling.

Wounded, bleeding, haggard and defeated, and expecting death, John Brown was the finest specimen of a man that I ever saw. His great gaunt form, his noble head and face, his iron-gray hair and patriarchal beard, with the patient endurance of his own suffering and his painful anxiety for the fate of his sons and welfare of his men, his reticence when jeered at, his readiness to turn away wrath with a kind answer, his whole appearance and manner, all impressed me with the deepest sense of reverence.

The Old Man raised his head, looked out at the crowd, and sank back with a tiny smile on his sooty face. The reporters began their questioning:

"Are you Captain John Brown of Kansas?"

"I am sometimes called so."

"Are you Osawatomie Brown?"

"I tried to do my duty there."

"What was your present object?"

"To free the slaves from bondage."

"Were there other persons besides those with you, now, connected with the movement?"

"No. There was no one connected with the movement but those who came with me."

"Did you expect to kill people in order to carry your point?"

"No, I did not wish to do so, but you forced us to it."

Challenged by the reporters, the Old Man seemed to gain strength. His voice again took on the metallic clang that people who argued with him never forgot. Characteristically, and magnificently, he began to berate the Virginians, whose town he had captured, whose citizens he had killed, and whose slaves he had armed

against them. The reporters were stunned, amused, and a little ex-
alted by the moral strength of this dying old revolutionary. The
reporter from the New York *Tribune* wrote: "He seemed fully
convinced that he was badly treated and had a right to complain.
His conversation bore the impression that whatever he had done to
free slaves was right and that in the warfare in which he was engaged, he was entitled to be treated with all the respect of a prisoner
of war."

The Old Man propped himself painfully up on his elbows, and
looked scornfully about at the numbers necessary to capture him.
"I had the town at my mercy," he said. "I could have burnt it and
murdered all of the inhabitants. I treated my prisoners with every
courtesy and yet I was hunted down like a beast. My son was shot
down bearing a flag of truce . . ." He fell back again, fainting.

There was a sudden fusillade of shots from across the river near
Maryland Heights, and the Militia again ran for cover amidst great
shouting and confusion. Mr. Unseld, the Old Man's neighbor from
the road to the Kennedy farm, shouted excitedly that Cook, Tidd,
and the slaves they had taken with them were still barricaded in the
schoolhouse and getting ready to attack the Ferry in force. Unseld
was partly right; the fire was coming from the black man with the
shotgun and the slaves he had kept together.

Colonel Lee, realizing that the Militia would rather lynch his
prisoners than face the unknown dangers across the river, had the
Old Man and Stevens put into the Superintendent's office, under
heavy guard. Unseld tried to get a body of men to clear the insurgents out of the woods, and later gave an account of his efforts to
an Investigating Committee in Washington.

> I asked Captain Butler of the Hamtrack Guards. He said his
> company was dismissed. I said to another Captain, "Please go
> over to the schoolhouse, the danger is over there." He said, "I
> will go if John Avis will go," pointing to still another Captain.
> John said, "I will see about it directly," and walked away. I saw
> Colonel Baylor, Commander of the Virginia Militia. He said he
> had no right to send a company into Maryland. Said I, "The devil
> you have not. I would send them anywhere at a time like this."

He said he would not do it. I spoke to Robert E. Lee who said the Baltimore Grays had gone over. Said I, "They have not, they are still at breakfast." I met Captain Sinn of the Frederick Company. I said, "Let us take your men and go over and capture those fellows in the schoolhouse." "I cannot go now," he said. I was beginning to get a little out of humor. I met a member of the House of Representatives. He said, "Colonel Lee says they have gone a half an hour ago." I said, "They have not. They are all at breakfast." Colonel Lee then told me, "I will get you a company and they will go with you if you will pilot them."

Rosengarten recalled that "little squads of regulars were sent out on the Maryland Heights to search for the stores accumulated there; and each foraging party was followed by a tail of stragglers from all the volunteers on the ground, who valiantly walked to the Maryland side of the bridge that crossed the Potomac, and then stopped there and waited for the return of the regulars."

But with that final fusillade, all opposition had ended. At the approach of the Marines, the armed slaves gave up the struggle, buried their weapons, and disappeared into the protective mass of their brothers and sisters. Back at the plantations, they told their masters that they had acted under duress, and the latter preferred to work the punishment out of them than to let them loaf around in Charlestown jail. They appeared docile, but Lewis Washington and the other local slaveholders took the precaution of not sleeping at home for a week or two.

The Marines found the schoolhouse deserted and in disarray, with several boxes of rifles still unopened. In a ravine a little south of the schoolhouse they found Colonel Washington's wagon and three of his horses. Unseld harnessed them up, loaded the wagon with the material in the schoolhouse, and drove back to the Ferry. "On the instant of his arrival," Rosengarten recorded, "the ragtag and bobtail party set to work to help themselves to the nearest articles and were soon seen making off homeward with their contraband of war on their backs."

Twenty more Marines were put under the command of J. E. B. Stuart and sent over the bridge. They were reinforced by the soldiers at the schoolhouse and sent up the winding road to the Kennedy farm. When they reached the buildings, Stuart placed them in strategic positions from which to attack the last bastion of the invaders. Safe behind him were some of the braver members of the Baltimore Grays.

The last of Brown's men to be at the Kennedy farm were not Owen and his party but Osborn Anderson and Hazlett, who had left the arsenal building under the cover of darkness just after the Marines moved into position around the Engine House. They had hoped that they could rally the rear guard into making a counterattack across the bridge. They walked up the railroad track alongside the Shenandoah, crossed Harper's Ferry to the Virginia side, and found an old boat tied to a tree at the shore of the Potomac. They crossed the river in this and went up to the farmhouse, which they found ransacked and deserted. They trudged back down to the schoolhouse. There was no food there either, and no sign of their comrades. They slept the rest of the night in the woods of the ravine, to be awakened by the sound of firing. Hoping it was Owen Brown and the rear guard, trying to force their way into town for a rescue, they started along the ridge to join them.

Osborn reported: "When we got in sight of the Ferry, we saw the troops firing across the river with considerable spirit. Looking closely, we saw they were firing on a few of the colored men who had been armed the day before by our men and stationed at the schoolhouse. They were in the bushes at the edge of the mountains, dodging about, occasionally exposing themselves to the enemy. The troops crossed the bridge in pursuit of them but they retreated in several directions. Some of the troops went into the schoolhouse and took possession of it. Our last hope of shelter, or of meeting our companions, now being destroyed, we concluded to make our escape North."

The Marines, concealed on the periphery of the Kennedy farm, poured several rounds of fire into the building, but there were no shots fired in return. Stuart then gave the orders to take the building by storm; they entered, bayonets ready, but there was no one there. The floors were littered with papers and articles of clothing, and the fire still smoldered in the stove. As one of the newspapers reported: "The most valuable discovery was a trunk and a carpetbag belonging to Captain Brown, containing a great number of highly important papers, documents and plans and letters from private individuals throughout the Union, revealing the existence of an extensive and thoroughly organized conspiracy."

The carpetbag, the greatest prize of the attack, was carried back to the Ferry and put into the hands of Governor Wise. The latter immediately went into private conference with Andrew Hunter, whom he had already appointed as special prosecutor at the trial of the invaders. After a hasty examination of the bag's contents, Wise called in the press to announce that he had indisputable proof, "of a knowledge and instigation of the raid by prominent persons and party leaders in the North."

The reporters then demanded a full-scale interview with Captain Brown, but the Old Man had slipped into a sleep so deep that his guards took it for a coma. Governor Wise gave orders that if Brown showed any signs of coming out of it, he was to be informed, and the Old Man given an opportunity to make his deathbed confession.

10

Complicity

The whole scheme is said to have been formed in Boston.

By telegraph
from Harper's Ferry

Franklin Benjamin Sanborn, the F. B. S. of the letters found in incriminating abundance in the carpetbag, was twenty-eight years old and the teacher of a school organized by Emerson at Concord. He had graduated from Harvard and made a point of becoming acquainted with the literary celebrities of his time. Hawthorne, Whitman, Lowell, Longfellow, Ellery Channing—he knew them all and was particularly intimate with Thoreau, Emerson, and Alcott, seeing them almost every day. He had become very involved in the Kansas struggle and, during part of 1856 and 1857, had taken a leave of absence from his school to serve as Secretary of the Massachusetts State Kansas Committee. In this capacity he had become responsible for the handling of the thousands of dollars of funds for Kansas raised in Massachusetts. (Concord, a town of little more than 2,000 people, had contributed more than a thousand dollars for arms alone.) He had been to Kansas during the turmoil and prided himself that he had read every available account written about its affairs. He considered himself a thoroughgoing abolitionist and transcendentalist and, along with Alcott, was to found, years later, the Concord School of Philosophy.

Sanborn was at work on a lazy, Indian summer afternoon, putting the children of Emerson and other notables through their Latin drill when a neighbor came in with the Boston papers. A column of dispatches received by the American Telegraph Company, 31 State Street, in Boston, was arranged in chronological order.

Monday: Oct. 17: A dispatch just received from Fredericksburg and dated this morning states that an insurrection has broken out at Harper's Ferry where an armed band of abolitionists have full possession of the Government arsenal. The insurrectionists number about 200 whites and they are aided by a gang of Negroes.

Baltimore: A later dispatch says the affair at Harper's Ferry greatly exaggerated. There is no insurrection, only a difficulty among the employees at the Armory, with which the Negroes have nothing to do.

Baltimore, 3 P.M.: It is apprehended that the affair at Harper's Ferry is more serious than our citizens can believe. The wires are out. The Southern train, due this morning, has not yet arrived.

The Telegraph Repaired. The announcement that the telegraph has been repaired provided the press representatives with abundant employment. It brings news of strange portent. An actual insurrection is said to be raging in Virginia. We are told that general terror prevails in the vicinity and the alarm is spreading in all directions. In such time of agitation, the inherent weakness of a society in which large numbers are held in a state of servitude is revealed. The President, the Secretary of War and the Secretary of State were in conference all day. Soldiers left on the 3:30 train from Washington, D.C.

Harper's Ferry, midnight, Oct. 17: The insurgents have declined to surrender. One taken prisoner is quoted as saying that the whole movement consists of 17 whites and 5 blacks. All agreed to the movement, which is one of philanthropy.

Morning: Oct. 18: The Marines have fought their way through a broken door in an Engine House where the insurrectionists have been entrenched. Two of them have been killed. Osawatomie Brown, leader of the rioters, was mortally wounded.

Harper's Ferry, noon: The Government has succeeded in suppressing the rioters, whose chief is represented as the gallant Brown, who did such good service at Osawatomie and elsewhere in Kansas, protecting the Free State settlers· against lawless aggressors. Brown's statements reveal a plot for establishing a new government in the United States. Papers found on the person and in the valise of the determined firebrand, known as Old

Brown of Osawatomie to the whole country, confirm reports
that his scheme had advocates in the various states, and that a
Provisional Government was to be attempted. The whole scheme
was said to have been formed in Boston.

Reading these dispatches, Sanborn was overcome with shock. He
had never prepared his mind for the Old Man's defeat and death,
and the inevitable exposure of his friends and associates to the
ordeals of investigation, accusation, and trial, perhaps for treason.
It was known locally that he was Brown's principal confidant, and
his Concord friends, Thoreau, Emerson, and Alcott, were aware
that he was in regular communication with the old revolutionary.
It was the Old Man's custom to write a single letter to advance a
stage of the conspiracy. That letter would be sent to Sanborn, and
he would show it to Samuel Gridley Howe, Theodore Parker,
George Luther Stearns, Thomas W. Higginson, and Gerrit Smith
who had severally pledged to provide Brown with money and arms.
Of all the backers, however, Sanborn had been the only one asked
by the Old Man to join the actual coup; Brown wanted him to
conduct a school for the black boys and girls, freed under the Provisional Government and thirsty for knowledge. "I must remember
my old friend," Sanborn thought, "lonely, poor, persecuted, making
a stand with his handful of followers on the outpost of Freedom,
our own batteries trained upon him as the furious enemy swept him
away in the storm of vengeance."

He dismissed his class and went at once to Emerson's house and
found Bronson Alcott and Henry Thoreau also there, reading the
dispatches from the South and fully as overwrought as he was.
Sanborn had been unsure of his welcome there, having involved
them all in public support of John Brown for more than two years
and thus exposed them to the dangers·of guilt by association. But
the three philosophers were filled with a mixture of sadness and
exultation, and Alcott kept repeating, "I knew from the first that he
was the man for the deed." When Emerson gently asked whether
the deed was a disaster, even if the disaster of a saint, Alcott vigorously disagreed. "I defend the deed under all circumstances, and
the *Man*. If alive, he should be rescued. If he dies a martyr, he will

be of greater service to the country and to the coming in of righteous
rule than years of agitation by the press, or the voices of partisans,
North and South. It was a bold stroke for justice universal and it
damages all political parties beyond repair. Even the Republicans,"
he concluded with political perception, "must in some sense claim
him as theirs in self-defense and to justify Republicanism in the
people's eyes as Freedom's defenders." According to Sanborn's
account, Thoreau talked that day in almost the same words he later
put into his famous essay on John Brown: "The thought of that
man's position and fate is spoiling many a man's day here in the
North for other thinking. If anyone who has seen John Brown here
in Concord can pursue successfully any other train of thought, I do
not know what he is made of. I am so absorbed in him as to be
surprised whenever I see the routine of the natural world surviving
still, or meet people going about their affairs, indifferent."

Sanborn said he was going to see his lawyer.

He went to Boston to see John Albion Andrew, a dedicated antislavery member of the Massachusetts Legislature, who had been
prominent in defending the would-be rescuers of two fugitive slaves,
Thomas Sims and Anthony Burns. Andrew also felt a complicity
with the Old Man, having given him twenty-five dollars before he
went to the Ferry. George L. Stearns, equally active in the conspiracy with Sanborn, went to Andrew's office with him. The latter
accurately assessed the direction of the inevitable government attack
on Brown's supporters. He told Sanborn and Stearns that evidence
was being accumulated, much of it, according to a later telegraph
dispatch, from "bushels of letters found at Brown's headquarters,"
to determine whether the invasion and seizure of the arsenal were
made by a bona fide revolutionary organization intending to overthrow the government of any state, and where the money was
raised, how the arms were obtained, who paid for them and arranged to have them transported to the base in Maryland.

This would make Sanborn and Stearns the country's most wanted
men, if the truth were known. Almost every dollar raised for the
Old Man had passed through Sanborn's hands, and George Stearns
had paid for the rifles and revolvers out of his own pocket. Sanborn

John Brown in His Kansas Days

was not ready to confess everything to a lawyer, in advance of any necessity for it, but Emerson, in his elliptical way, advised him to "state your liabilities, if any exist, to a counselor, on the contingency that there be something not known, or probable to the U.S. power."

Sanborn felt that the real liability in his case was his knowledge of how weak the movement really was, how few its informed partisans, and how devastating these facts would be in the hands of the press and the politicians who were now so obligingly blowing up Brown's thrifty little coup into an irrepressible conflict between the whole North and the whole South. He decided that he should not reveal to the lawyer the "full particulars of our complicity with Brown," but Andrew, who was to be chairman of the state Republican delegation to the National Convention only a few months away, was a shrewd questioner and very anxious to discover how deeply Brown's plot had penetrated the Republican hierarchy.

Sanborn had a huge packet of letters with him which he had hastily gathered and wanted to destroy, but the lawyer cautioned him that some of them could be helpful in establishing favorable evidence if he ever came to trial. They began to sort them out in order, and Sanborn started to tell them story of how he became involved in history.

He had been sitting in his office on School Street in Boston and had looked up to see a gaunt, erect man standing there with a face from which all traces of softness and accommodation had been burned away. The man said his name was John Brown and presented a letter of introduction from Sanborn's brother-in-law. Sanborn was impressed by such modesty, since Brown was known to him, and in fact to the whole coterie of Boston militants since his opposition to the ignoble peace at the first siege of Lawrence by the Border Ruffians.

The Old Man then ceremoniously presented another letter, an endorsement from Robinson of the Free State Party, with a flattering addition from Governor Chase. Sanborn indicated that such references were totally unnecessary in his case, and Brown dropped his carpetbag to the floor with a thud. Sanborn stooped politely to move the bag out of Brown's way and found it very difficult to lift. The Old Man opened it, revealing a long length of trace chain, and explained that it had manacled his son, John Jr., in Kansas as he was dragged on bleeding feet for miles over a dried-up riverbed by a mounted U.S. Dragoon. "This treatment," the Old Man said drily, pointing to the rusted blood still on the chain, "made my son a maniac, yes, a maniac."

Brown immediately put before Sanborn his written plan to arm and equip a party of one hundred men to continue the fighting in Kansas and occasionally carry the war into Missouri. He had

arrived at a very opportune time. The Massachusetts State Kansas
Committee was in vigorous disagreement with the National Kansas
Committee's plans to have a complete demilitarization of its forces
in Kansas and to depend fully upon the National Administration's
promises to keep the peace. The guns sequestered and rusting in
Tabor were, it was rumored, to be sold to liquidate outstanding
debts. Sanborn's first question to the Old Man was about the two
hundred Sharps rifles bought by the Massachusetts Committee and
turned over to the National Committee for shipment. They were
now missing somewhere between Chicago and Kansas and the
Committee members were quite disturbed. Brown told him that the
guns were now at Tabor. Sanborn asked if there were any possibility
of getting them into the hands of the Kansas settlers. The Old
Man answered tartly. "The immediate introduction of the supplies
is not of much consequence, compared to the danger of losing
them." He went on to describe how the last northern wagon train
had been stopped six miles over the border and every box, trunk,
and valise broken open in a search for arms. Ten Sharps rifles and
two dozen revolvers were confiscated and the men conducting the
train were marched off to appear before the Governor. "They were
warned that this might happen," Brown said, "Yet they traveled
without a defense organization. They had their teams strung out
over the prairie for a distance of three or four miles. Nearly all the
men were without arms and walking helplessly by the side of the
teams. They were, as I was informed by one of the good citizens of
Tabor, relying on their rights as American citizens, instead of keeping their powder dry."

Sanborn became excited about these revelations and asked the
Old Man to accompany him to the nearby office of George Stearns,
the Chairman of the Massachusetts Committee. They met him
coming up School Street and immediately launched into conversation. Stearns was a slight, rather strange-looking man with a black
beard that came to the middle of his chest. Sanborn asked the Old
Man to repeat to Stearns what he had just told him about the guns.
Stearns exploded angrily that he was fed up with the National Committee's idea "that everything that was passed to them for their
transportation became their property the moment it passed into

their hands." A successful businessman, a dealer in lead, who was used to playing hunches, Stearns said to the Old Man, there in the streets of Boston, on a cold January afternoon: "Captain, I would like to have you as our agent. Otherwise these guns will be entirely lost to us, and Kansas as well. I would like to put them entirely in your hands, to have you proceed there and reclaim them and take proper care of them."

Stearns went on to say that his offer would be made official by a vote of the Committee and he would ask them for an appropriation of five hundred dollars to pay the Old Man's expenses. Sanborn, delighted at the turn of events, told the Old Man that Thoreau wanted to meet him and brought him to Concord for a visit. Because of it, Thoreau was later able to write about Brown with intimacy, quoting him directly, and assessing him as "a transcendentalist above all, a man of ideas and principles." Emerson, equally impressed, invited him to his own house to spend the night. Sanborn made it clear to his lawyer that he had taken Brown to Concord to have him speak with the wisest judges of character he knew and that the Old Man had emerged from their questionings as the greatest man either of them had ever met.

A few days later, Stearns explained to Brown that over two hundred fifty thousand dollars had been contributed toward a free Kansas by the northern Republicans, at least one hundred thousand of which had been contributed by Massachusetts alone. All the arms sent there had been bought and paid for by the Massachusetts Committee, while domestic supplies had been handled by the National Committee. Stearns went into his money raising methods, which the Old Man had listened to with marked attention: "We would go into a town, announce a lecture, organize a committee in that town for subscriptions, and in the course of one week, go to every house in the town, every individual would be approached and asked to give any sum—five or ten cents, a dollar, or whatever he chose." Andrew asked Stearns if it was known that some of this money was going for the purchase of arms. The latter shrugged. "I don't think the question was ever asked. If it had been, I think the response would have been quite as large for arms as it would have been for other purposes." As for large donations from members of Congress or

prominent men in the Party, Stearns explained, "We did not go
about it in that way. Instead of getting money as you would in a
political contest, we went to the lower class of people. Our de-
pendence was on the laborers, the mechanics, the farmers, and such
persons."

Andrew then asked if the name John Brown had ever come up
during these collections. Stearns gave a very positive yes to this. "I
find that most of my customers, plumbers, tinsmiths, and workmen
of that order have a great admiration for John Brown." But had
Brown been questioned about what he was planning to do with
the guns? "He told me," said Stearns, "that it was the worst possible
policy for a man to reveal his plans. I recollect his taking several
scraps of paper from his pocket and saying, 'The United States
government immediately disclose their orders to their military officers. Before the orders leave Washington, they are published all
throughout the papers. Well, now, that is not the way; if a man is to
do anything, he must keep his plans to himself.' "

Going over his papers, Sanborn had found the document linking
the laborers, the mechanics, farmers, tinsmiths, and plumbers of
Massachusetts to the guns of Harper's Ferry:

> Boston, January 8, 1857
>
> Dear Sir:
>
> Enclosed we hand you our order for two hundred Sharps rifled
> carbines, with four thousand ball cartridges, as we suppose, now
> stored at Tabor, in the State of Iowa. We wish you to take
> possession of this property, either at Tabor or wherever it may be
> found, as our agent, and hold it subject to our order.
>
> George Stearns,
> Chairman of Massachusetts State Kansas Committee

"Testimony of this matter," the lawyer commented, "could in-
volve nearly every man in Massachusetts, I suppose." "If that is
true," Sanborn said, "there is a similar document, issued by the
National Kansas Committee, involving men in every Free State in
the Union." He produced a copy and laid it before the lawyer:

> Resolved, That such arms and supplies as the committee may
> have, and which may be needed by Captain Brown, are appro-

priated to his use, *provided* that the arms and supplies be not more than enough for one hundred men. Any person having property covered by the above resolution is requested to deliver the same to Mr. John Brown or his agent.

H. B. Hurd, Secretary National Kansas Committee

Andrew said that this did not prove that any of these people knew about Harper's Ferry, but they must have had some knowledge of Brown's intentions as a practical abolitionist, aiding the slaves by force, even at the risk of an armed encounter. None of the men involved in these arrangements should testify anywhere. Sanborn explained to Andrew that he had accompanied Brown to a meeting of the National Committee in New York on January 24; the Old Man had addressed the meeting and asked for the Tabor supplies to arm a hundred mounted volunteers in Kansas. There was heavy opposition, led by H. B. Hurd, the Chairman of the National Committee, who accused him of ultraviolence. "If you get the arms and money you desire, will you invade Missouri, or any slave territory?" he demanded. The Old Man's answer was characteristic. "I am no adventurer; you all know me; you are acquainted with history, you know what I have done in Kansas. I do not expose my plans, nobody knows them but myself, except, perhaps, one. I do not wish to be interrogated. If you wish to give me anything, I want you to give it freely. I have no other purpose but to serve the cause of liberty."

Brown's request was first voted down, and he angrily left the meeting, shouting that he was going to take his request "to the people." However, the next day, on the arrival of some of the more radical members, the resolutions were taken up again, and he not only got arms but an appropriation of $5,000, and the custody of the two hundred Sharps rifles was voted back to the Massachusetts Committee. It was on the strength of this that the Old Man sought out and engaged Colonel Forbes, who assumed that his employer had access to some of the richest men in the North.

At that moment, it seemed as if the Old Man, as the embodiment of northern militancy in Kansas, was about to win over the entire tier of Free States. When he got back to Boston, George Stearns initiated a bill in the Massachusetts Legislature to appropriate one hundred thousand dollars "to help make Kansas Free." He also began to send letters to other states advocating the same measure.

> To organize a secret force, well armed, and under the control of the famous John Brown, to repel Border Ruffians' outrage and defend the Free-State men from all alleged impositions. This organization is strictly to be a defensive one. I am personally acquainted with Captain Brown and have great confidence in his courage, prudence and good judgment. He has control of the whole affair, including contributions of arms, clothing, etc., to the amount of 13 thousand dollars. His presence in the Territory will give the Free-State men confidence in their cause, and also check the disposition of the Border Ruffians to impose on them. Many of the Free-State leaders being engaged in speculation are willing to accept peace on any terms. Brown and his friends will hold to the original principle of making Kansas Free, without regard to private interests.

Stearns, of course, did not know that the Old Man's private interest was to switch the whole Kansas campaign into black revolution, or that every time he mentioned arming settlers, he really meant slaves, free blacks, or "practical abolitionists."

Appearing before a large audience at the Massachusetts State House, Brown taunted the legislators, saying the Ruffians told him "the Yankees could not be coaxed, driven or whipped into a fight, and that one Southerner could whip a dozen abolitionists; they intended to drive out the whole Free-State population of Kansas. . . ."

The appropriation was turned down because of the financial panic of 1857, and the Old Man then gave a series of speeches trying to raise money in little towns and hamlets in western Massachusetts and Connecticut. It was then that, without informing his Boston friends, he ordered the thousand pikes, which he was to bring with him to the Ferry and which would have not been useful at all in Kansas. His campaign for funds from "the people" was cut short by a letter from his son Jason, saying that a U.S. Marshal with a murder warrant against Osawatomie Brown had just been looking for him in Cleveland. Sanborn took the Old Man to the home of a Boston judge, Thomas B. Russell, for concealment.

Brown informed the Russell family that he would not be taken alive, and that he "Should hate to spoil your carpet."

To explain his disappearance from the scene, he dispatched a fascinating letter to some of his supporters. "One of the U.S. hounds is on my track and I have kept myself hid for a few days to let my track get cold. I have no idea of being taken and intend to go back with irons *in,* rather than *upon* my hands." To make up for the loss of his money-raising capacity, Stearns bought him two hundred revolvers and paid for them out of his own pocket, but in the name of the Kansas Committee.

About the first of May Brown started back to Kansas, by way of Iowa. He had now taken the name of Nelson Hawkins, to throw the marshals off his track. Through a series of shrewd letters to Sanborn and Stearns, he managed to keep the rifles given him from ever getting to Kansas and to prepare the minds of his supporters for the acceptance of their transfer to his plan of attacking slavery head-on in Virginia. The letters spoke of sickness and ague, of teams breaking down and horses going lame. From time to time the men in Boston would receive a disquieting hint that the Old Man was up to something very different from the operation for which they had armed and financed him: a "Scotch Captain" was to come out and train his men in "the arts of peace." In one letter he revealed, as if by a casual afterthought, his purchase of the pikes, "a cheap but effectual weapon to place in the hands of entirely unskillful and unpracticed men, which will not easily get out of order and require no ammunition." Another declared that "I intend to put the supplies I have in a safe, secure place and then to put myself and such as go with me where we may get more speedy communication."

All that fall Stearns and the Kansas Committee got despairing letters from men in Kansas asking for the arms, or at least the appearance of the Old Man, who was putting them off with pleas of sickness, lack of transport, and other excuses. His Boston supporters could not understand the delays, but since winter was coming on and there had been no Missouri invasions, they began to feel that perhaps the Old Man had already done his work in Kansas and there was a real peace there.

Such illusions were shattered by a series of letters from Colonel Forbes, the first sent to Senator Charles Sumner, and others to Sanborn and Howe. Forbes said he had been severely criticized by the Old Man for his delay in arriving, and although promised a year's work at one hundred dollars a month, he received only six hundred dollars. Forbes bluntly revealed in one letter that the Old Man's real plan was to "make a dash at the Harper's Ferry arms manufactory." The letters were so personally abusive and so centered on demands for money that they irritated the Boston men more than they alarmed them, although it seemed that there indeed had been an agreement between Forbes and Brown. At first Forbes sent copies of the letters to the Old Man, who did not seem very disturbed by them, or by the fact that his Boston backers were getting some insight into his true intentions. Those whom Forbes informed were the very men of power in the Republican Party whom Brown would have liked to approach but didn't quite dare, for fear of betrayal. Having the matter put this way meant he could deny everything if things came to a dangerous crisis. Meanwhile, he was tremendously heartened by the fact that nobody did put the question to him, and he never had to deny it.

Brown now started to move the guns at Tabor to the east, to Ohio, where they were kept until just before the foray at the Ferry. He made one trip into Kansas, without bringing the weapons they were calling for, and recruited men for the raid. He told them—at one time, he had thirteen recruits—only that they were going to a school for guerrilla warfare somewhere in Iowa.

The mystery was finally cleared up, at least for Sanborn, when he got a letter from the Old Man, saying, "I am again out of Kansas and am at this time concealing my whereabouts; but for different reasons from those I had for doing so at Boston last spring. I have nearly perfected arrangements for carrying out an important measure in which the world has a deep interest, as well as Kansas, and only lack from five to eight hundred dollars to enable me to do so. It is my only errand here, and I cannot explain without my friends first committing themselves more than I know of them doing. Do you not know of some other parties whom you could induce to give their abolition theories a more practical shape?"

Brown sent almost identical letters to Theodore Parker, Stearns, and Thomas Wentworth Higginson. Sanborn and Stearns urged him to come to Boston, offering to pay expenses. He replied that he was "keeping quiet," as it was understood that "I am hiding somewhere in the Territory," but would they all come and consult with him at the home of Gerrit Smith, in Peterboro, New York? Smith's secretary, Edwin Morton, was a classmate of Sanborn's at Harvard, and Sanborn wrote him to see if he could throw some light on the matter. Morton answered that "Brown expects to overthrow slavery in a large part of the country. He is staying with Frederick Douglass." Sanborn had already surmised by the complaints and insinuations of Forbes that the Old Man had some plan for an uprising of slaves. He agreed to meet Brown and went there on February 22, 1858, alone, but with an agreement with Parker, Higginson, and Stearns that they were willing to discuss the matter later in strictest confidence.

Gerrit Smith, who was sixty-one years old, was the son of John Jacob Astor's partner and one of the richest men in America. He had been giving one thousand dollars a month to the Kansas fund, and at his death it was said that he had given away over eight million dollars to a variety of philanthropic causes. He was a freethinker, opposed to all organized sects, an abolitionist and nominally a pacifist, being president of the American Peace Society. Smith had been a Congressman, supported women's rights, and had given large tracts of land in the Adirondacks to blacks for them to colonize and develop as their own property.

When Sanborn got to Peterboro, he found that whatever Brown's plan was, Smith was going to back it all the way. There was a sumptuous dinner, during which Brown showed himself, as Thoreau later wrote admiringly, "scrupulous about his diet at your table, excusing himself by saying that he must eat sparingly and fare hard, as became one who was fitting himself for difficult enterprises, a life of exposure." Later, he wept quietly in the parlor while Mr. Morton played Schubert's "Serenade" on the piano; afterward, Sanborn, Smith, Morton, and the Old Man went to a small room in the attic, where, Sanborn said, "the whole outline of Brown's campaign in Virginia was laid before our little council to the astonishment, and almost the dismay, of those present." Brown showed them the constitution he had drawn up with the help of Frederick Douglass, gave the middle of May, 1858, as the time for the attack, and asked for only eight hundred dollars, saying he would consider himself rich with a thousand. He wanted their candid opinion of the proposal but freely declared that he had no consciousness of guilt about withholding the guns from the Kansas Wars. "I got tired of hearing about the sympathy and cooperation the white Kansas emigrants deserved from their friends back east. If such men were deserving of sympathy and ought to be supplied with arms, are not the crushed and bleeding slaves of the South a million times more deserving of their help? I have always felt this, but I did not state it and every time I asked for arms and supplies for the Kansas settlers, I said slaves in my heart."

This was the only time his voice broke from the calm cadence he adopted while outlining his most desperate moves, except when the question was asked: was he not "forcibly freeing the slaves, without asking their own choice in the matter?" "I am not forcing men to be free," he said. "I will bring arms to them, give them their choice, stand behind them so as to protect them in a free choice. If they choose to stay in slavery, let them, but if they choose to go out, sustain them in it."

The Old Man overcame all their arguments and literally wore them down. He had made all his arrangements, he had the guns and the men, all he wanted now was the money. What first seemed the height of madness gradually began to appeal to Sanborn's imagination. It was obvious that Brown didn't really care if they agreed with him; they must either stand by him or leave him to go it alone. The next day was spent in meditation; about sunset, Smith and Sanborn went for a walk. "You see how it is," Smith finally said, "our dear friend has made up his mind to this course and cannot be turned from it. We cannot give him up to die alone; we must support him. I will raise so many hundred dollars for him; you must lay the case before your friends in Massachusetts and ask them to do as much. I see no other way."

Sanborn made no promises but told Brown before leaving that he would speak to the other men. The choice of these other men

reveals the Old Man's uncanny capacity, with the notable exception of Forbes, to pick supporters of extraordinary quality. All
agreed, all contributed, none of them betrayed him. Theodore
Parker, forty-seven years old, most celebrated of the collaborators,
whose grandfather "fired the shot heard round the world" at Lexington, was considered at the time the greatest intellect in the
country, delivering intensely political sermons to from two to three
thousand persons every Sunday and lecturing during the week, far
and wide. A preacher, vying with Henry Ward Beecher for the top
honors in the country in this profession, he was America's profound-
est theologian. A daring abolitionist, he had been arrested and tried
for violently attempting to rescue the slave Anthony Burns. Higginson, a younger preacher and writer, had also been involved in
the Burns case, was wounded during an attack on the Boston
Courthouse, and later became the first colonel of a regiment of free
slaves in the Civil War. Dr. Howe, aged fifty-six, had been, as a
young man, chief surgeon of the Greek fleet in the Greek Revolution; later he was imprisoned in Germany for aiding Polish revolutionaries. Howe founded Perkins Institute, the great school for
the blind, initiated the use of raised type in teaching them to read,
was the first to educate a blind, deaf, and dumb person, Laura Bridg-
man, and pioneered in finding a social use and acceptance for idiotic
and feeble-minded children. His wife, Julia Ward Howe, is perhaps
even more famous. When one realizes that Brown revealed his
Virginia Plan to six men of this stature, let them argue every possible objection, and still won them over, it is hard to understand
those commentators who want to dismiss him as a fanatic or well-
meaning visionary. Long after the event, Dr. Howe insisted "that
the plan had been a very able one, and that its failure could not
have been a foregone conclusion."

Coming back from Peterboro, Sanborn experienced some doubts
—or perhaps simply fears—but they were swept away by a new
letter from the Old Man:

My dear Friend, Mr. Morton has taken the liberty of saying to
me that you felt half inclined to make a common cause with me.
I greatly rejoice in this: for I believe when you come to look

at the ample field I labor in, and the rich harvest which not only this entire country but the whole world during the present and future generations may reap from its successful cultivation, you may feel that you are entirely out of your element until you find you are in it, an entire unit. God has honored but comparatively a very small part of mankind with any possible chance for such mighty and soul-satisfying rewards. . . . I expect nothing but to endure hardness, but I expect to effect a mighty conquest, even though it be like the last victory of Samson. I felt for a number of years, in earlier life, a steady, strong desire to die; but since I saw any prospect of becoming a "reaper" in the great harvest, I have not only felt quite willing to live, but have enjoyed life much; and am now rather anxious to live for a few years more.

Sanborn read this letter aloud, becoming rather tearful at the end. Laying it carefully aside, as one piece of evidence that would never be destroyed, he held out his hands in appeal. "What could we do? We saw this lonely, ailing, and harassed old man, chosing poverty before wealth, renouncing the ties of affection, throwing away his ease, his reputation, and his life for a despised race and his country's ancient liberties. We were shamed by this example. . . . We did not question too much the reasonability of the Virginia Plan, we accepted it because it was his."

"It's not a question of its reasonability," said Andrew, with unprofessional frankness. "Whether the enterprise in Virginia was right or wrong, wise or foolish, I only know that John Brown himself is right. I sympathize with the man and I sympathize with the idea. I believe that there is an irresistible conflict between freedom and slavery and that he had a right to call on you, or me, or anyone else that professes to believe in the rights of man."

Sanborn said he had talked to Higginson and Dr. Howe, Brown having instructed him to leave Stearns for himself. Both were enthusiastic. "Had there been an insurrection every year since the French Revolution," Higginson declared, "I believe slavery would have been abolished long ago. The masters could not have plotted so much ahead had they been kept busy at home. The northern people would have been forced back on the fundamental question of liberty, instead of the partial and superficial aspect of the matter on which our politicians have dwelt. A single insurrection with decent temporary success would do more than anything else to explode our present political platforms."

Doctor Howe, however, took serious objection to the word "insurrection." The Abolitionists shrank from the spectacle of a blood bath in the South and were still dominated by a pacifist, nonviolent ideology, of which Garrison was the great advocate. The question had been raised earlier by Gerrit Smith, and Brown had answered it by reading his Provisional Constitution, but Sanborn took the time to explain it more fully: "He did not wish to begin with a great force, but with one that could be easily handled; he did not expect the slaves to come to him in great numbers, nor did he wish it, for he wanted no more followers than he could easily arm and discipline. . . . All this was to be governed by his constitution for the government of the territory he could wrest from slavery and into the control of his own little band." Dr. Howe and the others were satisfied by this explanation that the Old Man was opposed to promoting insurrection among the slaves and to shedding human blood except in self-defense. This gave Howe the assurance he needed to solicit funds for Brown, apart from their use in Kansas.

On March 4, 1858, Brown had come to Boston, taken a room at the American House, and met with Parker, Howe, Sanborn, Stearns, and Higginson. The Virginia Plan was fully discussed, the Provisional Constitution gone over, and general agreement reached. All this time, the conspirators were aware that Forbes knew of the plans and was threatening to expose them unless he was put in command, but there was something in their lofty, obtuse, Yankee minds that made them discount the threatenings of anyone so crass about money and so disgustingly unprincipled. Dr. Howe said, "I do not heed much Captain Forbes's information because it seems to me ill-natured and spiteful."

From Boston the Old Man had gone to Philadelphia to talk to Henry Highland Garnet, Stephen Smith, and other black militants. He conferred with William Still, the country's greatest authority on fugitive escape routes, on ways to get into, as well as out of, slave country. He instructed his son John to go about "hunting up every person and family of the reliable kind about, at, or near Bedford, Chambersburg, Gettysburg, and Carlisle in Pennsylvania, and also Hagerstown and vicinity, Maryland, and Harper's Ferry, Va." He had thus pinpointed the area of the attack to everyone in on his general plan. Having received a thousand dollars from the Secret Six, as his support committee was now called, Brown moved his men from Iowa to Canada and organized a convention at Chatham, Canada, in the midst of thirty or forty thousand escaped fugitives.

There on May 8, the Old Man carried out his convention with all the style and aplomb of the founding fathers in Philadelphia. A black minister, William Charles Monroe, presided, and there were thirty-four black delegates. The only white men present were those recruited by Brown for active service. Present were Dr. Martin Delaney, who became the highest-ranking black soldier in the Civil War, James H. Harris, later a Congressman from South Carolina, Richard Richardson (whom Brown had rescued in Kansas), I. D. Shadd, S. Hunton, James M. Bell, Osborn Anderson, Alfred Whipper, Isaac Holden, and other distinguished black intellectuals, editors, poets, and schoolteachers. During the discussion the only point of conflict came over Article 46, the key to Brown's coup! "The foregoing articles shall not be construed so as in any way to encourage the overthrow of any state government . . . or of the General Government, but simply to amendment and repeal. And our Flag shall be the same that our Fathers fought under in the Revolution."

Some of the black delegates objected violently to fighting under a flag under which they had been lashed and whose soldiers had fought under it to crush their pitiful little rebellions, but the Old Man stood firm. "Brown said the Old Flag was good enough for him; under it freedom had been won from the tyrants of the old world for white men, now he intended to make it do duty for black men. That settled the question."

Finally it was laid on the table for signature, an American Constitution at last which was a government for all the people. One of the delegates said, "This is treason and the first man who puts his name to it commits treason against his government. But when they got ready to sign every man was anxious to have his name at the head. Mine went on as seventh." The plan was to go directly into the slave country from there, back down the tortuous routes most of these black men had taken out of their land of bondage. There never was a revolutionary conspiracy with a background of more "decent respect for the opinions of mankind." The Old Man ordered copies of the Provisional Constitution to be printed in bulk and made his final plans to start the guns down from Ohio to a base to be established in Maryland.

Then, before the ink was dry on the new-printed copies, the Old Man heard from George Stearns. "You will recollect that you have the custody of the arms . . . to be used for the defense of Kansas, as agent of the Massachusetts State Kansas Committee. In consequence of information communicated to me, it becomes my duty to warn you not to use them for any other purpose and to hold them subject to order as Chairman of said Committee."

Enclosed with this absolutely crushing letter was a copy of one to Dr. Howe from Senator Henry Wilson of Massachusetts. As Stearns began to relate this, Andrew was again impressed with how Brown's "conspiracy" had penetrated the highest levels of the Republican Party, since he knew Wilson as one of its shrewdest and most devious leaders. The letter spoke for itself:

Dear Sir:

I write you to say that you had better talk to some of our friends who contributed money to aid old Brown to organize and arm some force in Kansas for defense, about the policy of getting those arms out of his hands. If they should be used for other purposes, as rumor says they may be, it might be of disadvantage to the men who were induced to contribute to that very foolish movement. If it can be done, get the arms out of his control and keep clear of him, at least for the present. This is in confidence.

Henry Wilson

The next day the Old Man got another letter, telling him to come to Boston for a conference. It was obvious the whole operation had to be called off and his men dispersed. He was forced to inform them that "owing to the panic on the part of *some* of our eastern friends, we may be compelled to hold on for months yet. *But what of that?*" Not only were his men expected to stand by under orders for the next call, but they were expected to support themselves during that time.

Sanborn was frank about this crisis in speaking to Andrew. "Wilson as well as Hale and Seward, and God knows how many more, had heard about the plot from Forbes. To go on in the face of this was madness." Sanborn conceded he had been greatly concerned; since the arms were officially the property of the Massachusetts State Kansas Committee, "it would expose the entire Committee, which comprised some of the richest and most important men in the state, to suspicions, if the arms were used by him in any expedition to Virginia." Arriving in Boston, Brown argued vigorously against postponement: "The knowledge that Forbes could give of his plans would be injurious, for he wished his opponents to underrate him, but still the increased terror produced would perhaps counterbalance this. If he had the means given him, even now, he would not lose a day."

Nevertheless, the Old Man conceded to Sanborn afterward it was essential that they should not think him reckless. He was powerless without them, having spent every available dollar setting up his convention. But they were not men of action and had been too easily intimidated by Wilson's letter.

Sanborn then showed him Forbes's letter to Dr. Howe, in which his exact plan of movement was traced out. "He even knows what very few do, that the Doctor, Smith, and myself are informed of it." Brown recognized deep personal anxieties in the support committee, and he appeared to acquiesce in a suggestion that the plan to be put off for another year.

Arriving the next day, however, Higginson warned, "If we give it up now, at the command of Forbes, it will be the same next year. The only way is to circumvent the man somehow. When the thing is well started, who cares what he says. A decent temporary success would do more than anything else to explode our present political platforms. Any betrayal afterward would only increase the panic which is one element in our speculation. If I had the wherewithal, I would buy out the other stockholders and tell the old veteran to go on . . ."

This vigorous support brought about a compromise: Stearns

would claim ownership of the arms as back payment of the money advanced by him to the Committee, and the Old Man would retain them and go off to Kansas, to throw Forbes off the scent. In a year they would support a reactivation of the plan, but "Brown should not tell us his plans in detail, we being willing to trust him with our money and wishing for no report of progress save by action."

The Old Man went back to Kansas, and along with some of his guerrillas, fortified himself on a troublesome section of the Kansas-Missouri border. He called himself Shubel Morgan, and his presence quickly became known, even to the Missouri slaves. One named Jim Daniels was on a farm where the master had died, and the estate was about to be broken up, he, his wife, and his children were to be sold apart. Daniels made up a bundle of brooms and begged the caretaker to let him go a short distance away to sell them. Encountering Gill, one of Brown's men patrolling the border, Daniels asked to be taken to see John Brown. Gill told Daniels to get the other slaves on the farm together and to prepare themselves for a quick liberation. The next night, John Brown rode into Missouri with a dozen men; eight others, under the command of his lieutenant, Aaron Stevens, went on a similar errand to another slave plantation.

At midnight, Brown and his men rode into the farm where Jim Daniels was enslaved, and told the caretaker that all the slaves, and all the property they had earned by their sweat and toil, were to be carried off. The man's personal property would not be molested, but the slaves had created most of the farm property and were entitled to it, for justice sake, and for their necessities. The farm manager was honest, and the slaves got their share: a yoke of oxen, two horses, and a huge old Conestoga wagon, loaded with all the things they felt they could rightly claim as earned.

This was done without snapping a gun. Farther down the road they liberated five more slaves. Unfortunately, the other party of liberators had only been able to free one slave, and Stevens had been forced to shoot the owner, who had drawn a gun.

John Brown armed the liberated slaves and told them to fight against being recaptured. But when he heard that conservative Free State men were angry at him for stirring up trouble, and were threatening to hand him over to the Missourians, he knew he had to get out of Kansas altogether. Delay was unavoidable when Jim Daniels's wife gave birth to a baby, named John Brown Daniels; it meant that the caravan could not move north for a few days.

Finally, late in January, Brown and Gill left with the eleven freed blacks, so suddenly made twelve. Every night of this perilous journey they had to be taken in, fed, and concealed. Many Free State families risked their lives in this, and the party had to travel through blizzards and freezing cold. Brown sold the oxen in Lawrence, Kansas, got another team of horses and a lighter wagon, and shepherded his precious freight across the bleak prairies, while the wind whipped the snow against their faces like icy sand. The Missouri Governor offered $3,000 and the U.S. Government, $250, for his capture, which meant that posses of greedy men would be lying in wait for him across every river and on the other side of every hill. But the Old Man pressed on indomitably, and as a joke, offered $2.50 for the President's head and then withdrew it, saying he was afraid his boys would go out and collect it.

John Brown had no winter clothes and hardly any money. Every bite of food, every bed and blanket had to be planned for ahead, and in enemy country. Only those with a true revolutionary morality could be trusted to take them in; sometimes they stayed in Indians' houses. At one point they came to a stream too high for the teams to ford. They waited a day, and the water froze over. The ice would support a man and one horse but not the wagon. They had to take the wagons apart and carry them over a piece at a time. Then they felled trees and covered them with brush to get the horses over.

One of the most affecting stories about the Old Man came out of this journey, told by a man named Jacob Willetts. "I lived on a farm a short distance from Topeka at the time Brown was last in Kansas. He wanted me to go into town on business for him. I came down with him that night to cross the river, and on the way he told me he had some colored people with him, who were in need, and asked me if I could do anything to help them. They had no shoes and but little to eat. I went among the houses and into several stores and got a number of pairs of shoes and some little money for the good cause. As we were going down to the river, I noticed Brown shivering and that his legs trembled a good deal. I suspected something, and as I sat beside him on my horse I reached down and felt of his pantaloons, and found they were of cotton, thin and suited to summer, not to the cold weather we had then. I asked him, 'Mr. Brown, have you no drawers?' He said he had not. 'Well,' I said, 'there is no time to go to the store now, but I have on a pair that were new today, and if you will take them you can have them and welcome.' After a few words he agreed to it. We got down beside the wagon; I took the drawers off and he put them on."

At a place called Holton, where another stream was made unfordable by high water coming downstream in torrents, eighty Border Ruffians lined up to halt Brown's company at this time which numbered twenty-two people, black and white. Advised to change his route, the Old Man proved stubborn: "I have set out on this route and I intend to travel it straight through and I will cross just here. Those afraid can turn back." But it was the Ruffians who panicked when Brown came down the grade to the creek, erect and dauntless, firing his guns and heading into them as if they could be scattered like dust. They left behind four horses, as well as some pistols and guns, helping to make Brown's party an even more dangerous objective for would-be captors.

After eluding two or three more posses, Brown entered Tabor, believing that he was at last in the clear. But the taking of slaves, cattle, and household goods, all private property, unsettled the townspeople, who looked on him as a horse thief, and because Stevens had shot a slaveowner, a murderer. They were afraid of southern reprisals and passed a resolution, saying, "We have no sympathy with those who go into slave states to entice away slaves and take property or lives when necessary to that end."

They did not dare do anything about their disapproval, but Brown knew now that even on Free soil he was in danger. However, when they reached Grinnell, Iowa, the man who founded the town welcomed the party with open arms, fed them well, raised money for them, and had prayers of thanksgiving offered for their safe delivery.

From then on, things went better. When they got to the town of Liberty where the railroad line began, a boxcar had been left, as if by accident, on a siding, and Brown, his party, and their redeemed property, got in, and the car was mysteriously hooked up between the engine and the express car of the next Chicago-bound train. After the fugitives were taken off and hidden safely in Chicago, Brown went on to Detroit to meet Frederick Douglass, who helped the liberated slaves on the last lap of their journey to Canada.

With a handful of brave guerrillas, the Old Man had freed eleven slaves and brought them eleven hundred miles over the western prairies in the dead of winter. Although there was a price on his head and enemies on every side, at no time did he show guilt or fear or act toward the freed slaves other than as a loving father or friend. Samuel Harper, one of the slaves, said afterward, "He was a very quiet man, awful quiet. He never even laughed. After we was free we was wild, of course, and we used to cut up all kinds of foolishness. But the Captain would always look solemn as a graveyard. Sometimes he just let out the tiniest bit of a smile and say, 'You'd better quit your foolin' and take to your book.' "

When the liberal press reported some of the more dramatic stages of the Old Man's desperate journey, the Secret Six began to stir with mingled fear and anticipation. Sanborn was not surprised to hear from Gerrit Smith that Brown had appeared at his home in April, quietly insisting on the fulfillment of the promise that his Virginia campaign be reactivated in a year's time. "Someone asked him if he not better apply himself in another direction and reminded him of his imminent peril, and that his life could not be spared. His replies were swift and most impressively tremendous. I was once doubtful in my own mind as to Captain Brown's course. I now approve it heartily, having given my mind to it more of late. He says he will not be trifled with and shall hold Boston to their word."

On Saturday, May 7, 1859, the Old Man appeared at the door of Sanborn's house in Concord, accompanied by Jere Anderson as his bodyguard. He was suffering from a malaria attack and had just been to his home at North Elba to recruit three of his sons, his daughter Annie, and two neighbor boys, William and Dauphin Thompson. Brown greeted Sanborn with affection but somewhat distantly; Sanborn felt that a shared greatness had been lost when the Secret Six had agreed the year before that "Brown should not tell us of his plans in detail, we being willing to trust him with our money and wishing for no report of progress save by action." This position had been worked out by Gerrit Smith, the least firm of the conspirators, but they all were aware of what Brown planned to do.

Sanborn had visited the little farmhouse at North Elba the previous year, aiding a project in which some of Brown's supporters bought the farm for his numerous family, since it was obvious that the Old Man was determined to give his life for his cause. He had been touched by the fact that Brown's three young daughters, Annie, fifteen, Sarah, twelve, and Ellen, only four, spoke confidently of their father's love and attention toward them, despite his almost continual absence. His wife, Mary, equally secure in her husband's affection. They had married when she was only fifteen, after he had lost his first wife; Mary, who was sixteen years younger than he was, had borne him thirteen children.

Sanborn thought of that frail, unpainted, unplastered little house, naked to the wintry Adirondack blasts, with the towering walls of snow-heavy mountains ringing it in. There was only one little road leading in, "so straight you could sight a U.S. Marshal for five miles." How could the Old Man have come back to make the demand he did? There was no oath to redeem, no curse to fulfill; there was only an old gravestone he had retrieved from vandalism in a Connecticut cemetery. On it was the name of Captain John Brown, his grandfather, who had died in the first Revolution, and under that, newly carved, the name of his son, Frederick, killed by slavery in Kansas. There was another monument resting there in a level field, a huge boulder, rounded but rough on its surface, monstrously inert, giving no feeling that it was split off from any other rock, or that it was a fission or fragment. Unique and indestructible, it stands there today, with the Old Man's name carved into it.

Sanborn had tried to comfort the family, touched by the loneliness and poverty of their lives. The children were quick to defend their father and explain that he was on some high and holy mission. Ruth, his oldest daughter, told Sanborn of how the Old Man had come home the last time, and his little girl had not known him. He told her "he had a little black lamb that had fallen into ditch and he could not come home until he had got it out." Then he had taken the child into his arms and sung "Blow Ye the Trumpet, Blow," and she still remembered it. Ruth told Sanborn her father was up every morning at three, working frantically to set things to right before he went away again. He had soothed the whole family with his lesson that "if any man not love his brother whom he hath seen, how can he love God whom he hath not seen?" Ruth told Sanborn the story of how she was washing one day when her father came in with a lamb in his arms. He threw out her washing and plunged the lamb into the hot, soapy water, and it came to life and frolicked about. It was plain that his daughters loved him.

When the Old Man arrived at Concord in May, Sanborn had the embarrassing job of telling him that no efforts had been made to raise money for him during his year's absence in Kansas. Parker had gone off to die in Italy, and Higginson was now saying that the whole scheme had begun "to seem to me rather chimerical." However, Gerrit Smith, overwhelmed by Brown's cross-country rescue of the slaves, promised him a thousand dollars, with no questions asked, and Stearns came forward with twelve hundred dollars. Nevertheless, raising money was difficult with the depression of 1857 still in effect, and the Old Man was forced to speak to small meetings, wherever they could be arranged, picking up nickels and dimes. He made no bones about his seizure of the slaves and the horses and made his political position clear. "Since 1855, it has been my deliberate judgment that the most ready and effectual way to retrieve this country would be to meddle directly with the peculiar system. Next, we have no way of supporting the rescued blacks without taking from the slaveholders a portion of their lawfully acquired earnings."

Andrew shook his head sadly during Sanborn's description of the Old Man's last days in Boston. He had met him at a friend's house around that time, and recalled the magnetism of Brown's personality: "I felt ashamed, after I had seen the old man and talked to him, that I had never contributed directly toward his assistance, as one who had sacrificed and suffered so much for the cause." Andrew had sent him twenty-five dollars.

Sanborn brought his account to a close with the admission that he, Stearns, and Garrit Smith had provided the Old Man with money up to within a few days of the attack, and Andrew gave his professional opinion: "If a man joins in a conspiracy to levy war, and war is, afterwards, in fact, levied, and he performs any act, which in the case of a felony, would render himself an accessory, he thereby renders himself a principle to the treason, since, in treason, all that are guilty at all are principles. Thus—if he gives arms, ammunition, horses or what not, to aid the war, pursuant to the conspiracy, such acts, when the war has been actually levied, will doubtless be deemed *overt acts* of treason, in themselves . . . but the parties committing them can only be tried in the district where they were committed."

Sanborn asked Andrew if they were liable to be arrested, and Andrew said that depended on the evidence against them. "If I were you, I would destroy every document or scrap of paper linking old Brown with you, or with the Kansas Committee. He cannot be known as having these relations without giving color to the charge that Republicans cooperated in his movement. If the government can establish through Brown's admissions or by papers found in his possession that arms were given him by the Massachusetts Kansas Committee or the National Kansas Committee there is no telling where the accusations of complicity might end."

"Then what are we to do?" asked Sanborn.

"I can't tell you what to do," said Andrew, "but I am afraid that you might be suddenly and secretly arrested and hurried out of the protection of Massachusetts law."

11

The
Press
Conference

Read his admirable answers to Mason and others. How they are dwarfed and defeated by the contrast! On the one side, half-brutish, half-timid questioning; On the other, truth, clear as lightning, crashing into their obscene temples. . . . And the New York *Herald* reports the conversation *verbatim!* It does not know of what undying words it is made the vehicle.

H. D. Thoreau
A Plea for John Brown

Word came in the afternoon that the Old Man was awake and could talk. A cortege of dignitaries, who had hurried from Washington and Ohio to join the Governor of Virginia, laid aside their excited reading of the carpetbag papers and gathered in the watch-house to hear Brown's last words. A whole covey of reporters followed Colonel Robert E. Lee, who was in charge of the ceremony and courteously informed the Old Man some men wanted to talk with him, but that he could refuse if he chose. Brown said no, he wanted to talk and was very anxious to convey to the country his purpose at the Ferry. "I will tell the whole truth," he said, "I have nothing to hide."

The great dignitaries came, almost tiptoeing into the room, hoping they would have the chance to raise their own particular questions before he expired. Looking down at the iron eyes of the Old Man, however, they suddenly felt like someone confronting a great bull, whose malevolent force was only lightly contained. The Old Man braced himself for an ordeal as critical as anything he had just gone through: the interview was to last more than three hours.

Standing about him, black-coated and hatted, frightened yet eager to peck at him, the dignitaries waited for the Governor to start the questioning. With him was Senator James Mason, author of the inflammatory Fugitive Slave Bill; A. R. Boteler, the Congress-

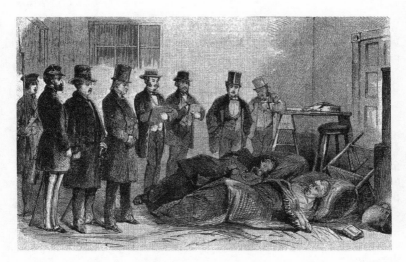

Governor Wise, Senator Mason, Congressman Vallandigham,
Colonel Robert E. Lee, and reporters interview John Brown

man from the Harper's Ferry district; Andrew Hunter, who was to
be Brown's prosecutor in the trial ahead; and Lewis Washington, his
late captive. They hoped to extract from a dying man a deathbed
confession that would incriminate the northern liberal politicians.

Some members of the Militia crowded in the doorway just behind them. "Ain't the ole turkey buzzard dead yet?" one asked,
provoking a raucous laugh. These men had been rewarded in the
general looting of Brown's effects with brand-new Sharps rifles. Seeing the anger on the Old Man's face as he noticed these roustabouts
with his precious guns, another Militiaman waved his rifle defiantly
at him. A third shouted, "Why listen to him, gentlemen? He is
nothing but a common robber and outlaw."

The Old Man bared his teeth at this. "You call me a robber," he
said, "standing there with a valuable gun you have filched from a
dying man. You Militiamen are worse than robbers; you steal the
property of a widow and her orphans—besides, you steal men . . ."

This outburst, so unexpected from the feeble, aged prisoner,
seemed to the Governor an insult to the honor of Virginia. He stepped
solemnly forward, raising his hand in a righteous rebuke. "Mr. Brown,

the silver of your hair is reddened by the blood of crime, and it is meet that you should eschew these hard allusions and think upon eternity."

The Old Man fixed his glittering eyes, like twin gunsights, on the Governor, and replied in a slow, dead-level but penetrating voice:

"Governor, I have from all appearances not more than fifteen or twenty years the start of you to that eternity of which you kindly warn me. And whether my tenure here shall be fifteen months or fifteen days, or fifteen *hours,* I am equally prepared to go. There is an eternity behind, and an eternity before, and the little speck in the center, however long, is but comparatively a minute. The difference between your tenure and mine is trifling, and I want, therefore, to tell *you* to be prepared. I *am* prepared. You slaveholders have a heavy responsibility, and it behooves *you* to prepare more than it does me."

The Governor, stunned by the philosophical power of this retort, turned suddenly to disruptive Militiamen standing at the back of the room, and ordered them out. He shut the office door and decided to avoid any further contests in homiletics with the Old Man.

Senator Mason, who lived in nearby Winchester, and was profoundly moved by the perils of a liberation movement, stepped forward to replace the Governor. Mason, a noted infighter in Congressional debates, with a talent for badgering and breaking down other senators in argument, began his questioning in a high, imperious voice.

"Can you tell us, at least, who furnished the money for your expedition?"

The Old Man looked back at him with the hint of a cold smile in his eyes. He answered calmly, almost affably, "I furnished most of it myself. I cannot implicate others. It is by my own folly that I have been taken. I could easily have saved myself from it had I exerted my own better judgment rather than yielded to my feelings."

Mason said, "You mean if you had escaped immediately?"

"No, I had the means to make myself secure without any escape, but I allowed myself to be surrounded by a force by being too tardy."

Caught up in the drama of the battle, Mason abandoned the censorious tone with which he had begun. "Tardy in getting away?"

The Old Man shook his head slightly. "I should have gone away, but I had thirty odd prisoners whose wives and daughters were in tears for their safety and I felt for them. Besides, I wanted to allay the fears of those who believed we came here to burn and kill. For this reason I allowed the train to cross the bridge, and gave them full liberty to pass on. I did it only to spare the feelings of those passengers and their families and to allay the apprehension that you had got in your vicinity a band of men who had no regard for life and property nor any feeling for humanity."

Mason became unshakably convinced that Brown represented a full-scale northern conspiracy. The man he was questioning could not answer with such assurance unless he had thousands, if not millions, of followers. Remembering what he had read of Brown's record in Congressional reports, he could not maintain his attitude of anger but spoke with the barely suppressed fear of one who has to know everything about his adversary in order to defend himself.

"But you killed some people passing along the streets quietly," he continued.

"Well, sir," said the Old Man, confidently, "if there was anything of that kind done, it was without my knowledge. Your own citizens, who were my prisoners, will tell you that every possible means were taken to prevent it. I did not allow my men to fire, or even to return any fire, when there was danger of killing those we regarded as innocent persons, if I could help it. They will tell you that we allowed ourselves to be fired at repeatedly and did not return."

A Militiaman at the back of the room who had been allowed to remain when the Governor had cleared out the troublemakers, shouted out, "That ain't so. You killed an unarmed man at the water tank and another besides."

"See here, my friend," the Old Man answered testily, "it is useless to dispute or contradict the report of your own neighbors who were my prisoners."

Senator Mason intervened in a soothing tone: "If you would tell us who sent you here—who provided the means—that would be information of some value."

Brown's steady eyes flashed with disbelief that the Senator would be so naïve. "I will answer freely and faithfully about what concerns *myself.* I will answer anything I can with honor, but not about others."

There was a bustling in the room as Clement L. Vallandigham, a Democratic Congressman from Ohio, came in. A man who called all abolitionists traitors, he had come across the name of his greatest political rival, Joshua Giddings, while going through Brown's carpetbag. Seeing his reelection guaranteed by what he conceived of as a plot almost totally the work of Ohio abolitionists, he came at the Old Man with a roar, "Mr. Brown, who sent you here?"

The Old Man again bared his teeth but spoke slowly and deliberately. "No man sent me here. It was my own prompting and that of my Maker, or of the devil, whichever you wish to ascribe it to. I acknowledge no master in human form."

"Did you get up this expedition yourself?" Vallandigham continued, a little more calmly.

"I did."

"Did you get up this document which is called a constitution?" Vallandigham asked, waving a sheaf of papers.

"I did," the Old Man replied firmly. "That is a constitution and ordinance of my own contriving and getting up."

"How long have you been engaged in this business?"

"From the breaking out of the difficulties in Kansas. Four of my sons had gone there to settle, and they induced me to go. I did not go there to settle, but because of the difficulties . . ."

Again there flashed into Senator Mason's mind fearful recollections of Black Jack, Osawatomie, and worst of all, Pottawatomie. Strangely subdued, he returned to his primary concern: "How many are engaged with you in this movement? I ask these questions for our own safety!"

The Old Man's answer took on an acid, rebuking quality. "Any questions that I can honorably answer I will, not otherwise. So far as I am, myself, concerned, I have told everything truthfully. I value my word, *sir.*"

There was a rather long pause among the interrogators. The interview was turning out to be dismayingly different from the successful fishing expedition anticipated. The Senator shifted his line of questioning, his voice heavy with deference and respect. "What was your object, sir, in coming?"

"We came here to free the slaves and only that."

The Militiaman at the back pushed his way forward. "How many men in all had you?"

The Old Man paused a moment, licking his lips. "I came to Virginia with eighteen men only, besides myself."

A groan of mortification escaped the Governor, standing in the back of the room. The Senator shook his head and looked at the uniformed Militiaman. The latter, flushing deeply, exclaimed, "What in the world did you suppose you could do here, in Virginia, with that amount of men?"

With only the slightest hint of a grin, Brown looked at him and then around the room at the dignitaries, the representatives of the U.S. Army, and the dozen or more reporters. "Young man," he said simply, "I don't wish to discuss that question here."

The Militiaman broke in hotly, "You could not do anything."

"Well, perhaps your ideas and mine on military subjects differ materially," said the Old Man, wryly, and Mason impatiently waved the Militiaman to the back of the room. The Senator took a more imposing stance, opened a new line of inquiry. "Now, sir, how do you justify your acts?"

The Old Man, matching the Senator's gravity with his own, answered with quiet dignity. "I think, my friend, you are guilty of a great wrong against God and humanity—I say it without wishing to be offensive—and that it would be perfectly right in anyone to interfere with you so far as to free those you wickedly and willfully hold in bondage. I do not say that insultingly."

"I understand that," said the Senator meekly.

"I think I did right," Brown went on, his voice full and strong with the assurance of a deacon in church. "And that others will do right who interfere with you at any time and at all times. I hold that the Golden Rule, 'Do unto others as you would that others should do unto you,' applies to all who would help others to gain their liberty."

Lieutenant J. E. B. Stuart, who was present as Lee's assistant, felt compelled to interrupt. An ardent churchgoer who knew every passage that could be used to justifiy slavery, Stuart exclaimed, "But you don't believe in the Bible."

"Certainly I do," said the Old Man quickly.

Congressman Vallandigham, unwilling to have the interview degenerate into a theological discussion, lunged in with his own obsession: "Where did your men come from? Did some of them come from Ohio?"

Brown answered coolly that some did and maintained his courtesy during a long interrogation exclusively on Ohio matters, skillfully fending off the Congressman without seeming to be denying anything. Senator Mason tried to refocus the dialogue on the higher issues. Seizing the Provisional Constitution out of Vallandigham's hands, he asked, "Did you consider this a military organization in this Constitution? I have not yet read it."

"I did in some sense. I wish you would give that paper close attention."

"You considered yourself the Commander in Chief of these Provisional military forces?" the Senator continued, more and more certain that the Old Man was a true revolutionary, with as considered a position as that which had inspired his own Virginia forebears.

"I was chosen agreeably to the ordinance of a certain document, Commander in Chief of that force."

"What wages did you offer?" asked the Senator.

"None," said the Old Man proudly.

J. E. B. Stuart, who had been meditating gloomily on the vast disparity between the biblical interpretations of a revolutionary Calvinist and a keeper of the status quo, said solemnly, "The wages of sin is death."

The Old Man shook his head sadly at the young man's brashness. "I would not have made such a remark to you if you had been a prisoner and wounded in my hands."

The Senator impatiently waved Stuart away, but had to endure another round of Vallandigham's pettifogging questions on Ohio: did the Old Man go to Dayton; where and how long did he live in the state; did he know another Brown, a noted counterfeiter there?

Mason finally broke in rudely, "Mr. Brown, does this talking annoy you?"

"Not in the least," the Old Man answered, determined not to show weakness, guilt, or impatience. He had answered Vallandigham meticulously, knowing the slightest misstep would bring disaster to himself and his followers still living, and to those who might have escaped. So far, his performance had been faultless but he was afraid Vallandigham would cause him to lose his temper and say what he should not say. He looked around for someone else to put a question, he caught the eye of the Militiaman at the back, who dutifully put another question.

"Did you go out to Kansas under the auspices of the Emigrant Aid Society?"

"No, sir. I went out under the auspices of John Brown and nobody else."

There was a half-suppressed murmur of admiration from the onlookers. The reporters were already won over, and the man from the New York *Herald* was straining every nerve to put down the exact wording of the dialogue, sensing that some great drama was being acted out. Annoyed at the crowd's growing sympathy for the Old Man, Vallandigham demanded roughly, "Did you talk with Joshua Giddings about your expedition here?"

"No, I won't answer that," Brown snapped back, struggling to contain an angry outburst. "Because a denial of it I would not make, and to make any affirmation of it I should be a great dunce."

There was a snicker among the reporters, and Vallandigham was forced to shift ground. "Have you had any correspondence with parties in the North on the subject of this movement?"

"I have had correspondence," Brown answered wearily, and the reporters snickered again. The Old Man began to search out another questioning face, to ask, mutely, for an interruption from Vallandigham's nagging. A young man standing at the back, beginning to understand the quality and commitment of the prisoner, asked the question Brown had been waiting for: "Do you consider this a religious movement?"

The Old Man's answer came from his depths. "It is, in my opinion, the greatest service a man can render to God."

"Upon what religious principle do you justify these acts?" the young man demanded, his voice breaking slightly.

"Upon the Golden Rule. That is why I am here. Not to gratify any personal animosity, revenge, or vindictiveness. It is my sympathy with the oppressed and the wronged—that are as good as you—and as precious in the sight of God."

"Certainly, certainly," said the young man. He sighed as if he wanted to believe in the Old Man, in spite of his southern training. But it was still hard to approve of anyone's tampering with slaves: "Why did you take the slaves against their will?"

"I did not, sir."

"You did in one instance, at least."

The concern and doubt in the young man's voice got to Aaron Stevens, who had been listening carefully, even though his eyes were closed. Suddenly he interrupted, in a high, clear boyish voice. "He is right, Captain. In one instance the Negro wanted to go back."

"Where did you come from?" demanded Vallandigham, reactivated at the sight of fresh prey.

"I lived in Ashtabula County, Ohio," answered Stevens.

Vallandigham began to hustle again. "How far did you live from Jefferson?"

Jefferson was where Joshua Giddings lived. The Old Man warned Stevens, "Be cautious, Aaron, about any answers that would commit any friend. I would not answer that." Stevens turned away with a heavy groan, and said nothing more. Vallandigham went on with his questions about Ohio until someone in the back of the room called out wearily, "Did you ever live in Washington City?"

"I did not," said the Old Man. He realized that everything of value to him had now been said, and he wanted to sum things up. He turned to look at the reporters, recognizable by their notebooks and their scribbling. "I want you to understand, gentlemen, and I want you to report that I respect the rights of the poorest and weakest of colored people, oppressed by the slave system, just as much as I do those of the most wealthy and powerful. That is the idea that has moved me, and that alone. We expect no reward, except the satisfaction of doing for those in distress and greatly oppressed, as we would be done by. The cry of distress of the oppressed is my reason, and the only thing that prompted me to come here."

He hoped that this would wind things up and the questioners would go away. He had not been examined yet by a doctor. His side was paining him badly, and there was a constant ringing in his ears which made it necessary to listen very hard to catch the meaning of the questions being fired at him. But the men standing around did not want the scene to end; they stayed, like someone coming in from the cold hangs about a fire, postponing the trials of dealing with the storm outside. "Why did you do it secretly?" someone finally asked, as if that was the real extent of the Old Man's crime and that everything else had been explained away.

"Because I thought that necessary to success; no other reason."

A reporter wanted to know if he had read a letter in the *Herald* by Gerrit Smith, one of his supporters, predicting the next movement for the slaves' emancipation would be an insurrection in the South.

"I have not read the *Herald* for some days now," said the Old Man, as if he were discussing the matter in a gentlemen's club. This was an area of discussion not yet covered and he wanted his sentiments to show on the record. "I agree with Mr. Smith that moral suasion is hopeless. I don't think the people of the South will ever consider the subject of slavery in its true light until some other argument is resorted to than moral suasion."

Vallandigham demanded to know if he expected "a general uprising of the slaves in case of your success."

"No, sir. And I did not wish it. I expected them to gather from time to time and set themselves free."

Vallandigham began another dreary round of questions, and this went on until the *Herald* reporter intervened. "I do not wish to annoy you, but if you have anything further you would like to say, I will report it."

The Old Man girded his fading strength for a summary; his voice was becoming shaky, and he was tiring fast. His first words showed how near to the end of his resistance he was getting. "I do not know that I ought to reveal my plans. I am here a prisoner and wounded because I foolishly allowed myself to be so . . ."

His voice trailed off, and the reporter came in closer, squatting down by his side, but after a minute or two of silence, the Old Man's voice again rang out like a clarion. "I have nothing to say, only that

I claim to be here carrying out a measure I believe perfectly justifiable and not to act the part of an incendiary or ruffian, but to aid those suffering great wrong. I wish to say, furthermore, that you had better . . . all you people at the South . . . prepare yourselves for a settlement of that question that must come up much sooner than you are prepared for. The sooner you are prepared, the better. You may dispose of me very easily; I am nearly disposed of now. But this question is still to be settled . . . this Negro Question, I mean . . . the end of that is not yet."

He stopped a moment; there was utter silence in the room. Even Vallandigham stood with his head bowed and his hands folded. Aware that the onlookers were taking note of the wounds on his head and in his side, Brown widened his attack: "These wounds were inflicted on me—both saber cuts on my head and bayonet stabs in different parts of my body—some minutes after I had ceased fighting and had consented to a surrender, for the benefit of others, not for my own."

This was clearly inaccurate, the first error the Old Man had made during the three hours of the interview, and struck a raw nerve in Lieutenant Stuart. "No, no," he shouted. "You did not surrender at any time. You ignored our offers."

"Tut, tut," Brown said, glaring at Stuart. "I believe the Major [Stuart] would not have been alive if I had not supposed he came to the door only to receive our surrender. I could have killed him just as easy as a mosquito. There had been long and loud calls of surrender from us—but in the confusion I suppose we were not heard. I do not think the Major, or anyone, meant to butcher us after we had surrendered."

"You should have surrendered long before," someone said. "If only out of consideration for your prisoners."

Brown shook his head. "I could not believe that these people here would wantonly sacrifice their own fellow citizens. We thought they would be a guarantee of our own safety. We did kill some men in defending ourselves, but fired at no one not in arms against us."

Here in summary was Brown's unshakable position: no aggression, simply self-defense against the oppressor and his power to enslave. The interview having come to its natural conclusion, there was a movement toward the door. One Militiaman, as he was leaving, called out, half in admiration, half in fear, "Brown, suppose you had every nigger in the United States, what would you do with them?"

"Set them free."

"Carry them off and free them?"

"Not at all. Free them here. The slaves should have this land, everything on it, the fruit of their labors."

Departures were arrested. An elderly man, dressed as a clergyman, announced in a deeply measured voice, "To set them free would sacrifice the life of every white man in this community."

"I don't think so!" shouted the Old Man.

"I know it, I know it," the elderly man insisted without rancor. "I think you are fanatical."

"And I think you are fanatical," Brown retorted. " 'Whom the Gods destroy they first make mad.' And you are mad!"

Colonel Lee began gently to push people out. This was the first direct exchange of insults, and he did not want any more trouble. But there was still a further question, seemingly as an anticlimax but revealing that the property question remained the core of the whole struggle between the sections, the states, and slavery versus free soil parties. "You say your object was to free the slaves and yet you tried to take Colonel Washington's watch and silver . . ."

The Old Man refused to offer the slightest tinge of apology. "Yes, we intended freely to appropriate the property of the slaveholders to carry out our object—but with no design to plunder."

He began to cough, groaned, and clasped his wounded side. Governor Wise made his way forward, and waved people out, signifying that the interview was over. "I will see that a doctor comes," he assured Brown, "and that you will have some refreshment."

As Lee stepped to the Governor's side, the Old Man had a question: "How many bodies did you take from the Engine House?"

"Three," Lee said.

"Then they are not both dead. There were three dead bodies there last night. Gentlemen, my boy Watson is living and in your power. I will ask for him what I would not ask for myself. Let him have kind treatment . . . he is a good son."

Governor Wise looked at Lee and then bent down to tell the intrepid father that Watson had died at three o'clock.

The Old Man closed his eyes and fell silent; only the guard of marines remained in the office, and Brown soon was deeply asleep.

At dark a burial party gathered up the mutilated and defiled bodies of the dead liberators, throwing them into an unmarked hole on the bank of the Shenandoah. In what they intended as a final act of defilement, the undertakers wrapped Oliver Brown in the arms of Dangerfield Newby and buried both bodies in this grisly embrace. If they had known John Brown's son, Oliver, they would have realized that he would have considered this the crowning accolade of his martyrdom.

The Burial of the Dead Revolutionaries in a Common Grave
at Midnight

12

The Trial

For more than thirty hours the Old Man and Aaron Stevens lay blood-soaked, unwashed, and on exhibition to their conquerors, on the floor of the Superintendent's office. The riotous gun-firing and drunken revelry went on constantly in the streets outside, and at the expense of the Old Man, himself. The gunpowder being shot off was from his Sharps rifles and revolvers, and most of the liquor was supplied by the selling and swapping off of the loot from the schoolhouse and the Farm.

There were only three other survivors of the raid in custody—Shields Green, John Copeland, and Edwin Coppoc—who were confined in the guardhouse. A young reporter from South Carolina wandered in and was very touched by the suffering of Watson Brown in his last hours of life:

> I improvised a couch for him out of a bench, with a pair of overalls for a pillow. I remember how he looked, singularly handsome, even through the grime of his all-day struggle, and the intense suffering which he must have endured. He was very calm, and of a tone and look very gentle. The look with which he searched my heart I can never forget. One sentence of our conversation will give you the very keynote of the whole. I asked him, "What brought you here?" He replied, very patiently, "Duty, sir." After a pause I again asked, "Is it then your idea of duty to shoot men down on their own hearth-stones for defending their rights?" He answered, "I am dying. I cannot discuss the question. I did my duty as I saw it."

Governor Wise, struggling with the task of bringing order back to Harper's Ferry and the state of Virginia, was closeted for a long time with Andrew Hunter, the lawyer who had been present during much of the event. Hunter had been formerly the chief legal counsel for the Baltimore and Ohio Railroad and was far more talented than the usual southern county prosecutor, whose sole legal obligation was to satisfy the neighbors who had elected him. The official Jefferson County prosecutor was a man named Charles D. Harding whose least failing was to fall asleep in court and snore loudly. He was quite capable of falling to the floor, intoxicated, while conducting an argument.

The strength displayed by the Old Man in defending his actions in front of the reporters had convinced the Governor that he had to be handled with great skill, avoiding both cruelty and callousness, which would only rebound to his advantage. Hunter, appointed Special Prosecutor with the entire conduct of the trial under his direction, agreed with Governor Wise, "that this John Brown raid was not the insignificant thing which it appeared to be before the public, but that it really and truly was the incipient movement of the great conflict between the North and South and that it evidently resulted in the war."

Hunter strongly advised the Governor to move Brown and the other prisoners immediately to the jail in Charlestown, since by then it was obvious the Old Man was not conveniently going to die from his wounds. Harper's Ferry was indefensible, and "there were a large number of Brown's followers and emissaries lurking in the angle of the mountain between the river and the mountain road ready to march down." He was convinced that the seizure of the arms held at the schoolhouse was the only factor preventing a rescue, and there was no time to lose before other arms were provided from unknown revolutionaries.

"We will send them up tonight in the Winchester cars," the Governor said. "You have Rowan's Company of the Militia to protect them from the depot to the jail."

Hunter disagreed. "That company will massacre every one of them before they reach the jail. Don't send the prisoners unless you go with them with a party of Colonel Lee's marines."

When the five o'clock train was ready to depart for Charlestown, a hollow square of marines was formed outside the office. Stevens and the Old Man were carried to a wagon. The other men were put inside the protective hollow square, while cries of "Lynch them, kill them" filled the air. The Governor stood valiantly at their side, trying to cool the crowd. Stevens was laid on the floor of the car; the Old Man was propped upright on a seat with some pillows from the hotel. There was further consternation when Brown asked that Shields Green be placed in the seat opposite him as a "member of Congress under the Provisional Government."

Governor Wise, irresistibly fascinated with his revolutionary captive, sat beside the Old Man, hoping to continue the questioning. He began graciously with the remark that Colonel Washington had described Brown as the "gamest man he ever saw," but Brown tartly commented that he was not flattered to be compared to a participant in a cock fight.

The Governor was meditating on what he would have to report on his return to Richmond. He very much wanted some "inside" information to show that he was now in control of the event, and knew more than the obiquitous reporters. The Old Man's remark that Shields Green was a Member of Congress had so upset Prosecutor Hunter that he told the Governor that if he had Brown as his client he would immediately offer a plea of insanity. Hunter advised the Governor to question the Old Man as closely as possible to see if such a defense would stand up. Certainly the Old Man's conduct during the interview had been lucid, but wanting ignorant slaves to take high positions in the government suggested a craziness which might allow the prisoner to cheat the gallows.

The Governor accordingly attempted to sooth the Old Man, saying how sorry he was to see someone of his age and station of life in a position like this. Brown, however, said he asked for no sympathy and had no apologies to make. "It is all my own fault that I was taken. I deserve to die for my bad generalship."

"There is a rumor abroad," said the Governor, "that someone had betrayed you to the Secretary of War. Do you think this is true?"

"Yes," said the Old Man, "and that is why I practiced that ruse to prevent suspicion."

"What ruse was that?" asked the Governor quickly, thinking at last that he had caught Brown in a damaging statement.

The Old Man glared back at him coldly, not answering. Then he said, "Governor, I know exactly in what position I have placed myself and I am prepared to suffer the consequences."

"Could you tell me who gave you the idea of taking over the Harper's Ferry arsenal?"

"Yes, I can do that." The Governor leaned forward eagerly. "It was you, Governor," the Old Man went on. "I read of a speech you had made in '56 at the time of the Presidential canvass in which you said if Fremont was elected Virginia would forcibly leave the Union and obtain the arms and munitions of war at Harper's Ferry."

There was a laugh at this from some who were within earshot, and one man added with a chuckle, "True, true, the Governor did say that. It got into all the Yankee papers."

"Brown," the Governor said scornfully, "what made you think with your corporal's guard of men that you could remove the thousands of guns in the arsenal? You would need more than ten freight cars and forty mule teams."

"I never intended to remove them," said the Old Man blandly. "I brought far better weapons of my own." He looked around at the guards on the train. "Weapons I now see stolen by your citizens —as they steal men and women, Governor."

"*I* have put your Sharps rifles into the hands of our people, Captain Brown. I intend to arm every slaveowner in the state and establish stations of munitions and supplies all along our border," declared the governor, indignantly.

"I had intended to do the same," Brown retorted. "If I had not been forced into error by my hostages, I would have been joined by many native-born Virginia gentlemen. I wasn't counting on the roughs and the rowdies of the North, but on your wealthy and educated classes who see the handwriting on the wall."

"Why don't you give me their names?"

"I did not mean to linger at the Ferry," said the Old Man, "but your citizens kept delaying me with their propositions for a cease-fire which were never intended to be carried out." Then, abruptly: "I do not want to discuss this anymore."

"Just one question," the Governor insisted. "I know you will not name any names, but tell me if you are a member of the Republican Party—unless you are ashamed of it."

"I despise the Republican Party. They talk against slavery and win their elections by it. But they never see the slave . . . walking in bloody chains down all your roads . . . starving in your cornfields . . . freezing at your firesides. . . . They never see the four million of your enemies that are intermingled with you . . . waiting for the word to start a backfire. I think they will have to see them now."

The cold ferocity of the Old Man's answer brought the Governor to his feet. "Regardless of your opinions, Captain Brown," he said nervously, "Virginia will promise you a fair trial."

"Spare me the mockery," said the Old Man bitterly, "of a public murder. Shoot me with one of my own Sharps guns and get it over. There are others to take up my work and bring it to a successful issue."

The Governor moved back to confer with Prosecutor Hunter, and the Old Man waved for Coppoc to come and talk to him. "Were you with Watson when he died?" he asked.

Coppoc, who had just been telling a reporter that he had not wanted to come to Harper's Ferry and had no idea it would result in treason, answered Brown in a shaky voice. "Watson was put in the guardhouse with me. He complained of the hardness of the bench they had him on. I begged them for a bed for him, or even a blanket, but they said they had none. I took off my coat and put him on that and held his head in my lap, and he died then without a groan or a struggle."

The Old Man groaned and turned away.

The Governor meanwhile reported his findings to Prosecutor Hunter. "No one can believe he is a madman. He is a bundle of the best nerves I have ever seen, cut and thrust, bleeding and in bonds. He has a clear head, courage, fortitude . . . simple ingenuousness . . . a man for truth . . ."

"Then why doesn't he say who sent him?" asked Hunter.

"Oh, let me tell you, sir," Wise declared, "he is remarkably sane in avoiding disclosures. He is more sane than his prompter and promoters skulking back there in the North—leaving him pinned down at the Ferry when a few more men could have got him out of there."

"Why didn't you work up his feelings against them?"

*Courthouse and Headquarters of Virginia Militia,
Charlestown*

"No, I could not. He is a master in concealing inferences of this
sort. But he does not conceal his contempt for the cowardice that
would not back him better—he is bitter against the whole Republican Party."

"Oh," said Hunter, disappointed.

After arriving in the Jefferson County seat at Charlestown, the
prisoners were carried off to the jail. Threats and execrations were
shouted at them all the way, and the only friendly faces the Old
Man saw were of northern reporters who had rushed in to cover one
of the greatest stories of their lives. When they began to clamor to
interview Brown and his men, however, they were quickly weeded
out and expelled from the town. They could not see Brown, they
were told, for fear "that he may put forth something calculated to
influence the public mind and to have a bad effect on the slaves."

The truth was that Hunter had already picked out a carefully
chosen group of favorites who were beginning to be called "his
suite." Within it were the only reporters who were allowed to have
any contact with Brown or the trial, or who were even tolerated in
Charlestown. Two men, from now on, were to put down the way

things were for the historical record—one, the Associated Press man from Baltimore; the other a Charlestown resident named Gallagher, correspondent for the reactionary New York *Herald*. Although much has been written about sentimental liberals making a legend out of John Brown, when it is considered that almost every public utterance coming out of Charlestown was transmitted through these sources, the scenes of his trial and his final days take on unusual credibility.

Hunter was determined to indict, try, and execute the Old Man and his followers within ten days at the most. He stated this frankly; he "had to, or the fears of the people of the whole country will be kept in an unhealthy state of excitement, and a large, expensive force will be required to prevent attempts at a rescue."

The commitment to jail was made on a complaint signed by Governor Wise himself that Brown and company had "conspired to make an abolition insurrection and open War against the Commonwealth of Virginia, were guilty of murder and conspiring with the slaves to rebel." The indictments were long and complicated, and it was not until five days later that the prisoners were brought

Jailhouse at Charlestown

into court for a five-day arraignment, trial, and hanging. According to Virginia law, persons involved in a slave insurrection deserved this accelerated justice.

The Old Man and Stevens were put into the same cell and their hands manacled. The jail was strong and the Old Man's window looked out on a wall fourteen feet high. In front of the cell block stood the jailer's house. The jailer, a Captain John Avis, had commanded a company at Harper's Ferry and had been an officer in the Mexican War; he recognized Stevens as the bugler for a Massachusetts Regiment. Avis was a just man, and it was not long before the Old Man had won him over.

After a good night's sleep, the Old Man began to feel much better. On the next day, however, he was assailed by the tremendous fear captured revolutionaries often have that their struggle and sacrifices will not be known by the people they are trying to serve. He agreed quickly, therefore, when asked by the jailer, to talk again with the newspapermen.

Three or four men came eagerly into the cell with their notebooks open. The Old Man asked if the reporter from the New York *Tribune* was there and was disturbed to learn that all Republican and suspected sympathetic newsmen had been expelled. In his last letter to them, he had told his family to "watch the *Tribune*"; now they would not know the truth of what he had done. But, unknown to Brown, the *Herald* reporter had been completely won over, though Gallagher gave no sign of this, except for the content of his dispatches. In fact, Gallagher later applied for extra work as a prison guard so that he could be close to Brown at all times.

The Old Man, lying prone on his cot, began to lecture the reporters, telling them to state the facts in his favor as well as those against him. "Otherwise, I will not answer." Asked why the affair had become such a slaughter, he replied, "I did not believe that the southern people would sacrifice eight of their own fellow citizens for the sake of killing my little party."

Stevens kept joining in to back up his leader's words. "We want the facts to go properly before the world," he declared. "I am willing to die and expect to die—a thousand deaths, ten thousand deaths, a million deaths, if I can benefit the cause."

Brown kept stressing that he cared nothing for fame, but he did not want to be represented as a thief and a murderer. He insisted that he had shed no blood, committed no violence, done no un-courteous act, uttered no unkind or vindictive saying, beyond what the furtherance of his plan demanded. Then he noticed, to his dismay, that Gallagher was the only one taking down exactly what he said; the others were merely making notes from time to time. He fell silent, therefore, and the reporters started to leave, but he caught Gallagher's eye and beckoned him to his side. He asked him why they did not put everything on record and was told that they were waiting for the testimony at the trial. "That will be a mock-ery," Brown groaned.

"Not if you have a good lawyer—someone to bring out testimony in your behalf," Gallagher argued. The Old Man then asked if he knew of a fair lawyer in the area, but Gallagher advised him to send a letter to his northern friends, offering to take it down for him, if his wounds prevented him from writing it himself. The Old Man sat up in his cot, took heart, and began to dictate.

Charlestown, Jefferson County, Va., Oct. 21, 1859
Hon. Thos. Russell.

Dear sir.

I am here a prisoner with several sabre cuts in my head and bayonet stabs in my body. My object in writing you is to obtain able and faithful counsel for myself and fellow prisoners, five in all. Without we can obtain such counsel from without the slave states: neither the facts in our case can come before the world; nor can we have the benefit of such facts (as might be considered mitigating in the view of others) upon our trial. I have money on hand here to the amount of $250 and personal property suffi-cient to pay a most liberal fee to yourself, or to any suitable man who will undertake our defense, if I can be allowed the benefit of said property. Can you or some other good man come immedi-ately for the sake of the young men prisoners at least? My wounds are doing well. Do not send an ultra Abolitionist.

Very respectfully yours,
John Brown

An identical letter was sent to a friend in Cleveland, Ohio. Both men addressed were Superior Court judges and underground abolitionists. Judge Russell had hidden him in his home for over a week while a U.S. Marshal was pursuing with a murder warrant; Brown felt they could both be trusted. When the letter was brought to the County Sheriff, who was to censor all communications going in and out of the jail, he added another line! "The trial is set for Wednesday next the 25th instant. J. W. Campbell, Sheriff, Jefferson County."

The tragic news had already reached North Elba. It was young Annie Brown who had to announce that Martha and Belle Brown were widows, her father was on the brink of death, and the Thompson family had lost two boys. Someone had brought the *Times,* containing the first accounts of Harper's Ferry: "Let Annie read it, for she can read faster than any of us can." As she recalled, later, "So I read the long account from beginning to end, aloud, without faltering. I was stunned and my senses so benumbed that I did not comprehend the meaning of the words I pronounced. There was very little weeping or wailing, or loud demonstration on the part of our brave household; we were most of us struck dumb, horror stricken with a grief too deep and hard to find expression in words or tears."

The blow fell heavily on Martha, Oliver's wife, who was soon to have a baby that Oliver was never to see. She and the baby died shortly afterward. Annie reported, "I never saw Martha smile but twice after the news was received, once when she came upstairs to see me when I was sick and I showed her some water and told her an angel sent it, and she smiled and said she was my angel. The other time was when her baby was born and she told me to 'write to Tidd and tell him he had a little sister.' Tidd used to call Martha and Oliver 'Mother and Father' to tease them, when we were at the Kennedy farm. The only time after that I saw her shed a tear was when I held her little baby at her bedside, for her to take a last look at it before they put it into the coffin. A few great scalding tears fell on its little face."

The story of the Old Man's titanic battle to establish justice in Virginia is buried among the daily stenographic reports of the trial,

Troop Formation Between Jail and Courthouse

which were published uniformly in most of the papers. Now and again, however, there would be some break in the thick curtain of suppression, revealing Brown in action; these usually appeared in the New York *Herald* on days when it printed what Gallagher sent out in his regular dispatches. It is from this source that we get the vivid picture of the men entering the court at the opening of the trial, six days after their capture. They had to walk from the jail across the street to the courthouse between files of troops holding bayoneted rifles.

"Old Brown marched in with head erect and cast a hasty and rather defiant look around him. His confinement has not at all tamed the daring of his spirit. His height, as he stood erect, appeared to be a full six feet. His eyes are both swollen, exhibiting the marks of bruises and contusions much more clearly than on the occasion of our last interview with him, and altogether he looked very haggard and suffering."

Prosecutor Hunter had agreed with the Governor to give the prisoners a fair trial, "but in double quick time." It was planned to go through all the motions of court, arraignment, indictment, trial and conviction, but each process following in rapid order, instead of, as is usually the case, allowing some days or even weeks, between these stages, so that the person on trial can prepare his defense, talk to his lawyers, arrange for defense witnesses and all those actions imperative for a man on trial for his life, regardless of how guilty he already appears to be.

The Old Man appeared shocked at the speed at which things were moving, especially since he had heard from neither Boston nor Cleveland in respect to his defense. He realized that his friends there, knowing his condition, and that of Stevens, would assume they had additional time to get the right lawyer. In Boston they were, in fact, attempting to carry out Brown's plea not to send an "ultra abolitionist" by engaging Ben Butler, the shrewdest of Massachusetts lawyers, a notorious abolitionist-baiter, and Democratic Party chieftain. Butler was trying to clear his cases in the local courts so that he could go to Virginia.

The Old Man was barely able to stand; Stevens, with three balls in his head, two in his breast, and one in his arm, could not, and was held up by two deputies. The Sheriff read the commitment

Shields Green, John Copeland, John Brown, Edwin Coppoc,
and Aaron Stevens at Their Arraignment

charges—treason, murder, and inciting the slaves to insurgence—
each carrying the death penalty. The Prosecutor, anxious to hurry
the trial along, asked the prisoners if they wanted a court-appointed
lawyer to defend them. Brown took fire at this:

"Virginians, I did not ask for quarter at the time I was taken. I
did not ask to have my life spared. The Governor has tendered me
his assurance that I should have a fair trial but it seems that under
no circumstances whatever, will I be able to have a fair trial. If
you seek my blood you can have it at any moment without this
mockery. I have had no counsel and I have not been able to advise
with anyone. I know nothing about the feelings of my fellow
prisoners and am utterly unable to attend in any way to my own
defense. My memory don't serve me. My health is insufficient, although improving. There are mitigating circumstances that I could
urge in our favor if a fair trial is to be allowed to us. But if we are
to be forced with a mere form—a trial for execution—you might
spare yourselves that trouble. I do not even know what the special
design of this examination is. I hope that I may not be foolishly
insulted as only cowardly barbarians insult those who fall into their
power."

The Court beckoned to two men standing in the crowd that
jammed the courtroom. They came forward and were introduced,
and the Prosecutor asked Brown if he would accept them as his
counsel.

"I have *sent* for counsel," said the Old Man. "They have not had
time to get here. I wish for counsel if I am to have a trial . . . but
if it is to be this mockery, I do not care. It is unnecessary to trouble
any gentleman with that duty."

The Prosecutor said, "You will have a fair trial."

The Old Man looked the two lawyers up and down and shook
his head doubtfully. "I am a stranger here; I do not know the disposition or the character of the gentlemen named. I have applied
for counsel of my own and doubtless could have them, if I am not,
as I have said before, to be hurried to execution before they can
reach me. But if that is the disposition to be made of me, all this
trouble and expense can be saved."

The Prosecutor, on the verge of losing his temper said, "The question is, do you desire the aid of these gentlemen as your counsel? Please to answer yes or no!"

Brown hesitated a long time before answering. "I cannot regard this as an examination, under any circumstances. It's a matter of very little account to me. If they *had* designed to assist me as counsel, I would have wanted an opportunity to consult them at my leisure."

The Prosecutor turned impatiently to Stevens. "Are you willing to take these gentlemen as your counsel?"

Aaron Stevens said weakly, and in despair, "I am willing to take them both." All the other prisoners also agreed, but the Old Man shrugged and clamped his mouth shut disapprovingly. Looking around the courtroom, he saw, pressing closely to the bar of the enclosure, the friendly face of Mr. Gallagher, the Reporter.

"Reporters," Brown said in stentorian tones, "you may put down my reason for refusing counsel is that I will not be allowed to speak for myself and the southern counsel will not be willing to express my views."

The Court gaveled him down, then ruled peremptorily that the press must not publish testimony "as it would render the getting of a jury before the Circuit Court, impossible."

The Old Man started to speak again, but with an awful groan, Stevens collapsed. A mattress was brought for him, and he was laid on the floor. The Old Man had to hold his peace, not wanting to upset Stevens any further.

Eight witnesses were then called. All but one had been hostages at Harper's Ferry, and as they looked at him, still controlled and strong in the midst of enemies thirsting for his death, they could not help saying that he had treated them with great courtesy and respect.

Due process went on, with blinding speed. The prisoners were remanded for trial, and the witnesses were kept in their places to testify next before the Grand Jury, which was to hand down indictments that same day. Judge Richard Parker, presiding at the trial, gave a masterly charge to the jury.

"I must remember, gentlemen, that as a minister of justice, bound to execute our laws faithfully, that I must hold that every one accused of crime is innocent until he be proven guilty by an honest, an independent, and impartial jury of his countrymen. And such laws are equally binding on you. These men are now in the hands of *justice*. They are to have a fair trial.

"I will not permit myself to give expression to those feelings which at once spring up in every breast when reflecting upon the enormity of guilt in which those are involved who invade by force a peaceful, unsuspecting portion of our common country, raise the standard of insurrection amongst us, and shoot down without mercy Virginia citizens defending Virginia soil against their invasion."

Predictably, a wave of murmured hatred stirred the courtroom, and the Judge held up his hand. "They are to have a fair and impartial trial. Let us remember that the law has charge of these alleged offenders, the law alone must deal with them to the last. It can tolerate no interference by others with duties it has assumed to itself."

Then smiling, ever so slightly and reassuringly, the Judge said, "If guilty, they will pay the extreme penalty of their guilt and this example of punishment will be more efficacious for our future protection than any torture to which mere passion could subject them." There would be no lynch law in Judge Parker's Court: it wasn't needed.

The fate of John Brown and his men rushed inexorably on to its ordained end. Only the Old Man, serving a common cause as no one else could or wanted to do, was able to deflect the onrush of total tragedy.

The prisoners were brought back the following morning, when the real trial began. The press continued its oddly sympathetic account:

> The prisoners were brought in, accompanied by a body of armed men. Cannon were stationed in front of the Court House and an armed guard were patrolling around the jail. Brown looked something better and his eyes were not so much swollen. Stevens had to be supported, and reclined on a mattress on the floor of the courtroom, evidently unable to sit. He has the appearance of a

dying man, breathing with great difficulty. The prisoners were compelled to stand during the indictment, but it was with difficulty, Stevens being held upright by two bailiffs.

The verdict the Old Man really wanted was that he had performed an act of principle and was neither an outlaw or a murderer. Death he was prepared to accept, but it had to be with honor. Consequently, he wanted to play out the trial as long as possible, believing that time and the truth might put public opinion on his side. He knew the only weakness in Virginia's case against him was the Governor's resolve that "her honor" not be further tainted by the memory of the drunken mob of Virginians at the Ferry, held at bay by a handful of men.

The Old Man had a pious look on his face as he said, "I do not intend to detain the Court but merely wish to say that, as I have been promised a fair trial, I am not now in circumstances that enable me to attend a trial, owing to the state of my health. I have a severe wound in the back, or rather in the kidney, which enfeebles me very much. But I am doing well and I only ask for a short delay of my trial and I think I will be able to listen to it. I merely ask that 'the devil may have his due.' My hearing is impaired and indistinct due to the wounds I have about my head. I could not hear what the Court said this morning and I would be glad to at least listen to my trial and hear what questions were asked of the citizens and what their answers were."

Prosecutor Hunter objected strenuously. Any delay would be dangerous because of the "exceeding pressure on the physical resources of the community." He asked the Court not to receive the "unimportant statements" of the prisoners as grounds for delay, but have the jailer and a physician examined on the question. The Judge said he would grant a delay, although reluctantly, if inability was shown, but it was necessary to finish up the trial by the end of the month, and the term the Court was sitting. His intention was that Brown and the rest should be hanged on the last day of October.

The Doctor then testified that Brown was able to go on and that his mind and recollection were not affected by his wounds. However, the jailer, Captain Avis, stated that he "had heard Brown frequently say to persons visiting him that his mind was confused and his hearing affected." He would not like to give any opinion as to Brown's ability to stand trial. The Judge ordered that the trial proceed without delay, with all prisoners tried separately, and Brown first.

There was a recess for lunch, and the prisoners were taken back to jail; the jury was to be selected that afternoon. Jailer Avis, whom Brown had won over, reported that the prisoner had taken to his bed and would not get up for his trial. Avis was told sternly the Old Man had to be there in Court, even if he had to be brought in on a cot. And so Osawatomie Brown lay there with his eyes closed during the questioning of the jury, offering no challenge or objection to any of them. At five o'clock he was brought back to his cell, and the Court adjourned until morning.

The next day, a Thursday, the Old Man was half carried into court between two bailiffs and long lines of armed men. He lay down on his cot as Mr. Green, one of the court-assigned lawyers, approached the bench and asked permission to read a telegram just received from Akron, Ohio. It said that the Old Man was insane—more specifically, that there was insanity in his family.

This was the answer of his Ohio supporters: the destruction of the whole meaning of his effort. Ironically, it might have achieved what he desperately wanted—a delay of the trial while a medical examination was made. But Brown had already instructed Mr. Green to tell the Court that he "disdained to put in that plea." After the lawyer had stated this, the Old Man raised himself on his elbows, and elaborated at length:

"I will add, if the Court will allow me, that I look upon it as a miserable artifice and pretext of those who ought to take a different course in regard to me. I view it with contempt more than otherwise. As I remarked to Mr. Green, insane persons, so far as my experience goes, have but little ability to judge of their own sanity, and if I am insane, of course, I should think I know more than all the rest of the world. But I do not think so. I am perfectly unconscious of insanity and I reject, so far as I am capable, any attempt to interfere in my behalf on that score."

His lawyer then informed the Court that Brown still wanted a delay of the trial, since he had received a telegram from an Ohio attorney asking if he should leave that night for Charlestown. A reply had been sent, requesting this man to come at once.

Hunter again objected, concluding sarcastically: "The prisoner has made open, repeated, and constant acknowledgment of everything charged against him. He has gloried in it and shows the same spirit and purpose in not wanting the defense of insanity put in. We know not whether this lawyer is to come here as counsel to the prisoner or whether he wants to head a band of desperadoes."

After a lengthy wrangling between the lawyers, the Judge refused any delay. The Prosecution began its case, asking the jury to cast aside prejudices and be fair, and "not allow their hatred of Abolitionists to influence them against those who have raised the black flag on the soil of this Commonwealth." Witnesses were called, and they recited with a commendable accuracy the events at the Ferry. All the defense could bring out in cross-examination was that no one was harmed at close quarters.

The most damning testimony against Brown, and the high point of the prosecution's case came in the testimony of Conductor Phelps. "Brown told Governor Wise that he had books in his trunk that would explain to him his whole proceedings, and what the purpose of his business was. Colonel Lee said he had one, and handed it to Governor Wise. Brown asked him to read two of its first preambles and four of the last sections, which he did, and Brown said that was a correct copy. In reply to a question of Governor Wise, he said he was Commander-in-Chief of the forces under the Provisional Government, and that he then held that position. He said that the Constitution was adopted in a place called Chatham, in Canada. Brown said there was a Secretary of War, Secretary of State, Judge of the Supreme Court, and all the officers for a general government. He said there was a House of Representatives, and there was an intelligent colored man elected as one of the members of the House."

This created a massive sensation in the Courtroom, particularly among the members of the Jury. If the statement stood up under cross examination, the prosecutor needed no other evidence to prove that Brown had "conspired to make insurrection" and his case came under the statute authorizing "immediate execution of the death sentence in cases of insurrection or rebellion."

Lewis Washington was called to the stand. He testified that "Governor Wise asked Brown if he had not selected Harper's Ferry as a border place between Maryland and Virginia for the establishment of his Provisional Government, and he answered 'certainly.' " Washington then "detailed the conversation respecting the Provisional Government substantially as did Conductor Phelps." The greatest sensation was caused when a witness said Brown "had all the officers for a general government and there was an intelligent colored men elected as a member of the House."

This witness was Dr. Starry. Brown asked Green to try for a delay again, so his counsel, who would surely arrive that night, could cross-question the Prosecution's most important witness. Again the motion was denied, and at seven in the evening, the trial was recessed to the following day. It seemed that the Prosecution could complete its case the next day, and Brown could be sentenced, perhaps hanged, before the end of the month, four days away. The courtroom was filled every day with four or five hundred people. They constantly chomped chestnuts and peanuts. The floor was covered with discarded shells and tobacco chaws.

During the night a lawyer finally arrived from Boston. He looked very young, had just passed his bar examination, and his name was George Hoyt. When the news of the Old Man's capture had reached Boston, certain radical Republicans, led by a man named John Le Barnes, having no doubts that Brown would be summarily hanged, had decided that he must be rescued. A plot was quickly set in motion at Republican headquarters for Hoyt to go to Charlestown as Brown's lawyer. His youth and obvious inexperience would throw off suspicion and animosity, and he would be allowed to confer with Brown.

Le Barnes wrote: "The purposes for which I wanted him to go were: first, to watch and be able to report proceedings, to talk to Brown and communicate anything Brown might want to say, and second, to send me an accurate and detailed account of the military situation at Charlestown, the number of troops, the location and defenses of the jail, the nature of the approaches to the town, the opportunities for a sudden attack, with the location and situation of the room in which Brown was confined, and all other particulars as to some plan of escape."

Hoyt was not allowed to see the Old Man, however, even though he pleaded with the Sheriff and the Prosecutor. He was only able to get into the trial the next morning by attaching himself to Senator Mason and walking in with him. Brown's court-appointed counsel refused to appear with him in the case. The Prosecutor was immediately suspicious and in his daily report to Governor Wise wrote, "A beardless boy came in last night as Brown's Counsel. I think he is a spy."

When the Old Man saw this callow and frightened youth being introduced to the Judge as his Boston attorney, he groaned disbelief and sank back on his cot. Brown was an expert on lawyers, having been involved in many court cases during his career as an unsuccessful businessman. His associates had obtained the most eminent lawyers in the country to defend him on a trivial matter of who owed fifty or sixty thousand dollars; now, when his life and the lives of other brave men were at stake, they sent a boy.

When Hunter demanded proof that Hoyt was a Member of the Bar, the latter replied lamely that he had no credentials with him. Judge Parker, not wanting such quibbles to interfere with the rapid conclusion of the trial, said he would accept Hoyt on his word. The young lawyer, darting a quick, sheepish glance at Brown, said that for the moment he would not participate, but only act as an observer. "Good," the Old Man thought, "now I can defend myself." But first he had to find a way to get rid of his southern counsel, who, he had to admit, were doing a very fair job under the circumstances.

13

*Two
Preambles
and
Three
Articles*

PROVISIONAL

CONSTITUTION

AND

ORDINANCES

FOR THE

PEOPLE OF THE UNITED STATES

PREAMBLE

Whereas, Slavery, throughout its entire existence in the United States, is none other than a most barbarous, unprovoked, and unjustifiable War of one portion of its citizens upon another portion; the only conditions of which are perpetual imprisonment, and hopeless servitude or absolute extermination; in utter disregard and violation of those eternal and self-evident truths set forth in our Declaration of Independence: Therefore,

We, Citizens of the United States, and the Oppressed People, who, by a recent decision of the Supreme Court are declared to have no rights which the White Man is bound to respect; together with all other people degraded by the laws thereof, Do, for the time being ordain and establish for ourselves, the following PROVISIONAL CONSTITUTION and ORDINANCES, the better to protect our Persons, Property, Lives, and Liberties; and to govern our actions:

When the court next assembled, the reporters were titillated by the presence of Senator Mason. It was freely speculated that the Senator's observance of the trial would lead directly to some action in Washington against the high-ranking Republicans whose names had been repeatedly mentioned in connection with Brown's attempt to establish a revolutionary Provisional Government.

The Old Man, now quite openly carrying on his own defense, had Conductor Phelps and hostage Washington recalled for cross-examination. Lewis Washington admitted that he "heard Brown give frequent orders not to fire on unarmed men" and that "the first firing was *against* the engine house." Brown had then observed to Washington that "the people out there seem to pay little regard to the lives of citizens and we must take our chances with them." The Old Man heard this testimony with satisfaction, as reinforcing his position that all his firing was done in self-defense.

Then, with a meaningful glance at Senator Mason, the carpetbag material was offered as evidence by the Prosecutor. He then read the Preamble of the Provisional Constitution and articles seven, forty-five, and forty-eight. The seventh article stated that a Commander-in-Chief "shall be chosen by the officials of the government." Article forty-five stated that "Persons within the limits of the territory holden by this organization, not connected with the organization, having arms, will be seized." Article forty-eight stated that all persons connected with the organization should take an oath or affirmation to support it.

As each letter was produced and identified by Sheriff Campbell, the Old Man nodded his head and said in a loud voice, "That is mine." A letter from Congressman Giddings and one from Gerrit Smith was read. Brown asked his lawyer to examine each of the letters but did not dispute his connection with them. The Prosecutor began to get uneasy over the time being consumed by this technicality and decided privately not to use them as direct evidence in the trial.

Under shrewd questioning by the Old Man, almost every one of the Prosecution witnesses had something to say in his favor. Armstead Ball said that when he was captured, he "was conducted to Captain Brown, who told me his object was to free the slaves, and not the making of war on the people; that my person and my private property would be safe, he then gave me permission to return to my family and assure them of my safety and get my breakfast. I started back home accompanied by two armed men, who stopped at my door. My breakfast not being ready, I went back and was allowed to return home again, under escort, at a later hour. On returning again, I heard Captain Brown say it was his determination to seize the arms and munitions of the Government to arm the slaves to defend themselves against their masters."

The Old Man's hearing was better but he still had to strain to catch the remarks of the witnesses. He was encouraged by the honesty of the government witnesses who, he felt, were building solid evidence for the defense he wanted to make: the right of revolution, a right sustained by a morality that tries not to shed blood except in the last resort, and then the blood only of the oppressor.

Suddenly he heard the Prosecutor say, "The prosecution rests." He looked questioningly at his lawyers, Mr. Botts and Mr. Green, to whom he had given a carefully written out plan for his defense.

We gave to the prisoners perfect liberty.
Get all their names.
We allowed numerous other prisoners to visit their families to quiet their fears.
Get all their names.
We allowed the conductor to pass his train over the bridge with all his passengers, I, myself, crossing the bridge with him, and assuring all the passengers of their perfect safety.
Get the conductor's name and the names of the passengers, so far as may be.
We treated all our prisoners with utmost kindness and humanity.
Get their names as far as may be.
Our orders, from the first and throughout, were that no unarmed person should be injured, under any circumstances whatever.
Prove that by all the prisoners.

Brown's lawyers called first, for the defense, Mr. Brua, who testified about the aborted negotiations before the killing took place. Mr. Kitzmiller told how Watson and Stevens were shot down: "Stevens was shot before he fired back; Thompson, of Brown's men, was a prisoner on the bridge."

The Old Man sat up in great agitation: "Tell the Court how William Thompson was disposed of!" he cried out in a terrible voice.

Kitzmiller said, "I was not there and did not see the last."

The Old Man shook his head, remained erect, and seemed about to take over the trial. His lawyer called a James Beller, who said he was with Chambers when he had fired on and shot Stevens and Watson Brown while negotiating under a flag of truce.

The courtroom was charged with a sense of coming crisis. Brown swung his trembling legs to the floor, beckoned to one of his lawyers, Mr. Green, and whispered in his ear. Mr. Green told the witness Beller to stand down and said he desired to bring out testimony regarding the shooting of Thompson. Prosecutor Hunter strenuously objected—Thompson had been shot by his son, Henry. He said, rather incoherently, "That had no more to do with this case than the dead languages." Green pressed the issue, and the Judge said he would allow it.

Young Henry Hunter came to the witness stand, while Brown crouched as if ready to spring at him. Hunter testified, in a rush of words, "After Mr. Beckham, who was my granduncle, was shot, I was much exasperated, and started with Mr. Chambers [the killer of Watson Brown] to the room where Thompson was confined, with the purpose of shooting him. We found several persons in the room and had levelled our guns at him when Mrs. Foulke's sister threw herself before him, and begged us to leave him to the laws. We then caught hold of him and dragged him out by the throat, he saying, 'Though you may take my life, eight million will rise up to avenge me and carry out my purpose of giving liberty to the slaves.' We took him to the bridge, and two of us, levelling our guns in this moment of wild exasperation, fired, and before he fell, a dozen balls were buried in him. We then threw his body off the trestlework and returned to the hotel to bring out the prisoner Stevens and serve him in the same way. We found him suffering from his wounds and probably dying. We concluded to spare him and start after others and shoot all we could find. I had just seen my loved uncle and the best friend I ever had shot down by those villainous Abolitionists, and felt justified in shooting any that I could find. I felt it was my duty and have no regrets."

There was a warm murmur of agreement from the spectators, but the Old Man smiled broadly, feeling that this might serve as the capstone of his argument against the inhumanity of the slaveholding society. William Williams, the watchman, was called. He said he had not seen the shooting of the black man, Heywood.

Brown, now openly functioning as his own counsel with the tacit agreement of the Court, pressed him. "State what was said by myself and not about his being shot."

"I think you said that if he had taken care of himself, he would not have suffered," Williams conceded, and Brown gave a curt nod of satisfaction.

The Old Man's personality began to pervade the courtroom. Everyone was watching him, and the Judge, who had been reading a newspaper during much of the testimony, now laid all distractions aside. Reason Cross testified that attempts were made by Brown to arrange a cease-fire, and Brown asked him to state that there were two written propositions drawn up while he was a prisoner. The Old Man could see his lawyers whispering uneasily to one another as the conduct of the trial was passing from their hands. His eye fell on a document lying under Green's chair, obviously cast aside and covered with tobacco juice and boot scuffs. He caught young Hoyt's eye, and motioned for him to pick it up: it was the plan of defense he had drawn up for his lawyers.

At this point the clerk began to call out the names of Brown's other witnesses. They did not answer. The Judge smiled with relief and indicated that the defense should now rest its case, and the final speeches could be given to the jury. It was the end of the trial, he thought, and Brown could be convicted and hanged within the ten-day period.

The Old Man rose to his feet. "May it please the court," he said in his harsh, iron voice, "I discover that, notwithstanding all the assertions that I would receive a fair trial, nothing like a fair trial is to be given me, as it would seem. I gave the names as soon as I could get them, of the persons I wished to have called as witnesses, and was assured that they would be subpoenaed. I wrote down a memorandum to that effect, saying where those parties were, but it appears that they have not been subpoenaed, so far as I can learn. And now I ask, if I am to have anything at all deserving the name and shadow of a fair trial, that this proceeding be deferred until tomorrow morning; for I have no counsel, as I have before stated, in whom I feel that I can rely, but I am in hopes counsel may arrive who will see that I get the witnesses necessary for my defense. I am,

myself, unable to attend to it. I have given all the attention I possibly could to it, but I am unable to see or know about them and
can't even find out their names; and I have nobody to do my errands, for my money was all taken from me when I was hacked
and stabbed, and I have not a dime. I had two hundred and fifty
or sixty dollars in gold and silver taken from my pocket, and now I
have no possible means of getting anybody to do my errands for
me, and I have not had all the witnesses subpoenaed. They are not
within reach, and are not here. I ask at least until tomorrow morning to have something done, if anything is designed. If not, I am
ready for anything that may come up."

The Court was thrown into an uproar. Brown's court-appointed
lawyers stood up and resigned from the case, saying they had no
choice, "when the accused whom we have been laboring to defend,
declares in open court that he had no confidence in his counsel."
Young Hoyt struggled to his feet and announced that he had "come
from Boston, traveling day and night, to volunteer his services," but
needed time to study the case and asked a continuance until the
next day.

Prosecutor Hunter, goaded into high anger that his tight time
schedule for the case had been blown apart by the Old Man's
verbal bomb, made an amazing concession: "So far as the evidence
of the conduct of Captain Brown in the treating of his prisoners
with leniency, respect, and courtesy, and that his flags of truce—if
you choose to regard them so—were not respected by the citizens
and that some of his men were shot, we are perfectly willing to
admit these facts in any form they desire . . ."

The Judge declared that he could not give a delay for Hoyt to
study the case, but since Brown had asked for witnesses, and the
summonses for witnesses had not been returned, he had no choice,
under the law, but to carry the case over another day.

Brown walked erectly back to his cell. There he learned that
Cook had been captured. He was sorry for Cook but rejoiced in the
implication that the other men, including his son Owen, had gotten
free.

After a while, Mr. Hoyt came to the Old Man's cell, where he
still had to sit in chains, accompanied by the jailer. They talked

over the Old Man's plan of defense and Hoyt said he would try to carry it out to the letter but that he had been informed that two widely experienced lawyers would be there in the morning. As he left, he managed to put a note in the Old Man's manacled hands. Now, at last, the Old Man understood why such an innocent, inexperienced boy had been sent down from Boston. The note said, "Captain Brown, delay the trial all you can. We are organizing to rescue you."

The next morning, the 29th, the last day that would permit the Court to summarily hang the Old Man without delay, he was enormously cheered by the appearance of two real lawyers to undertake his last chance at a defense. Mr. Samuel Chilton appeared at his cell and informed him that a committee of prominent Bostonians, headed by John A. Andrew, had arranged for him to defend him. Mr. Chilton assured him that he had many supporters in Massachusetts who considered the hasty trial "a judicial outrage" and had offered Mr. Chilton a handsome fee to see that John Brown had a "complete and appropriate defense, according to the laws of jurisdiction where he was indicted, and raising whatever questions of law that ought to be raised and having them heard before a tribunal of ultimate resort."

Mr. Chilton assured the Old Man that he was thoroughly familiar with the Virginia code and practice, having been born and raised in the Commonwealth. He was unfamiliar with the case, but with frequent consultation with the Old Man he felt he could make some effective points. When the Old Man questioned him about his appearance, Chilton told him he had actually been hired by Montgomery Blair, a prominent border state Republican leader. The Old Man sensed, with some elation, that the Republican Party was now entering his cause, and it might be construed that it was adopting it. The men setting up this intervention were far too sophisticated politically to be paying Mr. Chilton a fee of one thousand dollars to carry out the defense of some abstract question of justice.

The second man, Mr. Griswold, had come directly from the Old Man's appeal to Judge Tilden of Ohio. He was from Cleveland and acted toward the Old Man, as did Mr. Chilton, with graciousness and respect. They assured him that the indictments and charges as drawn could not stand up to competent legal scrutiny. It was obvious that these men had absolutely nothing to do with the escape plans carried by Mr. Hoyt.

When Court began, Judge Parker qualified the two new lawyers as counsel for the prisoners, but would not agree to a postponement for them to discuss the case with him. The Judge agreed, however, not to admit Brown's carpetbag papers other than the Provisional Constitution, with the concurrence of the prosecutor. Mr. Hoyt, acting for the Old Man, called for the defense witnesses, to prove "the absence of malicious intent." When the witnesses testified, the first being Mr. Daingerfield, "a general colloquy ensued between the prisoner, lying on his cot, and the witnesses, as to the part taken by the prisoner in not unnecessarily exposing his hostages to danger. No objection was made to Brown's asking these questions in his own way, and interposing verbal explanations relative to his conduct."

After the noon recess, Mr. Griswold sat beside the Old Man "prepared to question the witnesses and received from him such suggestions in the course of examination as he had to make" because of the presence of Brown's new and important lawyers. The whole atmosphere of the trial was changing. The Prosecution did not even attempt to cross examine the witnesses making important points for the Old Man. "He did not have any malicious feelings. . . . Witness's wife and daughter were permitted to visit him unmolested, and free verbal communications were allowed with those outside, all the firing they saw from Brown's party could be considered purely defensive. . . ."

The defense closed its testimony on this note, nonmalice and self-defense. Mr. Chilton rose and asked the Court to elect one count of the indictment and abandon the others. He gave a sound argument for this. The Judge insisted that the trial go on and such matters be discussed after the verdict. With the help of Mr. Griswold, Chilton began to tie the Court up with such a profusion of red tape that all hope was disappearing of ending the trial that day, or that week, as it was now Saturday.

The Prosecutor insisted that such wrangling was unnecessary;

that it was the devious work of the prisoner in continually delaying the trial. "We should go on and bring this case to a close tonight. We have until twelve o'clock to do it in."

The Judge made a desperate effort to conclude the trial. He complained the jurors were exhausted and wanted to be sent home. Prosecutor Hunter said he would submit the case to them without a closing argument. Mr. Chilton objected: "Mr. Brown wants his case argued." Mr. Harding, the other prosecutor, said he was going to give his closing speech anyway, and "dwelt for some time on the absurdity of the claim of the prisoner that he be treated according the rules of honorable warfare. He seemed to lose sight of the fact that he was in command of a band of murderers and thieves, and forfeited all title to protection of this kind."

This statement seemed so ridiculous to Judge Parker after the array of witnesses put on by the Old Man that he threw up his hands and called for an adjournment until Monday morning.

Every day of the Old Man's trial, the streets were full of angry, violent men, held in check only by the armed military. His jailer, Captain Avis, was a subject of insult and execrations almost as much as the Old Man himself. But he was a brave and stubborn man, and the more he was pushed by the angry mob, the more he favored the prisoners. While Hoyt reported to Boston that Brown may "die by the rough hand of violence," his jailer permitted him to write letters, to read all available newspapers, and even encouraged visitors to his cell, who could not help but come away with a favorable view of the prisoner.

There was an amusing incident Sunday afternoon, while reporter Gallagher was helping clean up the Old Man's cell. The Old Man had a surprising sense of humor, which often expressed itself as a kind of pompous "put-on." A company of the uniformed Virginia guard, dressed in fringed buckskin, came to see him. He shook hands, Gallagher reported, with "much of his old self-possession and commanding manner." "Gentlemen," he greeted them, "I am very glad to see you, yes indeed. I served, though not enrolled, with a company of yours at one time. It was in the late war with England, as it was called, in 1812. [Brown would have been twelve at the time!] But very few of the poor fellows returned to their homes. They were a picked body of men and I remained near them for a time on the Northeast Frontier and it was my happiness on several occasions to render them aid and assistance in their suffering. They were mostly all of them from Petersburg in this state, and they were so equal-sized that when any small party of men were together, I would recognize them at any distance. The Virginia Companies were then the finest I had ever seen.

"Gentlemen, how many of you have arrived here?"

The Captain of the Winchester Volunteers answered effusively, "Some thirty of us, Captain Brown."

The Old Man could not suppress a bit of a wink, "Gentlemen, I would very much like to see you out of doors and at your evolutions, but I am not in a position to do this at the moment."

The Volunteers laughed heartily at this, and Brown said, "However, I am glad to see you as it is."

That evening the three lawyers for the defense came to see the Old Man; the callow boy, Hoyt, who had little more to offer than his intense hero worship, and the two professionals, smelling opulently of bay rum and fine barbering and exuding that wiliness and supreme self-confidence that puts the hearts of accused men at peace. Brown had been thinking about the connection of John A. Andrew with his case and rightly concluded that he was acting for the Secret Six. This meant that he had to consider them, as well as his soldiers, in the presentation of the case. It raised for him, a huge dilemma. While Hoyt sat silently by, the two lawyers went to work on Brown to accept the customary accommodation of pleading guilty to a lesser charge, for the sake of unidentified friends still free. They outlined a defense for him that would not badly demean his intentions, merely belittle them, a defense that could conceivably save his life, and the lives of others, and achieve the support, and perhaps the covert approval of the Republican Party. The lawyers' credentials in this respect were impeccable, and Brown began to see them more and more as evidence of the intervention of strong and favorable political forces into his act and his trial. He did not give them a ready answer, but after they left, he said to Hoyt, who had nervously remained behind, hoping that the Old Man would not give too much ground to the demands of the party, "I am almost fully persuaded that I am worth more to hang than for any other purpose."

Hoyt took this to mean that the Old Man was opposed to a rescue. Nevertheless he made a careful drawing of the jail and sent it on to his principals in Boston.

The last day of the trial, Griswold and Chilton made their pleas for the Old Man's life. Mr. Griswold fervently declared his abhor-

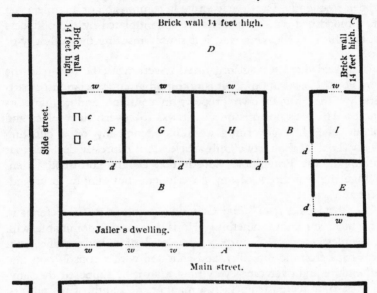

A Main entrance; *B* Space between walls, Avis's house, and the jail building; *C* Point of wall which Cook and Coppoc reached on the night of Dec. 15th in their attempt to escape; *D* Jail yard *d d d d*, cell doors; *E* Reception-room; *F* Cell occupied by Brown and Stevens, afterwards by the latter and Hazlett; *G* Cell of Green and Copeland; *H* Cell of Coppoc and Cook; *I* Cell first occupied by Albert Hazlett, *w w w, w w,* windows, those of cells look into the jail yard; *c c* cots of Brown and Stevens.

Plan of Brown's Prison Printed in the New York TRIBUNE
to Encourage a Rescue

rence of the crime his client was charged with, but insisted that the Old Man had no intention of trying to overthrow the government of Virginia. "For the purpose of carrying away slaves from the state, he had taken temporary possession of the arsenal and while there, attempts were made by the citizens to attack him and drive him off. In a sort of self-defense, blood was shed and lives were taken, but that is not levying war against the state of Virginia. Such things happen frequently. Death may ensue in commission of a crime, even when bloodshed was not necessarily contemplated by the offenders . . . but this is not levying war, it is simply resisting the authority of law.

"It is said there was an organized government; he had read the Provisional Constitution . . . it is nothing but an association or partnership. They are to own property in common and regulate its tenures. This was not treason . . . it was to govern themselves and nobody else, like governing a military company or a debating society. Look at the forty-eighth article . . . it expressly declares that nothing in the Provisional Constitution can be construed to encourage the overthrow of any government, but simply to amendment and repeal.

"Here stands a man," said Griswold, pointing to the defendant, "of which you know something. He is a man of indominable will, of sleepless energy, of purpose, possessed of a perseverance that turns back from no difficulty, and endowed with a constitution that will endure and overcome everything. Can it be supposed that anything is to be feared from such a man, at the zenith of his powers, when he had a name in history, and when something might be hoped for the cause in which he was engaged, could only, throughout the Union, raise twenty-one men?

"Frame your indictment against him today, charging him with enticing away your slaves, with interfering with that species of property, and his confessions are as thick as the leaves upon your forest trees that he was among you for that purpose. Frame your indictment and the moment it is read he will plead guilty to it, and submit to the penalty of his crime without a murmur."

And with this de-revolutionizing of the Old Man's intents, his lawyers rested his case.

Mr. Hunter gave his summary, based on his honest notion of the Old Man's intentions. It represented very accurately what was in the mind of the South at that time.

"His provisional government was a real thing, and no debating society, as his counsel would have us believe, and in holding office under it, and exercising its functions, he was clearly guilty of treason. His purposes were well matured and he and his party declared that there were thousands in the North ready to join him. The forty-sixth section has been referred to, as showing it was not treasonable, but all that meant was that the new government was to be a union of separate states like the present, with the difference that all were to be free states."

The jury agreed with Prosecutor Hunter. After a recess of three quarters of an hour, they came back with a verdict. Every newspaper in the country carried a report of it. "At this moment the crowd filled all the space from the couch inside the bar, around the prisoner, beyond the railing in the body of the court, out through the wide hall and beyond the doors. There stood the anxious but perfectly silent populace, stretching head and neck to witness the closing scene of Old Brown's trial. It was terrible to look upon such a crowd of human faces, moved and agitated with but one dreadful expectancy, then to let the eyes rest for a moment upon the only calm and unruffled countenance there . . . and to think, that he alone of all present, was the doomed one . . . above whose head hung the sword of fate. But there he stood, a man of indomitable will and iron nerves, all collected and unmoved, even while the verdict that consigned him to an ignominious doom was pronounced upon him."

He was found guilty of treason and conspiring and advising with slaves and others to rebel and murder in the first degree.

His lawyers filed exceptions and errors. Brown, who had been standing during the verdict, turned to straighten his blanket and laid down again on his pallet. The trial of Coppoc began immediately. For a while nobody wanted to ask the Old Man to leave the courtroom and return to his cell.

The next day, the trial of Coppoc was whisked away in a morning, and Brown was brought in for sentencing, "to save time," while the jury was deliberating Coppoc's guilt. He came walking wearily and painfully, at the point of exhaustion. He had not been able to draw a breath without suspense and impending disaster filling every moment since he had left the Kennedy farm eighteen days ago. He did not go to his cot, but sat as uprightly as he could beside young Hoyt, like any criminal awaiting sentence.

But the lawyers had to argue out their technicalities, upholding the laws, as officers of the court themselves. Brown's lawyer closed his case by saying, "Unless the majesty of the law (even Virginia law) was upheld, dissolution of the Union must soon ensue with all the evils that must necessarily follow in its train."

While the Judge reviewed the exceptions in Brown's favor, and turned them down, the gas lights in the courtroom—it was a dark, gloomy day—cut huge hollows in the Old Man's face. The clerk asked him to rise and say why sentence should not be passed upon him.

The Old Man painfully rose, trying to shake the stiffness out of his joints, trying to restrain the slightest tendency to tremble. The paper said, "He was like a block of stone." With his hands resting on the table before him he gave a speech which became the best known of all his utterances.

I have, may it please the Court, a few words to say. In the first place, I deny everything but what I have all along freely admitted—the design on my part to free the slaves. I intended certainly to have made a clean thing of that matter, as I did last winter, when I went into Missouri and took slaves without the snapping of a gun on either side, moved them through the country, and finally left them in Canada. I designed to have done the same thing again, on a larger scale. That is all I intended. I never did intend murder or treason or the destruction of property, or to excite slaves to rebellion, or to make insurrection.

I have another objection: and that is, it is unjust that I should suffer such a penalty, had I interfered in the manner which I admit, and which I admit had been fairly proved (for I admit the truthfulness and candor of the greater portion of the witnesses who have testified in this case), had I so interfered in

Trial of Captain John Brown

behalf of the rich, the powerful, the intelligent, the so-called great, or in behalf of any of their friends—either father, mother, brother, sister, wife, or children, or any of that class—and suffered and sacrificed what I have in this interference, it would have been all right; and every man in this court would have deemed it an act worthy of reward rather than punishment.

This court acknowledges, as I suppose, the validity of the law of God. I see a book kissed here which I suppose is the Bible, or at least the New Testament. That teaches me further, to "remember them that are in bonds, as bound with them." I endeavored to act up to that instruction. I say, I am yet too young to understand that God is any respecter of persons. I believe that to have interfered as I have done—as I have always freely admitted I have done—in behalf of His despised poor, was not wrong, but right. Now if it is deemed necessary that I should forfeit my life for the furtherance of the ends of justice, and mingle my blood further with the blood of my children and with the blood of millions in this slave country whose rights are disregarded by wicked, cruel, and unjust enactments, I submit; so let it be done.

Let me say one word further.

I feel entirely satisfied with the treatment I have received on my trial. Considering all the circumstances, it has been more generous than I expected. But I feel no consciousness of guilt. I have stated from the first what was my intention, and what was not. I never had any design against the life of any person, nor any disposition to commit treason, or excite slaves to rebel, or make any general insurrection. I never encouraged any man to do so, but always discouraged any idea of the kind.

Let me say, also, a word in regard to the statements made by some of those connected with me. I hear it has been stated by some of them that I have induced them to join me. But the contrary is true. I do not say this to injure them but as regarding their weakness. There is not one of them but joined me of his own accord, and the greater part of them at their own expense.

John Brown Walking Back to His Cell After Day in Court

A number of them I never saw, and never had a word of conversation with, till the day they came to me; and that was for the purpose I have stated. Now I have done!

Calmly he resumed his seat. The clerk ordered him to stand again. The Judge told him he was to be hanged by the neck until he was dead on the second of December, next.

The courtroom was silent but for one man, standing behind the Judge, who began to clap vigorously. When no one joined him, his enthusiasm petered out, haltingly, and there was a long, dead pause. The man turned to leave the courtroom. The nutshells crunched beneath his feet with the sound of broken glass. One of the jailers asked Brown if he wanted to be taken back to the jail on his cot. He said he would prefer to walk.

14

The Whole World Is Watching

John Brown, upon a wretched pallet, with six half-gaping wounds, a gunshot wound in his arm, another in his loins, and two in his head, scarcely conscious of surrounding sounds, bathing his mattress in blood, and with the ghostly presence of his two dead sons ever beside him; his four fellow sufferers wounded, dragging themselves along at his side; Stevens bleeding from four saber wounds; justice in a hurry and overleaping all obstacles; an attorney, Hunter, who wished to proceed hastily, and a judge, Parker, who suffers him to have his way; the hearing cut short, almost every application for delay refused; forged and mutilated documents produced, the witnesses for the defense kidnapped, every obstacle thrown in the way of the prisoner's counsel, two cannon, loaded with canister stationed in the court, orders given to the jailers to shoot the prisoners if they sought to escape, forty minutes of deliberation and three men sentenced to die. I declare on my honor that this took place, not in Turkey, but in America. Such things cannot be done with impunity in the face of the civilized world. The universal conscience of humanity is an ever watchful eye. Let the judges of Charlestown and Hunter and the slaveholding jurors and the whole population of Virginia, ponder on it well; they are watched! There is something more terrible than Cain slaying Abel: It is Washington slaying Spartacus.

Letter of Victor Hugo to the *London Daily News,* New York *Tribune* and the St. Petersburg, Russia, *Northern Bee*

During the next thirty days, while the Old Man remained caged and in chains, he was still able to continue his life and death struggle against slavery. In the national press, and consequently in the minds of its millions of readers, the ebb and flow of the tides generated at Harper's Ferry were featured every day. Readers sometimes wrote in to complain that a "nigger rebellion" should take up so much space. But editorials replied that there had been no more important matter in the history of the country. The New York *Herald,* which had covered the trial more completely than any other paper, in hopes of keeping the connections between the Old Man and the radical Republicans before the public eye, carefully explained that unless the whole and frightening truth of the Old Man's action be told, "his gallows will be the emblem of a second Savior, whose sacrificial blood has ransomed the black race. His words and acts will become a new gospel and the evangelists of revolution will present it from Maine to Virginia."

The newspaper accounts became so unwittingly sympathetic that *Leslie's Magazine* had three artists expelled from Charlestown in a week. Some interdicted Republican correspondents went to Richmond, enlisted and returned in the gray uniforms of the Virginia State Militia. Others set themselves up as rewrite men on the northern periphery of the restricted zone and bribed acceptable reporters to send them copy from the fortified city.

Everything the Old Man wrote was read by the Sheriff and passed on to certain favored newsmen to copy and publish. After his sentencing, a writing table was set up in his cell and he sat down to write a postscript to a letter he had already started to the family at North Elba, telling the saddest news a man ever had to deliver.

My Dear Wife and Children, every one,

I suppose you have learned before this by the newspapers that two weeks ago today we were fighting for our lives at Harper's Ferry: that during the fight Watson was mortally wounded; Oliver killed, Wm. Thompson killed, and Dauphin slightly wounded. That on the following day I was taken prisoner immediately after which I received several saber cuts in my head; and bayonet stabs in my body. As nearly as I can learn, Watson died of his wound on Wednesday the 2nd or on Thursday the 3rd day after I was taken.

Dauphin was killed when I was taken; and Anderson I suppose, also. I have since been tried, and found guilty of Treason, etc., and of murder in the first degree. I have not yet received my sentence. No others of my company with whom you were acquainted were, so far as I can learn, either killed or taken. Under all these terrible calamities; I feel quite cheerful in the assurance that God reigns; and will overrule all for his glory; and the best possible good. I feel no consciousness of guilt in the matter; nor even mortification on account of my imprisonment; and irons; and I feel perfectly sure that very soon no member of my family will feel any possible disposition to "blush on my account."

I am in charge of a jailer like the one who took charge of "Paul and Silas" and you may rest assured that both kind hearts and kind faces are more or less about me; whilst thousands are thirsting for my blood. These light afflictions which are but for a moment shall work out for us a far more exceeding and eternal weight of Glory.

Your Affectionate Husband, & Father,
John Brown

P.S. Nov. 2nd I was sentenced to be hanged on Dec. 2nd next. Do not grieve on my account. I am still quite cheerful. God bless you all.

Yours ever,
J. Brown

As he was writing, two significant visitors were allowed into his cell—Judge Thomas Russell and his wife, the daughter of the famous seaman's preacher, "Father" Taylor. Mrs. Russell threw herself into the Old Man's arms, sobbing uncontrollably. Judge Russell told him he had not been prepared for the unusual haste in which the trial had been carried out. He had received Brown's letter and intended to defend him but had not been able to clear his docket in his own court before now.

They had been present in the Virginia Court when the sentence of death was given. Judge Russell spoke calmly to the Old Man.

sensing that any overt display of emotional sympathy, like that of his wife, would be too upsetting. He congratulated Brown on his speech, talking like one lawyer to another after a hard day's trial. "I liked it when instead of assuming your hearers were Christians, you said, 'I see a book kissed here which I suppose to be the Bible, or at least the New Testament,' from which you inferred that Christianity was not quite unknown to these barbarians."

It did the Old Man a great deal of good to know that the Russells had come to stand at his side while others were calling him a madman and crying out for his lynching. Mrs. Russell wept again on seeing the pillow on the Old Man's cot wet with fresh blood and his coat stained with the grime of battle and the blood of his dead sons. She made him take it off and handed it to one of the watching guards. "Clean this coat," she ordered, in her quick, Yankee voice. It soon came back, meticulously sponged and pressed.

The Old Man was rather taken aback by this. He had not asked for clean clothes or for any such comforts. He was, in fact, overwhelmed by what he considered the excessive kindness of his jailer in letting him write and receive letters, read the daily papers and see visitors. He had expected a dark dungeon somewhere in the bowels of the earth, and at the very least, solitary confinement. He knew Jailer Avis was "now being abused for his humanity."

Meanwhile an angry mob was building up in the street outside. Allowing a woman to visit the Old Man was particularly infuriating to the Virginians, partly because they were afraid he would attempt an escape in disguise. But mostly because the total identification of Brown and his men with the enslaved blacks brought all their sick, sexual fear into focus. When it was reported that Mrs. Russell, a very beautiful young woman, had thrown herself into the Old Man's arms and kissed him, there was a sense of shock: "Strange sympathy this, for a scoundrel whose purpose was to place those of her own sex in Virginia in the power of the unbridled passions of cutthroats and villains. Her presence does violence to our wives, mothers, sisters. Her stay must be a short one." Lewis Washington was needed to calm the mob. Escorting her later back to the train, he told her that if she had not been "a lady," she and the Judge would not have left Charlestown alive.

Judge Russell was really there to arrange for the Old Man's escape. He carefully measured the chimney in the cell and said quietly, "Two good Yankees could get your men out of that and away *so* easily." Brown offered him indirect discouragement by calling in his jailer and saying, "Have you any objection to my adding a postscript to my letter to my wife, saying I am to be hanged the second of December?" Avis said no, and the Old Man turned back to his friends with a shrug.

The Russells walked back to their hotel in tears, moved by the Old Man's lack of self-pity and his unconsciousness of guilt. On the train platform as they were leaving, Lewis Washington questioned them suspiciously regarding their intimacy with the prisoner. "I am not sure I am doing the right thing," he said, "letting you get out of here." He asked Mrs. Russell why John Brown had come to her house. "To bring maple sugar to my children," she answered. He could not understand, he conceded, her attitude toward such a "miserable man." She responded through her tears: "I did not talk about this raid with Captain Brown. I never sympathized with him on such subjects . . . but I love John Brown. He could never do a weak or mean deed, nor a cruel one unless he felt some great good required the sacrifice."

Judge Russell had brought a brilliant young Boston lawyer named George Sennott to defend the other men. However, Edwin Coppoc was found guilty the day the Old Man made his last speech, and Copeland and Shields Green were found guilty with equal speed. None of these trials was extensively reported. After the Old Man was sentenced, the telegraph station, newly brought to Charlestown, was quickly dismantled and taken away. Sennott tried to sustain interest in the fates of the others, but the best he could do for the blacks was to have the treason charge against them dropped. Even Prosecutor Hunter agreed that to charge a persecuted black man, free or enslaved, with disloyalty to the United States was nonsensical. The Supreme Court, in the recent Dred Scott decision, had ruled that Negroes could not be citizens; historically, they had no rights that white people needed to respect. The three blacks conducted themselves with nobility and calm and were sentenced to die on the gallows December sixteenth. The highlight of these trials for

the American press was an interchange between Sennott and the
Marine Lieutenant who had wounded the Old Man at the Engine
House:

> Sennott: You say that when Brown was down you struck him
> in the face with your saber.
> Lieutenant: Yes sir.
> Sennott: This was after he was down?
> Lieutenant: Yes sir, he was down.
> Sennott: How many times, Lieutenant Green, did you strike
> Brown in the face with the saber after he was down?
> Lieutenant: Why, he was defending himself with his gun!
> Prosecutor Hunter: I hope counsel for the defense will not
> press such questions as these.
> Sennott: Yes sir.

The "hard news" after the trial was of the fugitives known to be
still free and making their way north through the mountains.
Cook, of course, had been captured and immediately hinted he
would confess everything. His mother-in-law, a lifelong resident of
Harper's Ferry, delivered a trunk to Prosecutor Hunter. It was
Tidd's and contained the letters which had disturbed the Old Man at
the Kennedy farm. After Tidd and the Old Man had had their set-to
at the farmhouse, Tidd had brought them to Cook's house; now, as
Brown had predicted, they were finding their way into the New
York *Herald*.

The country knew that Owen Brown, Charles Tidd, Francis
Meriam, Albert Hazlett, Osborn Anderson, and Barclay Coppoc
were still at large in the mountains between Virginia and the
Mason-Dixon line. They were thought to be part of a five-hundred-
man force circling Charlestown, getting ready to swoop down for
the rescue. There were alarms and reports from the little villages
in the valleys nearby that a party of men were seen, and even that
inhabitants had been murdered by these invaders. Companies of
Virginia Militia were sent out on mounted patrols. All reports
were found to be false.

There was, of course, no concentration of men, only Owen
Brown, doggedly trying to get the tattered remnant of the Old

Man's band safely back to the North. After leaving the Ferry haunted by the "only answer that came to us out of the rain and the darkness"—that his father had been gunned down in a tempest of rifle fire—he started through the thick laurel bush of the mountainsides to Pennsylvania. His worst problem was Cook, who "in his fiery, quick-thinking way, was always proposing hazardous measures." Cook's rhetoric often swayed Coppoc and Tidd—for example, in suggesting that they steal horses and ride down the road, a plan which seemed to Owen certain death. Again and again, Owen was barely able to overturn some wild notion of Cook's by convincing him that his wife and child, waiting for him at Chambersburg, deserved the most cautious of survival tactics.

Owen did not want to go anywhere near Chambersburg, which had been linked with the raid and was alert for any appearance of the raiders. Meriam was physically so weak that Owen had to carry him much of the way, along with two Sharps guns, two sacks of food, and other armament. Sometimes Owen would lose control over the route and be forced to follow Tidd and Cook to the easy walking at the edge of clearing. On one occasion squirrels set up such a chattering over their hiding place that Tidd and Cook wanted to shoot them with their revolvers. While they were walking along the clearings at dusk, a horseman saw the armed party—five men, each carrying two guns—and rode off at a gallop to alarm the valley.

There was nothing for them to do but press on as fast and as invisibly as possible. Cook still insisted on traveling the roads and stopping for provisions. Owen gave him and Tidd the rest of the sugar and biscuits, while he began to live on dry Indian corn left standing in the fields. As the cold rain changed to snow, they left telltale signatures of their tortuous passage. They had to cross a gap in the mountains, traveling on bare ground with high visibility. Just as they came to it, they heard the baying of hounds, more than they could count, nuzzling around for their scent. There were a hundred campfires flaring out in the night, as the hosts of hunters warmed themselves while waiting for their prey.

They had to walk all night to get away from the gap to the mountains beyond. Sometimes Meriam would drop back and be lost. Once Owen and Tidd went after him, and Tidd dragged him roughly along, bruising him against protruding roots. Always they heard the dogs baying behind them and the clatter of hoofs along the fatally inviting road. Finally, they had to sleep; exhaustion overcame them on a bare spot of the ridge. Owen said, "Tired as I was, I spent an hour cutting laurel bushes and sticking them into the ground around us." Laurel will not wilt, and the shrubs looked as if they were growing there, and they made a good concealment.

From a farmhouse that morning came the smell of doughnuts frying. Miserable with hunger, Tidd felt he must have some. "You'll be here all winter and never get through," he told Owen. "You'll starve or freeze to death. It's just as well to expose ourselves in one way as another." Owen pleaded with him to remain as concealed as possible until they got three or four miles beyond Chambersburg. When Tidd still maintained that he was willing to run great risk for the doughnuts, Owen gave in but insisted that Cook, who had the glibbest tongue, should be sent for food. He went and came back safe, smacking his lips and declaring he had been treated to a delicious dinner. He also had a sack of doughnuts. But what could have been a tiny moment of relief from the agony of flight was ruined when Cook goaded Tidd into a temper tantrum. Cook still had an old flintlock horse pistol once carried by George Washington. He started firing it, saying that he had told the people at the farmhouse that he was with a hunting party, and that they would be expecting to hear shots. Tidd ordered him to stop. They shouted at each other, and in a moment they had drawn guns. Owen rushed between them and got them to agree to hold the shoot-out they were both demanding somewhere else, where the others would not be exposed and captured. They both sulked apart, and Owen dreaded the next day's travel.

They had to cross a creek. Owen, who had to carry Cook across on his back, dropped him in the water to cool him off. Nevertheless, Cook kept maneuvering to walk alone with Owen, telling him he wanted to shoot it out with Tidd. Finally Cook insisted that they were near enough to Chambersburg for him to break away and see his wife. He begged Owen to make the others wait for him to return. Owen had to let him go; otherwise the shoot-out would have taken place.

Just after Cook left, two ravens flew over their heads. They waited perilously until dusk, but Cook did not come back. They waited until nine, until midnight; still he did not come, and the sounds of the dogs seemed nearer. They waited until half the night was over and then pushed on. Cook was captured that night.

Owen decided to take to the public roads, hoping to find Cook again. Tidd wanted to go to the house of Mrs. Ritter, who had sheltered Kagi and the others in the early days of the conspiracy. Owen begged him not to expose her, but Tidd went anyway, taking Coppoc along. Owen argued that he was exposing the rest of the party as much as himself. He pleaded with them to hide out for a while in a brier patch he had used when bringing Shields Green to the Kennedy farm. But Tidd went stubbornly down the road, and Owen felt compelled to follow him "to see if he could find Cook," knowing that if Tidd found him first he might have killed him.

When Tidd got to Mrs. Ritter's place, he knocked on her upstairs window with a long bean pole from her garden. She opened her window and whispered, "Leave, leave; for God's sake." "I'm hungry," said Tidd.

"I couldn't help you if you were starving . . . go away . . . this house is guarded by armed men."

The first streaks of daylight were coming. Owen had to get everyone back under cover. Meriam had fallen asleep in the middle of the street. Owen jerked him awake, saying, "Walk, your life depends on it." Someone with a wagonload of milk was plodding toward them; Owen marveled at how much he felt like killing that innocent man.

Sudden clouds of morning fog enveloped them, and they got safely out of town. Owen still hoped they would find Cook at the old hiding place, but he was not there; in spite of himself, Owen felt a wrench of conscience as they finally abandoned him and pushed on in a northwesterly direction. They were hoping to find some old friends, conductors in the Underground in that region of Pennsylvania. If they could not stay there, they would continue on to Ohio, or even to Canada.

Such a journey would have been impossible for Meriam. They brought him to an obscure railroad station in a driving snowstorm; somehow, alone and defenseless, he made it to Philadelphia and freedom. Owen, Tidd, and Coppoc pushed on. Their corn ran out and they had to live on stolen chickens. Tidd recklessly made a fire and roasted them; he was so hungry that he mashed up the bones and ate them as well. Men and teams passed them as they crouched in the bush; every day there were alarms and terrors. Desperation finally overcame them: one sunny morning they washed their clothes and mended them, cut their beards and hair, rolled their guns and ammunition in blankets, and decided to face the world.

All day they walked the roads unmolested and stopped at a friendly farmhouse for the night. The farmer seemed completely unsuspicious. After they finished a meal of flapjacks, the farmer took up his weekly *Tribune.* Owen writes, "Perhaps you can have some idea how painful was the suspense, waiting until we could decently arise from the table and lay our hands on that paper." At last Tidd seized the paper, and the farmer said, "Old Brown's son is still on the loose." Owen could see Tidd reacting breathlessly to what he was reading. "Old Brown is still alive," Tidd muttered between clenched teeth. "But he will be hanged, for he has been tried and found guilty." Owen later wrote, "To me, who thought my father was dead, this somehow had the effect of good news."

When Tidd read how his crony Stevens and Watson Brown had been shot down while carrying a flag of truce, he could stand it no longer and passed the paper to Barclay Coppoc. As Barclay, staring fixedly into the fire, held the paper unread in his hands, the farmer suddenly commented, "The latest news is that the man Coppoc has been tried too and found guilty." Owen, assuming that the farmer had found them out, picked up the paper and, in a show of bravado, began to read aloud in a steady, dispassionate voice. Before he realized what he was doing, he was halfway through a detailed description of himself, but did not dare stop, even at the recital of the extravagant rewards for his capture. On he went through the whole action at the Ferry. "But when I came to the well-known passage from Governor Wise's speech—'And Colonel Washington said that he [Brown] was the coolest man he ever saw in defying death and danger. With one son dead by his side, and another shot through, he felt the pulse of his dying son with one hand and held his rifle with the other, and commanded his men with the utmost composure, encouraging them to be firm, and spend their lives as dearly as possible'—well, that told me too much, my voice trembled and I passed the paper to Coppoc."

Owen began to wonder about the source of his description and how much it would affect chances of escape. Looking over Coppoc's shoulder, he read that Cook had been captured and was in the Charlestown jail selling everyone out. "Cook continues to spread the belief that he was deluded by Brown. His brother-in-law, the Governor of Indiana, is moving heaven and earth to secure a commutation of sentence. Cook has promised a full confession."

Cook's recklessness and bravado had inevitably brought him to betray his comrades. After leaving Owen and the others, he had blundered into a field where some men were hunting game birds. They recognized him at once—his description, along with the announcement of a $1,000 reward for his head, had already been well circulated. With casual effrontery Cook went up to one of the men, asked him how the hunting was and where he could "replenish my store of bread and bacon." This man, a mountaineer who had picked up many a bounty tracking and capturing fugitive slaves, got Cook in between himself and another man and seized him. Cook was known as a very fast draw with a revolver but found himself helpless. When he asked why he was being held, the answer was, "Because you are Captain Cook and worth a thousand dollars."

As he was being led away, Cook said confidently that his brother-in-law was a rich politician and if the $1,000 was all that was wanted, he could get it for him, in exchange for an escape. His captor, a steely-eyed opportunist named Logan, said neither slavery nor freedom was worth dying for. He hinted that a deal could be arranged. Cook went meekly along, even telling some of the details of his escape and who had been with him. There was a well-known Republican lawyer in Chambersburg, and Logan agreed to put the matter of Cook's ransom in his hands. Then began a typical Cook episode, so self-destructive that it may have been that Cook felt so guilty about his conduct at the Ferry that he wanted to be captured.

After several hours, when no one had made any serious effort to find this Republican lawyer, Logan got nervous about his reward and turned Cook over to the Sheriff. Then the lawyer appeared, and the deal for Cook's release again appeared to be set. The Sheriff half-agreed to let Cook escape if he would stay around a few hours to make it look good. Thinking he had won over the Sheriff and Logan, Cook turned down an invitation from his lawyer's wife to escape in her dress and cape. Luxuriating in a circle of new listeners, he inferred that to escape at that moment would be an abandonment of the Movement. "No, the battle must be fought to the bitter end and we must triumph, or God is not just." His Republican lawyer had assured him that it would take at least twenty-four hours for a legal requisition for his removal into Virginia to reach Chambersburg. Accordingly, Cook believed that he had considerable time to go on with his romanticizing, overcoming the humiliation of being captured without a shot fired. The flyer sent out for his arrest had described him as "reckless and expert in the use of weapons and his capture alive is not to be expected."

But the explosive action of even so small a number of men as John Brown's band creates a succession of unpredictable results. The event spread like a charge of buckshot with every pellet having a destiny of its own. Something that had already happened was closing off Cook's chances for survival.

Osborn Anderson and Albert Hazlett had also escaped from the Ferry. They too had come north through the laurel thickets on the mountainside. The rains and the snow on the ground had soaked Hazlett's feet into a tender surface of open sores. He could barely walk. He convinced Anderson that they should break up. If the latter were seen traveling in company with a white man, it would be assumed he was a fugitive, and he could be shot on sight.

"I was loth to leave him," wrote Anderson, "as we both knew the danger was worse there than in the mountains around Harper's Ferry. In the latter place the ignorant slaveholder was not acquainted with the topography of his own hills . . . in Pennsylvania the cupidity of the proslavery class would induce them to seize a stranger on suspicion, or go hunting for our party, for the bribe." They agreed to meet later farther north, after getting around Chambersburg. Anderson got to the town some two hours after midnight and went to the home of a black compatriot. The man told him the place was crawling with U.S. Marshals, his house had already been illegally searched, and the Marshal was coming back to do it again with a warrant.

He fed Anderson, and the fugitive was barely able to escape, going out the back door as the Marshal was pounding on the front. He heard the Marshal say, "You are suspected of harboring persons who were engaged in the Harper's Ferry outbreak." The warrant was brandished and the house more thoroughly searched, but Anderson managed to get some distance down the road toward the north, hiding in a haystack as soon as it was daylight. He made his way to York, Pennsylvania, and from there on, his black comrades got him safely to Canada.

Poor Hazlett, nearly out of his mind with the pain of simply walking, went desperately to the road and hailed the first stagecoach to come down the Pike to Chambersburg. He went to Mrs. Ritter's house, which had already been searched and was under surveillance. She warned him off. He begged her for some bandages and ointment for his feet. He hobbled down the railroad ties to Carlisle, where the Old Man had another friend. He hoped that once he was a little farther north, he would be taken in and given sanctuary.

The agent at the railroad station, however, noticed him walk past. His clothing could almost be considered a uniform for Brown's guerrillas—a black frock coat, a striped calico shirt, light woolen trousers, heavy cowhide boots, and a Sharps rifle. The agent, who had been listening to such a description on the telegraph wires for days, arranged to have somebody follow Hazlett at a safe distance all the way into Carlisle, where he was captured. Papers for his arrest were prepared, but the agent had taken him for Cook, a much shorter man, and the description did not fit him. He was held on suspicion and then sent back to Virginia, although up to the day of his trial he was never betrayed nor his identity properly established.

Thus the ironies of history had so arranged things that legal papers for the removal of Cook were already prepared in Pennsylvania. The papers wrongly prepared for Hazlett were served by Virginia officers on Cook, who was easily identified and still had his captain's commission, signed by the Old Man, in his pocket. After a transaction of twenty minutes, Cook fell into the hands of Virginia and was taken back to Charlestown. His lawyer had "never dreamed of a requisition reaching him before the second day," and was sleeping soundly at the time of the rendition.

True to form, he began talking to reporters as soon as he arrived. His first remark was to slander Frederick Douglass, asserting that the latter had promised to meet him at the schoolhouse with five hundred men. "I conveyed the arms there for him and waited until nearly night and the coward did not come."

It looked for a while as if the trial of John E. Cook would be as newsworthy as that of the Old Man. His talkativeness and name-dropping, along with his fear and guilt, made him someone for the Democratic Party to use against those Republicans unable to conceal their sympathy for John Brown's antislavery convictions. Cook's brother-in-law, Ashbel P. Willard, the Governor of Indiana, came to Charleston with the State's Attorney General, McDonald, and the Federal District Attorney for the Indiana region, Daniel Voorhees, all powerful Democratic Party officials. The rumor was that Cook had been pressured into making a startling confession and that, in return, Governor Wise would commute his sentence. Cook would then be free to stump for the Democrats, exposing the great Republican conspiracy at Harper's Ferry.

Cook was put into a separate cell to write his confession. He came to trial with five lawyers, the Governor and the two other Indiana officials, both of whom became U.S. Senators, and Botts and Green, the local attorneys whom the Old Man had rejected. He pleaded guilty, but when his confession was read to the Court by Hunter, it did not prove very revealing. It exposed only Frederick Douglass, Gerrit Smith, Samuel Gridley Howe, Frank Sanborn, and some lesser-known among the humanitarians. Those friendly to Cook argued that he had suppressed the real betrayal; others felt that he had told all he knew.

The arrangements to get him off without the treason charge, so that the Virginia Governor could pardon him, were so obvious that Harding, the drunken second Prosecutor, began to object. He had not been informed of the secret arrangements, although even the press knew about them beforehand: "Harding, not in the secret, objected to testimony at the top of his voice, but while stopping to pick up a large and valuable deposit of tobacco, which had unfortunately dropped out of his mouth, he was interrupted by Cook's lawyer, Botts."

But the resentment of the local citizens against Cook was even greater than against the Old Man. He was accused of seducing the Harper's Ferry girl who became his wife, solely for the purpose of advancing the conspiracy, and also viewed contemptuously for abandoning his leader when there was a chance to save him. In any case, the jury had already implacably marked him down for a hanging, and he was sentenced to die, along with Coppoc, Shields Green, and Copeland, on December 16. The trials of Stevens and Hazlett were put off indefinitely. Shields Green and John Copeland also had their day in court, the black men braving the ordeal magnifi-

*Cook and His Distinguished Counsel, A. P. Willard, James
Ewing McDonald, and Daniel Voorhees*

cently, unwavering in their consciousness of doing right. Shortly after the trial, Copeland, the Oberlin student, made a prophetic statement:

It is true that the outbreak at Harper's Ferry did not give immediate freedom to the slaves of this country, but it is the prelude to that great event. Remember, the first commencement of the struggle of the independence of this country and the Harper's Ferry outbreak are in every point of view the same. For at the commencement of the struggle, the first blood spilt was that of a Negro, Crispus Attucks . . . and in this commencement of the struggle for the Negro slaves, the first death was that of a Negro, one who had come to free his wife from the cruel hands of her master, Dangerfield Newby.

The trials over, the condemned waited in their cells, remaining dignified and calm, even under the pressures of probing and baiting questions from a steady stream of visitors. Hazlett was put into the cell with John Copeland and Shields Green, and they were all kept under close observation. Not once was a remark made which allowed the Virginia authorities positively to identify Hazlett as one of the party that had stormed Harper's Ferry.

Brown's startling connections with Governors and Senators added credibility to the accusations that the Old Man had tried to stage a coup in concert with highly placed Republican Party radicals. The Governor of Vermont had promised him guns, the ex-Governor of Pennsylvania had entertained him a few months before Harper's Ferry. The Republican Party fought desperately to fend off this attack. It fell not only on front-runner Seward, but on Salmon Chase, who was second in line as a Presidential prospect. Even the rumored "dark horse," Abraham Lincoln, was not spared as a suspect. His speech declaring that "a house divided cannot stand" was cited as a threat of anti-slavery warfare second only to Seward's.

Horace Greeley poured scorn on the accusations:

Nothing is more absurd than John Brown, assuming the character of chief of a provisional government, and expecting, at the head of an army of seventeen white men and five Negroes, to set on foot a great social and political revolution, and by the bold stroke of seizing the arsenal at Harper's Ferry, to bring about, as it were, in a moment, that which all the care, thoughts, prayers and arguments of a century failed to accomplish . . . namely, the abolition of slavery. But he seems to have infected the citizens of Virginia with a delusion as great as his own. It seems impossible for them to get over the terror his bold seizure of Harper's Ferry inspired . . . or their expectation that a grand army of abolitionists were about to invade them from the North.

In the fall elections, which came only a few days after Brown's conviction, the Democrats' strategy was to insist that every vote for a Republican candidate was a vote for John Brown and a slave insurrection. The Republican Party was constantly referred to as the "Black Republican Revolutionary Party" and assertions made that "if Seward is elected, the inference will be that his traitorous doctrines have been endorsed by the voters." To find out how a man in going to vote, said the *Tribune,* just say "Old Brown" to him.

But this whole strategy of fear backfired. The voters went to the polls and produced Republican victories in New York, Massachusetts, Wisconsin, Michigan, Indiana, and Illinois, under what the Democrats had called "the auspices of John Brown."

The real test of a revolutionary is not the number or prestige of his recruits but how he influences the millions. People may not declare openly for him, or his program but if they only tolerate him, it may be a sign of their adjustment to his giant step. As Emerson said, "All people, in proportion to their sensibility and self-respect, sympathize with John Brown." The onslaught of twenty-three men on slavery at Harper's Ferry had driven so deeply into the consciousness of America that nothing would remain untouched by their sacrifice. The Republican victory came as a tacit endorsement of John Brown and his men.

15

"High Noon, Thank God!"

... whereas, ten years since, there were thousands that could not endure my lightest word of rebuke of the South, they can now easily swallow John Brown whole, and his rifle into the bargain. In firing his gun, he has merely told us what time of day it is. It is high noon, thank God.

William Lloyd Garrison
Liberator, January 30, 1860

Even after the elections, the effect of Harper's Ferry swept on like an uncontrollable forest fire. Virginia was officially put on a war footing. Militia companies swelling with new recruits came pouring into Charlestown. The country seemed on the brink of a Civil War, if indeed it had not already begun.

Prosecutor Hunter set up an intelligence system, sending agents North with forged letters of introduction to try to penetrate groups of radical young abolitionists. The Old Man's mail was carefully read and all suspicious items, as well as some contributions of money, confiscated. As Hunter said, "I suspected from Brown's intercepted correspondence that there were combinations being formed in all parts of the United States, chiefly in Pennsylvania, Ohio, and Kentucky, for the purpose of coming here and releasing the prisoner."

The military defenses were to cost Virginia more than two hundred fifty thousand dollars. The Governor easily justified this in a report to the State Legislature by claiming it was "not alone for the protection of the jail and preventing Brown's rescue, but for the purpose of *coming events*."

These *coming events* were clearly spelled out in the Democratic papers, South and North. The election was said to have proved that no southerner could now be elected President, and that the real power of the Democrats had been driven south of the Mason-Dixon line. The New York *Herald,* still trying to instill fear into its readers, said that if in the year ahead political loyalties did not shift away from antislavery, and Seward was not stopped, the South would "Call a convention in a Southern city, refuse to send representatives to Congress, declare a separate state, organize an army to defend its borders, make a treaty of recognition with England and set up a Confederation of her own."

Virginia appeared to be acting prematurely but was really arming out of fear of a rescue attempt. Hunter's spies sent him a report that there were "9,000 desperate men led by John Brown, Jr., coming in from Ohio." Men from Harrisburg, Pennsylvania, "all armed with Colt's six-shooters and homemade bowie knives," were on their way. Eight thousand desperate men from Detroit and five thousand from Philadelphia, armed with "Pike's rifles and four cannon" were to join twenty-five hundred New Yorkers, "armed to the teeth and prepared to fire ten shots a minute at the jail guards and rescue Brown," were also reported.

Governor Wise's agents, meanwhile, were said to be collecting evidence for the extradition from the North of Senator Seward, Gerrit Smith, Horace Greeley, Frederick Douglass, and Joshua Giddings, a former Congressman from Ohio. After they were hauled in, a bigger and better treason trial was to be staged on evidence supplied by Hugh Forbes.

Rescue plans were so vividly presented that Wise wrote frantically to Hunter: "Information from every quarter leads to the conviction that there is an organized plan to harass our whole slave border at every point. I tell you these Devils are trained in the Indian art of predatory war! Keep a full guard on the line of frontier from Martinsburg to Harper's Ferry."

Wise began to worry that two separate days were set for the hangings and wrote again, "Brown ought to be hung between the two Negroes and there oughtn't to be two days of excitement." A reporter explained that the hangings were to be made into a five-act tragedy: "First, two acts in the morning, when the Negroes Copeland and Green are to be strangled. Second, two in the afternoon,

Cartoon of Celebrities Implicated in the Raid

after a suitable intermission for the imagination to feast on the recollection of what has passed, and to anticipate what is to come, Cook and Coppoc are to yield their lives. Finally, at a late hour, for the crowning climax, they demand that Brown shall expire before them, the curtains of night to fall on the old man's death struggles, and the light of the firmament to guide the retiring footsteps of the vast audience."

There were those in the North who were planning to rescue the Old Man, whether he wanted it or not. This could be the high climax of the event . . . thousands of Virginians defending Charlestown and a horde of radical abolitionists from the North, fighting it out, muzzle to muzzle, over the majestic person of their revolutionary leader. John W. Le Barnes, a young Bostonian, whose name had never been connected with either Brown or abolitionism, was arranging for this grand climacteric to the raid. While this operation was being developed, a philosopher named Lysander Spooner came up with a plan to kidnap Governor Wise in Richmond, carry him off to sea in a tugboat, and hold him as a hostage until the Old Man and his followers were released. Fifteen thousand dollars would be needed. A tugboat was to be purchased near Richmond, the Governor picked up, put aboard, and then transferred to the yacht *Flirt,* which was owned by militant abolitionists. The yacht was kept near Boston Harbor and had already been used for two or three simple acts of piracy, in which coasting vessels carrying slaves had been approached and fugitives taken from them by force. Le Barnes was intrigued and agreed to find men, a pilot, and a boat for the operation. The pilot, who knew "all the rivers of the Richmond region thoroughly," was actually hired. But raising money became too time-consuming, and the plan was abandoned for a direct overland onslaught on Charlestown from a base at Harrisburg.

The final decision was to rendezvous in the mountains a few miles from Charlestown on November 27. On the morning of the hanging, a rush would be made on the Old Man's escort, the horses of the Virginia Cavalry would be seized, and an escape made. The attackers were to be armed with "Orsini bombs" and hand grenades. The jail walls would be breached and the other prisoners let go at the same time. Four men were to pull this scheme together—Le Barnes, Thomas Wentworth Higginson, and Brown's later biographers, James Redpath and Richard Hinton. John Brown, Jr., was to spearhead the attack with a company of Ohio men, while more than a hundred German revolutionaries, veterans of 1848, were grouping in New York.

To overcome the Old Man's objections to a rescue, Higginson was sent first to North Elba to enlist Brown's wife, Mary. She was to visit him in Charlestown and talk him into agreeing. However, when the Old Man heard his wife might be coming, he strenuously objected and had his lawyer, Sennott, send a sharp telegram north. "Mr. Brown says for God's sake don't let Mrs. Brown come. Send her word by telegram wherever she is."

The New York *Herald* gave a dire warning that was echoed all over the North. "If Brown is rescued, fierce war will follow. This dire catastrophe hangs over the Union like two dark thunder clouds approaching each other, and at any moment may explode. Nothing can prevent this but conservative forces, using firmness and discretion and rallying around itself, the public virtue and patriotism of the country."

General W. B. Taliaferro, Chief of Staff of the Virginia State Militia, took command of the defense of Charlestown in anticipa-

Officers of the Virginia Militia

tion of a rescue attempt. He immediately set up a military screening board before which every stranger in Charlestown had to be cleared. He and his officers sat in Napoleonic splendor in the finest room of the hotel, and reporters had to shape up before these majestic figures. One said it was like being court-martialed. Those found unreliable on the subject of slavery were escorted far from town by a company of Calvary.

The security got so tight that Colonel Robert Baylor, the Militia Commander at the time of the fight at the Engine House, and the largest slaveholder in western Virginia, was thrown into jail as a possible defector. Even Edmund Ruffin, a rabid secessionist who stood in front of the courthouse every day haranguing his fellow Virginians to leave the Union, was arrested and jailed briefly for not having proper identification. He pleaded unsuccessfully with the authorities for the honor of putting the noose around the Old Man's neck but less than five hundred days later was allowed to fire the mortar shell which burst over the parade ground of Fort Sumter. Governor Wise himself was detained for three hours outside town in a driving rain because he did not have the password of the day. Finally an officer came to relieve him, and Wise told the sentry, if he had not detained him under those conditions, he would have been court-martialed and shot.

The more the military buildup continued, the more calm and genial the Old Man seemed to become. The Virginians could not believe he would act like this if he did not expect a certain rescue, and their panic grew in rough proportion to Brown's serenity.

16

The Little Speck in the Center

In respect to politics, Mrs. Brown told me he thought that politics merely followed the condition of public sentiment on the slavery question, and that public sentiment was mainly created by actual collisions between slavery and freedom . . . he had a profound conviction of the importance of bringing all questions to a direct issue, and subjecting every theory to the test of direct action.

James Redpath
Life of Captain John Brown

In my opinion, the biggest things that are happening in the world today are on the one hand the movement of the slaves in America, started by the death of John Brown . . .

Karl Marx to Frederick Engels,
"The Correspondence of Marx and Engels"

The time to the hanging was getting short now and when he woke up one morning there was snow. His thoughts went more and more to the existentialist answer he had given Governor Wise when he was first dragged, stabbed and bloody, out of the Engine House. "There is an eternity behind, and an eternity before, and the little speck in the center is but comparatively a minute." He thought much of the eternity behind, and how his trajectory had been sighted long before. With this profound sense of predestination he had very little regret for what had happened. He was constantly composed and cheerful in his mind.

The "acceptable" reporters visited him almost daily, as did many others . . . mostly sight-seers. He was polite to all, although he sometimes complained he did not want to be made into a "monkey-show." The atmosphere in the cell was so pleasant that hardly an unkind word was said about him in the papers.

"Brown's conversation is singuarly attractive. His manner is magnetic. It attracts every one who approaches him, and while he talks, he reigns. The other prisoners venerate him. Stevens sits on his bed, usually with his face away from the window, and listens all day to the Captain's words, seldom offering a syllable except when called upon. As for the other men . . . Copeland, Green, and Coppoc . . . they are always sending messages to 'the Captain,' assuring him that it was not they who confessed and he mustn't growl at them, but at Cook."

The Old Man seldom mentioned the raid or the trial. He talked a lot with Stevens of the fighting in Kansas. One day he began to mention an old comrade there, Charlie Kaiser, who had been killed at the battle of Osawatomie. Brown felt responsible for his death, since he had left Kaiser to reconnoiter and ordered him to hold the point. Before he could get back, the enemy had got in between them, Kaiser had stayed there, waiting, and was taken prisoner rather than desert his post. "If he had only disobeyed, or if I had only told him to run, instead of staying there, he might be alive today."

"That's what happened to Kagi," Stevens murmured thoughtlessly, and the Old Man doubled up in pain and lay silently on his cot the rest of the day.

The only other time the fighting was discussed was during an argument over the Bible. The Old Man was saying that Samson, though blinded, was able to tear down the temple of the obscene heathen. "What was he doing fooling around with Delilah?" asked Stevens. "If he left her alone he would have done better. He let himself get betrayed and others had to die for it."

Brown went white at this but managed to answer in a shaky voice: "Had Samson kept to his determination of not telling Delilah, wherein his great strength lay, he would probably never have overturned the house. I did not tell Delilah; but I was induced to act very contrary to my better judgement, and I have lost my two noble boys, and other friends, if not my two eyes."

His painful sensitivity was most apparent when he heard that his wife was on her way to visit him and was already at Baltimore. The Old Man could not bear the thought of having to talk to her about the deaths of Oliver and Watson. Fearful that the experience would break him, he wrote a highly charged letter to Thomas Wentworth Higginson, who was arranging the trip.

"If my wife were to come here just now it would only tend to distract her mind ten fold and would only add to my affliction and could not possibly do me any good. It will also use up the scanty means she has to supply bread and cheap but comfortable clothing, fuel, etc. for herself and children through the winter. Do persuade her to remain at home for a time, at least, till she can learn further from me. She will receive a thousand times the consolation at home that she can possibly find elsewhere. I have just written her there and will write her constantly. Her presence here would deepen my affliction a thousand fold. I beg of her to be calm and submissive and not to go wild on my account. I lack for nothing and was quite cheerful before I heard she talked of coming on. I asked her to compose her mind and to remain quiet 'til the last of this month, out of pity for me. I can certainly judge better in this matter than anyone else."

The Old Man was proving himself a consummate revolutionary to the end. Knowing that his letters were being published, he used every communication to defend his position and his life-style. He could not be openly revolutionary. "There are objections to my writing many things while here that I might be disposed to write were I under different circumstances. Prison rules require that all I write or receive should be examined by the sheriff or state's attorney, and that all company I see should be attended by the jailer or some of his assistants."

Edward Luttwak observed in *Coup d'Etat,* "The older technology of God is still of paramount importance. This can be a source of very considerable political power to the organizations which are identified with the appropriate beliefs and are able to channel the sentiments of the believers."

The Old Man used the libertarian idioms in the scriptures to mask his insurrectionary message from his prison cell. It allowed him to maintain his revolutionary position without yielding a superior humanism or patriotism to the other side.

A Quaker woman wrote to say, "You can never know how very many dear friends love thee with all their hearts, for thy brave efforts in behalf of the poor oppressed, and although we are non-resistants, and could not approve of bloodshed, thousands pray for you every day."

He answered her in kind: "You know Christ once armed Peter. So also in my case; I think he put a sword in my hand and there continued it, so long as he saw best, and then kindly took it from me. I wish you could know with what cheerfulness I am now wielding the 'sword of the spirit.' I bless God that it proves mighty to the pulling down of strongholds. I always loved my Quaker friends and I commend to their kind regard my poor wife and my daughters and daughters-in-law, whose husbands fell by my side. One is a mother and the other likely to become one soon."

From the other end of the spectrum came the letter from a man signing himself, "A conservative Christian": "While I cannot approve of all your acts, I stand in awe of your position since your capture, and dare not oppose you lest I be found fighting against God; for you speak as one having authority, and seem to be strengthened from on high."

This must have pleased the Old Man very much, and he responded in his confident, vaulting tone: "I am conscious that you do me no more than justice. I cannot feel that God will suffer even the poorest service we may any of us render to him or his cause to be lost, or in vain. I do feel, dear brother, that I am wonderfully strengthened from on high. May the same grace enable me to serve him in a *new obedience* through my little remainder of this life."

Not all the letters he received were sympathetic. A pious cousin complained bitterly about the great mortification that had been given to the Brown family by having one of its members hanged for the triple crimes of treason, murder, and insurrection. Charitably, the writer decided the Old Man must have been sadly "infatuated" or "mad" to have done this. Brown's reply, which appeared in the national press, was masterly:

> You will allow me to say that I deeply sympathize with you and all my sorrowing friends in their grief and terrible mortifications. I feel ten times more afflicted on their account than on account of my own circumstances. But I must say I am neither conscious of being "infatuated" or "mad." You will doubtless agree

with me that neither imprisonment, irons or gallows falling to one's lot are of themselves evidence of either guilt, "infatuation" or madness.

I discover you labor under a mistaken impression as to some important facts, which my peculiar circumstances will in all probability prevent the possibility of my removing; and I do not propose to take up any argument to prove that any motion or act of my life is right. But I will here state that I know it to be wholly my own fault as a leader that caused our disaster. Of this you have no means of judging, not being on the ground or a practical soldier. I will only add that it was in yielding to my feelings of humanity in leaving my proper place and mingling with my prisoners to quiet their fears, that occasioned our being caught. If you do not believe that I had a murderous intention (while I *know* I did not), why grieve so terribly on my account? The scaffold has but few terrors for me. God has often covered my head in the day of battle and granted me many times deliverances that were almost so miraculous I can scarce realize their truth; and now, when it seems quite certain he intends to use me in a *different way,* shall I not most cheerfully go?

I have no reason to be ashamed of it, and indeed I cannot now, after more than a month for reflection, find in my heart (before God in whose presence I expect to stand within another week) any cause for shame.

The Old Man's sister was equally indignant on reading of the "mortification" of the pious cousin: "Do not let the evil spirit suggest such a thought as this to mar your peace. No! I rejoice that a brother of mine is accounted worthy to suffer and die in His cause, and I feel myself impelled to cy out, THE LORD REIGNETH, LET THE EARTH REJOICE!"

Those southern clergymen who came to use their Calvinist training in order to convict and convert him were given a tongue-lashing they never forgot. He quickly disposed of them by asking if they were ready to fight, if necessary, for the freedom of the slave. They would say no, of course, and he would say "I will thank you to retire from my cell. Your prayers would be an abomination to my God. You insult God, coming here with the blood of slaves on your skirts.

Mind you, I respect you as gentlemen . . . but as *heathen* gentlemen."

And when he got down to practical matters, his letters were no
less admirable. For example, the famous Lydia Maria Child, hoping
to nurse him in his cell, wrote, "Believing in Peace principles, I cannot sympathize with the method you chose to advance the cause of
Freedom, but I honor your generous intentions; I admire your
courage, moral and physical. In brief, I love you and bless you. I
think of you night and day, bleeding in prison, surrounded by hostile
faces, sustained only by trust in God and your own strong heart. . . . I
long to nurse you. . . . I have asked the permission of Governor
Wise to do so."

Brown's answer was prompt and diplomatic: "I should certainly
be greatly pleased to become personally acquainted with one so
gifted and so kind; but I cannot avoid seeing some objections to it,
under the present circumstances. First, I am in charge of a most
humane gentleman, who with his family, have rendered me every
possible attention I have desired, and I am so far recovered from
my wounds as to no longer require nursing. Then again, it would
subject you to great personal inconvenience and heavy expense,
without doing me any good. Allow me to name to you another
channel through which you may reach me with your sympathies
much more effectually. I have at home a wife and three young
daughters . . ."

Despite such prudent diplomacy, one such northern sympathizer,
Mrs. Rebecca Spring, did visit his cell on November 5 to nurse him.
"While he was talking to me with deepest solicitude of his family,
the rabble, ever hanging about the Court House and prison, fearful
that we were plotting treason inside, became restless. The Sheriff
was frightened and called the jailer, so that I had only a moment to
speak with Stevens and say farewell to Mr. Brown." This episode
was widely publicized and presented the Old Man favorably but led
Mrs. Brown to write him a most troublesome letter: "I am here with
Mrs. Spring, the kind lady who came to see you and minister to
your wants, which I am deprived of doing. You have nursed and
taken care of me a great deal, but I cannot even come and look at
you. O, it is hard. . . . When you were home last June I did not think
that I took your hand for the last time. I do not want to do or say

anything to disturb your peace of mind, but Oh, I would serve you gladly if I could. . . ."

This was just another one of "those light afflictions" the Old Man had to endure on his way to the gallows, but he could not bear the thought of Mary being exposed to the threats, the venom, and the insults of the permanent southern lynch mob hanging around the streets of Charlestown. It would be hard enough back home, in her own neighborhood, but he knew that the younger children could stand up to their suffering as imperviously as he could. A letter from young Annie testified to this: "Father, you said you were cheerful. But why should you be otherwise? All you were guilty of was, doing your duty to your fellow men. Would that we were all guilty of the same." But he knew that his wife and his older sons, belonging to a middle generation, did not have the revolutionary faith that he and the young shared so triumphantly. He was particularly worried about his son Jason, who had been very disturbed in Kansas by the hostility of his neighbors. He was trying very hard to get Jason into a community where he could live without feeling guilt. The Old Man's letter about this to Mrs. Spring reveals what kind of a tender, loving father John Brown was:

I have a son in Akron Ohio
that I greatly desire to have located in a neighborhood such as Yours;
and you will pardon me for giving you some account of him,
making all needful allowance for the source the account came from.
His name is Jason; he is about thirty-six years old,
has a wife and one little boy.
He is a very laborious, ingenious, temperate, honest and truthful man
He is very expert as a gardener, vine-dresser, and manager of fruit-trees
but does not pride himself on account of his skill in anything;
always has underrated himself; is bashful and retiring in his habits,
is not (like his father) too much inclined to assume and dictate;
is too conscientious in his dealings, and too tender of
other people's feelings to get from them his just deserts,
and is very poor.
He suffered almost everything on the way to and while in Kansas
but death, and returned to Ohio not a spoiled,
but next to a ruined man.
He never quarrels,
And yet I know he is both morally and physically brave.

He will not deny his principles to save his life,
and he turned not back on the day of battle.
At the Battle of Osawatomie he fought by my side.
He is a most tender, loving and steadfast friend,
and on the right side of things in general,
A practical Samaritan (if not Christian)
and could I know that he was located with a population who were
disposed to encourage him,
without expecting him to pay too dearly in the end for it,
I should feel greatly relieved.

For the girls he wanted a "plain but perfectly practical education. . . . I mean enough of the learning of the schools to enable
them to transact the common business of life, comfortable, and
respectably . . . which prepares both men and women to be useful
though poor and meet the stern realities of life with a good grace.
You well know I have always claimed that the music of the broom,
washtub, needle, spindle, loom, axe, scythe, hoe, flail, etc. should
first be learned in all events, and that of the piano etc., afterwards."

He needed to have no fear about this. People all over the country
wanted to educate the Brown girls, who chose, characteristically and
appropriately, to go to Mr. Sanborn's school in Concord, Massachusetts. Henry James, Sr., father of the novelist, had his children
there, and as he brought them in, he noted "a daughter of John
Brown, tall, erect, and freckled, as John Brown's daughter has a
right to be. I kissed her (inwardly) between the eyes, and inwardly
heard the martyred Johannes chuckle over the fat inheritance of
love and tenderness he had, after all, bequeathed to his children in
all good men's minds."

Governor Wise, a gentleman to the last, came to Charlestown to
inform the Old Man that the customary legal appeals to hold off the
execution had been turned down by the higher courts. The Old
Man took the opportunity to clear up another matter that was
bothering him. The Governor complained, in all honesty, that the
last speech to the Court had been completely at variance with what
Brown had told him just after his capture. He hinted that it smacked
of inconsistency, perhaps cowardice.

The speech was hurting the South, and seen as a brilliant political
stroke on the Old Man's part. It far surpassed anything his lawyers

had said in his defense and the Republican Party, forced to claim him, or tolerate him, for the sake of their crucial antislavery following, found it made their association with him unexpectedly advantageous. But Wise's complaints made the Old Man realize how much the speech had obscured his purpose. He told Wise bluntly that he had been taken by surprise at the end of Coppoc's trial and that he still adhered to his original revolutionary statement of purpose.

He was so troubled by the misunderstanding that he sent for the Prosecutor to come to his cell and help him "vindicate his memory and his consistency." Hunter told him to put his revision in a letter and he would see that it was properly circulated. "I have just had my attention called to a seeming confliction between the statement I first made to Governor Wise and that which I made at the time I received my sentence, regarding my intentions respecting the slaves we took about the Ferry. I had given Governor Wise a full and particular account of that and when called in court to say whether I had anything further to urge, I was taken wholly by surprise, as I did not expect my sentence before the others. In the hurry of the moment, I forgot much that I had before *intended to say* and did not consider the full bearing of what I *then said.* I intended to convey this idea, that it was my object to place the slaves in a condition to defend their liberties, if they would, without any bloodshed, but not that I intend to run them out of the slave States."

The shrewd Prosecutor read this over, remarking that while it was an excellent explanation, he did not believe that Brown was taken by surprise that day in court but had worked out the statement to be consistent with Coppoc's defense and was "Deliberate, cool and evidently prepared before-hand."

The Old Man was annoyed at this, as he was when anybody questioned, even for a moment, his absolute veracity. He said, tartly, "I was not aware of any inconsistency until my attention was *called* to it. I do not suppose that a man in *my then circumstances* should be *superhuman* in respect to the *exact purport* of every word he might utter." The Prosecutor left with a smile, saying that he never knew a man who more carefully calculated the exact purport of every word he uttered.

The Old Man both gained and lost by this maneuver. The papers opposed to him were quick to say that he had now lost whatever sympathy remained for him. They hoped if another party entered Virginia with John Brown's avowed purpose, that "they may be caught and, without jury, burned alive in a fire made of green fagots." But now that the trials were over and the defense strategy of the lawyers was no longer valid, Brown preferred to let his purpose stand for all time as a revolutionary one.

Such vicious squibs in the papers no longer bothered him. He was confident that, one way and another, pushing and pulling on the American conscience, he was triumphing over the wooden-headed insensitivity of America to the slave and the oppressed black everywhere. He had only to pick up the daily paper and read of slave stampedes, threats of disunion, and comments such as this: "Brown knows, almost as well as anyone in the country the extent of the shock he had given. He has been told how Virginia quakes and that almost the whole South trembled in sympathy. He cannot fail to understand, for many have made it plain for him, what great events have sprung from his weak and ill-advised attempt. All this Brown knows and is consoled by, but he shows no exultation over it, simply speaking of it earnestly and tranquilly, as a successful result beyond everything to which he had aspired. People are questioning the institution far more than they ever did . . . the slave stampede is taking place if only on a more gradual way than expected."

During this same period, a liberal named Arny, who had known Brown for many years, came to his cell to get him to deny that he had been involved in the so-called Pottawatomie Massacre, which the opposition was emphasizing in order to destroy sympathy for him. Glad to get this matter off his conscience, Brown would not deny it, although his son Salmon had rushed into print, for the sake of the family, to say his father was twenty miles away at the time. (The irony was that it was Salmon who did some of the actual killing.) Arny said in a half-apologetic, half-accusing way, "There is a different version being given to your Kansas exploits. Your reputation demands an explanation."

Brown glared at him. "I understand your illusion but you are mistaken in thinking it needs any refutation from me. Time and posterity will approve every act of mine to prevent slavery from being extended in Kansas. I never shed the blood of any man except in self-defense or in the promotion of a righteous cause." The Old Man went to his grave on that statement.

As his last days approached, he began to wish he could see Mary again and sent her a letter of reluctant yearning:

In regard to your coming here; if you feel sure that you can endure the trials and the shock, which will be unavoidable, I should be most glad to see you once more; but when I think of your being insulted on the road, and perhaps while here, and of only seeing your wretchedness made complete, I shrink from it. Your composure and fortitude of mind may be quite equal to it all, but I am in dreadful doubt of it. If you do come, the scenes which you will have to pass through on coming here will be anything but those you now pass, with tender, kind-hearted friends and kind faces to meet you everywhere. Do consider the matter well before you make the plunge. I think I had better say no more on this dreadful subject.

Mary Brown received this letter while at the Philadelphia home of William Grant Still, a black conductor of the Underground Railroad. It was one of many abortive stops she had made in an uncertain journey to Charlestown, undertaken after a visit from T. W. Higginson, who felt almost personally responsible for the Old Man's defeat at the Ferry. He was ashamed that "the men who gave him money and arms should not have been actually at his side." In spite of Brown's indication that he did not want to be rescued, Higginson hoped that if he got Mary Brown to talk to him, the Old Man would still consent to a rescue attempt.

Higginson found the North Elba farm a wild, bleak place but a good one for the family of a revolutionary. His task was a sensitive one, going into a family in which four young men had been killed within two weeks and asking support for a project in which more might be sacrificed. Mary Brown agreed to go to Charlestown, if only to bring back the bodies of her boys and her husband.

Higginson was awed by the stoic calm of the household: "As I sat that evening with the women busily sewing around me, preparing the mother for her sudden departure with me on the morrow, some daguerreotypes were brought out to show me and someone said, 'This is Oliver, one of those who were killed at Harper's Ferry.' I glanced up sidelong at the young, fair-headed girl, who sat near me by the little table . . . a wife at fifteen, a widow at sixteen; and this was her husband and he was killed. As the words were spoken in her hearing, not a muscle quivered, and her fingers did not tremble as she drew the thread. Her life had become too real to leave room for wincing at mere words. She had lived beyond the word, to the sterner fact, and having confronted that, language was an empty shell."

Higginson tried, in his ministerial way, to estimate how desperate the family needs were. He found out that they had subsistence but absolutely no money with which to face the winter. They had a few pennies to pay postage for letters to their father, which the girls had earned by picking berries. Higginson said, "The reason of these privations simply was that it cost money to live in adherence to the cause of freedom." Mary Brown assured Higginson that her widowed daughters were not destitute. Oliver had left his wife a property of five sheep. Higginson inquired further into this and found the sheep were worth two dollars apiece, "a child of sixteen, left a widow in the world with an estate amounting to ten dollars." Probing further, Mary Brown confessed to him she had a major financial problem about the taxes for the farm. She had put the ten dollars by for this but had to lend it suddenly to a poor black woman, with no hope of repayment.

It was no wonder that the Old Man fought off his consuming desire to see Mary again. It was the cost, the terrible cost such innocent desires wreak upon the poor. His fears of exhausting the last family resources stained his bravest letters with the painful stigmata of poverty. He reminded her that she was riding on the crest of temporary sympathy that would soon fade away. "There is but little more of the romantic about helping a poor widow and her children than there is about helping the poor niggers."

Many people, however, assured Mary Brown that there was money available for John Brown's wife to see her husband and provide for his decent burial and that of his sons and comrades. They urged her to write to Governor Wise, asking at least for the dead bodies. Wise replied with an order on General Taliaferro, in Charlestown, to "deliver the mortal remains of your husband when all 'shall be over,' " as he put it, with southern gallantry. Nothing was said about her sons or the others. Most of them were tangled in decay in a mass grave, and Watson had been taken to a nearby medical college for use as an anatomical specimen. The body was skinned and the skin varnished, after which a dispute arose about whether it should be stuffed by a taxidermist, or cut up into game pouches.

Governor Wise's gallantry went a step further to guarantee "if you attend the reception in person, to guard you sacredly in your solemn mission." Mary was encouraged to think that she could be at her husband's side before, as well as after the ordeal. Two days before the execution she was at Harper's Ferry.

She was escorted there by an abolitionist couple, Mr. and Mrs. J. Miller McKim, and a young lawyer named Hector Tyndale, who was involved in the rescue plot and spying out the defenses. He was appalled at their complexity. When they boarded the train at Baltimore, they discovered that every person on it had to have a passport or a letter from Governor Wise. No Republicans or antislavery sympathizers were allowed to board, and the passengers were almost entirely newspapermen. At every stop, the Brown party could see troops guarding the stations. When they got to Harper's Ferry, they learned that Colonel Robert E. Lee was back on duty there. This time he commanded two hundred and fifty artillerymen from Fort Monroe who had set up cannons on both sides of the bridges and at the ends of all the streets.

After a complicated exchange of telegrams, she was permitted, the next day, to go alone to Charlestown to see her husband. A closed carriage was sent to the Ferry under escort by eight cavalrymen and a sergeant. Riding back with her in the coach was a Captain Moore of the Militia. She left on the dreary ride the morning of December 1 and arrived at Charlestown about 3:30 in the afternoon.

The Old Man was told that she was coming. He spent the interval watching preparation being made at the field in which he was to be hanged, only a half mile away. Stakes were driven, marking the positions the military companies were to hold, and white papers placed on top of them. Then, the site of the gallows was marked off and the lumber brought in for the construction. The wood was borrowed from the construction of a Baptist church taking place nearby. The gallows was designed so that it could be knocked down and reused for the hanging of Coppoc and Cook. A completely new one was to be constructed for the hanging of the blacks.

The Old Man was extremely nervous about his wife's reception. The day before, no visitors were allowed because of an ugly incident in which a man had jostled him, shouting, "I want to be the buck to put the rope around your miserable neck." However, the crowds in the streets were not threatening; there was even an air of festivity because of the imminent hanging. A miliary band had been parading all day, serenading the dignitaries. The Militiamen had celebrated with such gusto they were confined to quarters at night and ordered to sleep on their arms.

It was into this street carnival that Mary Brown was brought from Harper's Ferry. In the jail she was searched by the jailer's wife, just in case she was trying to smuggle a knife or "some strychnine with which to cheat the gallows." The Old Man's leg chains were taken off, and he was brought into the jailer's parlor for this last visit. He had been having severe pains in his infected kidney; it was with great difficulty that he could stand erect, or stand at all. He immediately clasped Mary in his arms, however, and they stood for a long moment, quietly weeping. The jailer, the Sheriff, and General Taliaferro remained as witnesses, keeping the Old Man under surveillance during the entire meeting.

For a brief moment he lost the iron control he had established over his feeling for the forty odd days he had just spent in actual chains. They both cried a little, and then he led her to a little sofa, where they sat for these last hours. Brown scorned to mumble or keep his voice down and at times directed his remarks particularly to the ears of the intruders. His first comment to her was a low one, of deep contrition:

"Mary, I have had my dark days, laboring and waiting these twenty years, and at last believing that the day of fulfillment had come. But I have failed, and instead of being free on the mountain

John Brown's Farewell to His Wife, Charlestown Jail

to break every yoke and let the oppressed go free, I am shorn of my strength with a prison wall about me and . . ."

"No, father," said Mary, in a clear voice, strong enough so that those lurking by the doorways could hear her. "I had often thought I should rather hear you were dead than fallen into the hands of these enemies. But I don't think so now. The good that is growing out of it is wonderful. If you had preached in the pulpit ten such lives as you have lived, you could have not done so much good as in that one speech to the court. It is talked about and preached about everywhere in all places."

Taking his cue from her, the Old Man's voice assumed its vaulting, metallic tone.

"And that is why, Mary, I am awaiting the hour of my *public murder* with great composure of mind and cheerfulness. That is why I feel the strongest assurance that in no other possible way could I be used to advance the cause of God and humanity. I know that *nothing* that either I or all my family have sacrificed or suffered ... *will be lost!*"

Then, proceeding to business, he began a long, calm disposition of his complicated affairs. He showed her his will, leaving everything to her with the exception of a few presents to his sons and Bibles for his daughters. He called the Sheriff over to the sofa and asked him to witness it. Money had been sent to him enclosed in the sympathetic letters. He signed checks and endorsed them over to his wife, the largest for one hundred dollars. Time passed, the grim old warrior setting things to rights without a quaver in his hand or voice, a display of coolness which impressed onlookers more than any possible speech, however poetic or devout. After his estate and his prospects had been disposed of down to the last dollar and grandchild, he brought up the subject of his sons.

"When you secure the bodies of Watson and Oliver, and I would include also, Dauphin and Will Thompson, take my body and these others and get a pile of pine logs and burn them all together. It will be much less expensive to gather up the ashes in this way, and take them to their final resting place."

Mary moaned no, no, and started to weep and the Sheriff, who had returned to his perch, leaped to his feet and said the laws of the state of Virginia would not permit such an act of sacrilege.

With feigned innocence, the Old Man remarked, "I only thought after hearing what has happened to Watson and others that this might be the only way of getting us all together."

"I really cannot consent to this," Mary said in anguish. "I hope you will change your mind on this subject."

"Do not fret about it, Mary," said the Old Man, mildly. "I thought the plan would save money and was the best."

The Sheriff, made nervous by this shocking display of unorthodoxy, wanted to know what religious ceremonies or comforts

Brown would care to have in his final moments. His voice, again hard and dissonant, the Old Man declared "I want no prayer, nor religious services, whatever, in the jail or at the gallows from ministers who consent to the enslavement of their fellow Christians. I would prefer, Sheriff, to be accompanied by a dozen little ragged slave children and their black mother. I prefer their appeal to God for a blessing on my soul than the appeal of the whole clergy of the Commonwealth combined."

General Taliaferro, very much shaken by this sentiment, said in a severe, warning tone, "Captain Brown, I have orders that you will not be allowed to make any speeches tomorrow, here or anywhere else!" The prisoner shrugged; he had already *made* his speech and knew it would be well reported in the papers.

Here the jailer intervened, serving a small supper for the condemned man and his wife. After this, they sat in silence, hand in hand. The General began pacing impatiently, his spurs jingling; finally he turned and bowed to the couple on the sofa and said, "This is going on too long. Mrs. Brown has to go back to Harper's Ferry tonight. I am responsible for her safety."

"I would like to have Mary stay all night," said the Old Man, simply.

"That is out of the question," said the General.

"Well," Brown answered, "I want no favors from the state of Virginia."

The time for parting had come. He had no more words, he was very tired, and his back was paining unbearably. They stood for a moment shaking hands shyly, without the emotional strength for a final embrace. Mary Brown asked if she could say good-by to the other prisoners. This was refused. She asked if she could have the chain that was kept around the Old Man's ankles. This was also refused. Her husband said, "God bless you, Mary, and the children," and she was gone.

The Old Man was too tired to sleep, or pray, very much that night; mainly he wrote letters, which perhaps were his prayers. He sat at the window, looking out from time to time into that dark quadrant of space where his life was to end.

"I should be sixty years old were I to live till May 9, 1860. I have enjoyed life very much as it is. I have never, since I can remember, required a great amount of sleep. By that I conclude I have already enjoyed fully an average number of waking hours with those who reach their three score and ten. I have not as yet been driven to the use of glasses but can still see to read and write quite comfortably. But more than that I have generally enjoyed remarkably good health. I might go on to recount unnumbered and un-merited blessings among which would be some very severe afflic-tions, and those the most needed blessings of all. And now when I think how easily I might be left to spoil all I have done or suffered in the cause of freedom, I hardly dare risk another voyage, if I even had the opportunity."

The thing that bothered him most was the rejection by his children of formal religion and the teachings of the Bible. He could not seem to realize that by accepting him as an example of man's service of his fellowman, they might not need the orthodoxy that he cherished. Ironically, it was in great measure his teachings that had made them reject the slavery-tainted American church. They had told him long before that they thought the Bible was all a fiction, but on that last night he appealed to them again: "Make the Bible your daily and nightly study, with a childlike, candid, teachable spirit, and out of love and respect for your father."

It was almost dawn as he finished his last letter to the family and found, singing in his mind, the things he wanted them to remember most about him. "My dear and shattered family, do not feel ashamed on my account, nor for one moment despair of the cause, or grow weary of well-doing. I never felt a stronger confidence in the cer-tain and near approach of a bright morning and a glorious day, than I have felt, and now feel, since my confinement here. I am endeavoring to return like a poor prodigal, as I am, to my Father, against whom I have always sinned, in the hope that he may kindly meet me though a very great way off. Oh, my dear wife and child-ren, would to God you could know how I have been traveling in birth for you all. Try to build again your broken walls and make the utmost of every stone that is left. Nothing can so tend to make life a blessing as the consciousness that you *love* and are *beloved* and love the stranger still. It is ground of the utmost comfort to my mind, to know that so many of you as have had the opportunity, have given full proof of your fidelity to the great family of man. Be faithful until death. From the exercise of habitual love to man, it cannot be very hard to learn to love his *Maker.*"

The bright morning revealed outside his window also showed troops arriving already to take up their positions on the field. In addition, there were backup pickets and patrols as much as five miles away. The artillery arrived with a huge brass cannon placed so that if a rescue was attempted from the scaffold, a charge of grapeshot would tear Brown's body to shreds. Mingled with the shouted military orders came sounds of heavy hammering as the carpenters raised the roof beams of John Brown's house of death. His cellmate Stevens, stirring, heard this and whimpered in his far-off dreams. Five hundred troops had now assembled on the field; in the town itself, there were more than twenty-five hundred.

The Old Man continued to write, finishing a letter to an old Ohio friend an hour before his execution. At 10:30, the Sheriff and the jailer came for him. He was wearing the same clothes he had been cut down in, but they brought him a new black slouch hat. He asked them if he could say good-by to his boys, and they agreed.

He was led first to the cells of Copeland and Shields Green. He shook hands with them solemnly and gave them each a quarter, saying he had no more use for money, adding, "God bless you. Stand by your friends." When he got to the cell where Cook and Coppoc were confined together, he said, "Cook, you have made false statements, both about the prospect of getting reinforcements and some of the orders you were given." Cook started to argue and the Old Man waved him away. "Coppoc, you also made false statements, but I am glad to hear you have contradicted them. Stand up like a man." He then gave Coppoc a quarter and shook hands with them both.

Hazlett was in the next cell, and they started to lead him there. He pulled away, saying, "No, I do not know that man. He was not one of my men." The Old Man knew that Hazlett had not been properly identified as yet and so would not betray him, going to his death with this one lie on his lips.

At last he was brought back to Stevens. The Old Man embraced him and kissed his cheek. Stevens said, "Good-by, Captain, I know you are going to a better land." "I know I am," said the Old Man. "Bear up, Stevens, and don't betray your friends." He gave him a quarter, put on his new hat and walked to the door.

The day was shocking in its brightness. As he recoiled from the glare, a jailer put a piece of paper and a quarter in his hand. He wanted his autograph, which was now selling for one to five dollars apiece. The Old Man started to hand it back, but when he saw General Taliaferro sitting out there on his big white horse, he decided he would make his speech from the scaffold in spite of him. With a steady hand he wrote:

> Charlestown, Va, 2nd December, 1859.
> I John Brown am now quite certain that the crimes of this guilty, land: will never be purged away; but with Blood. I had as I now think: vainly flattered myself that without very much bloodshed; it might be done.

He handed back the quarter and walked, painfully bent but trying to stand erect, to a wagon, in which rested his coffin. He was to ride this, as a seat, to the place of execution. The streets were crowded with troops, mostly mounted. The procession, a climax of military pomp, proceeded him down the half mile of road. There were not many onlookers, since they had been warned to stay home and watch out for another slave insurrection.

"Where are the citizens?" the Old Man asked.

Jailer Avis, sitting nervously on the coffin with him, explained, "They are being kept away by the military."

"Too bad," said the Old Man. "Why all this military? I had no idea Governor Wise considered my execution so important."

"You are more cheerful than I am," Avis observed.

"Yes," replied the Old Man, looking grimly at the troops in battle array. "I ought to be."

He looked over to the southeast, where the blue mountains which had denied him their strength stood in their shielding haze. "This is a beautiful country," he said. "I never had the pleasure of seeing it before."

The two white horses drew the wagon in their stately way to the steps of the scaffold. The Old Man was lifted out and taken, his arms pinioned behind him, to stand waiting near the well-hinged trap. Looking up at him from the files of troops were Thomas Jackson, later known as Stonewall Jackson, commanding cadets from Virginia Military Institute, and John Wilkes Booth. Brown nudged off his hat and tried to straighten up. The Sheriff came to his side with the black cap of the to-be-hanged. Before he put it on, the Old Man spoke quickly to Jailer Avis. "I have no words to thank you for all your kindness to me."

The Sheriff dropped the black cap, cone-shaped, like a candle extinguisher, over the victim's head.

"Captain Brown," cried the Sheriff, "You are not standing on the drop. Come forward, please."

"I can't see, gentlemen," said the Old Man, in a smothered voice. "You must lead me."

Gingerly, as if they were almost afraid to touch him, the Sheriff and the jailer led him to the exact center of the drop. It gave slightly under the Old Man's weight and the young cadets from V. M. I. heaved an involuntary sigh. The cap was lifted lightly and the noose slipped over his head. A shameful delay ensued, as for nearly ten minutes troops were marching, turning, reversing, countermarching, trying to get into a preordered position to provide maximum defense. It went on so long that the embarrassed Sheriff would lift Brown's cap from time to time, and try to wave some air into it, so that he would not be smothered instead of hanged.

"Can't you be quick?" mumbled the Old Man, his last request. Finally, the masses of glittering forms stayed still, and the Sheriff took the ax and cut the rope. The drop gave way and the Old Man dangled to his death. At this exact moment, the slaves on Colonel Turner's plantation, in nearby Halltown, set their master's mansion and barns on fire.

Beneath the platform, the black-garbed doctors gathered, putting stethoscopes to the Old Man's still living body. For thirty-five min-

The Hanging

utes he dangled there, his fierce, strong heart fighting against silence and the grave. Finally he was pronounced dead and his body laid in a crumpled heap on the scaffold. It was then taken to the jail for the doctors to sign a death certificate. They clustered around the body, disturbed by its appearance. He did not look like a hanged man: his face was not blackened, his eyes did not protrude, nor were there discharges from the nose and mouth. None of the doctors wanted to sign. One suggested they make sure of his death by amputating his head, another by administering a massive dose of strychnine. They decided to come back after lunch. At 3:30, the document of Brown's death was signed, after much muttering that it was not inconceivable that his partisans in the North could revive him with a galvanic battery. The doctors could not believe he was dead, and they were right.

17

Body in Transit

Date of passage, Dec. 4: name, John Brown: age, 59: place of death, Charlestown, Vir: disease, hanging: remarks, hung for murder, treason and inciting slaves to escape from Virginia and Maryland.

From records, City Inspector's office
New York City

The rigid body of the hanged man traveling north was like an electrode plunged into battery acid; the North became charged by it. His first stop in a northern city was in Philadelphia at twenty minutes to one, on Saturday, December 3. There had been many meetings the day before. The hours and then the minutes before his execution were counted off in a crowded prayer meeting at the Shiloh Presbyterian Church, conducted by the Reverend Henry Highland Garnet. Nine black preachers joined him in hymns and lamentations rising to a climax at the very moment when the rope was biting into the Old Man's jugular vein. The white people had their observance at the National Hall, at which the principal speaker was Lucretia Mott, the Quaker abolitionist and women's rights leader.

The Mayor and Chief of Police, taking due notice of an uncontrollable excitement building up in a city of a border state, to be touched off by the intrusion of the most egregious violator of borders, arranged to have the body pass in and out with the greatest possible secrecy and speed. The coffin, swathed in an old blanket, was taken off the train from Baltimore and put without ceremony on a rickety wagon, drawn by a spavined old horse. The disguise did not work. A silent but emotional crowd, mostly blacks, gathered at the station, and the police, who had been concealed, had to form a barrier between the crowd and the coffin. A police driver whipped the horse out of the station yard, but the crowd ran after the wagon. There was a bigger crowd on the next corner, which also began racing behind the wagon, trying to touch it. As the fleeing cortege went rattling down factory-lined Washington Street, the operators, men and women, black and white, left their benches and rushed to the sidewalks. Many of them followed the wagon to its destination at the Walnut Street wharf, where a large crowd was waiting to show their grief and gratitude.

The Old Man's spectral intrusion into Washington, D.C., was far worse. On Saturday trains began to disgorge Senators and Representatives, who were hurrying to urgent party caucuses to develop tactics of assault and defense for the opening of Congress the following Monday. The representatives of southern constituencies were in a mood of despair. Henry Adams, there at the time, saw this as the madness of decadence; it became one of the crucial experiences of his *"Education."* He broke from the skeptical detachment of his usual prose to declare that "The Southern Secessionists were certainly unbalanced in mind—fit for medical treatment, like other victims of hallucination—haunted by suspicions, by *idées fixes,* by violent, morbid excitement; but this was not all. They were stupendously ignorant of the world. As a class, the cotton planters were mentally one sided—ill-balanced and provincial to a degree rarely known. They were a close society on whom the new fountains of power had powered a stream of wealth and slaves that acted like oil on flames."

The Old Man had an effect on their fiery consciousnesses more like high octane gasoline. But they thought they were great statesmen and could run the country and solve all crises by smothering them in constitutional prose. Henry Adams thought their statesmenship consisted of "bad temper, bad manners, poker and treason," but it was far more than that. They felt they had the one formula for national control which could not be overcome: the threat to break up the union and go it alone, taking the land in the southern half of the country all the way out to the Pacific and expropriating all federal property below the Mason-Dixon line. It had worked for years, for generations, and they were going to use it again, this time reasonably, even ethically, motivated by the John Brown raid in all its bloody realities.

After the first southern caucus, a press release was given out saying the South stood united in a drastic policy. "In view of the Harper's Ferry abolition invasion, and its extension and alarming ramifications, and in view of the sympathies of the abolitionized Republican Party for old Brown, and the threat of the party to reduce the South to submission, a special law shall be demanded for the future protection of the Southern States against all abolition conspirators, emissaries and incendiaries. In default of some such Congressional protection, the Southern Members of both houses shall withdraw and meet in a body in Richmond, Virginia, for the initial steps for an independent Southern Confederacy." Specifically, they were asking for the outlawing of the abolition movement, the purging of radical Republicans from the Party, and the guarantee that the presidential nominee would be a "national man" whose program would appeal to the old Whigs in the southern states.

The Republicans came to the capital in a mood of wary confidence. They had been winning elections at a surprising rate since the coup, but they knew the Party would be under heavy attack as conspirators with the Old Man at the Ferry. John Andrew, who had read the incriminating notes before they were destroyed that had passed between the Old Man and the Secret Six, wrote a warning letter to a Republican Senator. "I am confident that there are some half dozen men who ought not to testify *anywhere,* and who never will, with my consent, do so. Their relations with Brown were such, and their knowledge of his movements, and his intentions as a practical abolitionist to aid the escape of slaves by force, even at the risk of armed encounter, that they could not, without personal danger, say anything. Nor could they be known as having those relations without giving some color to the charge that Republicans co-operate in such movements."

But the Party figured that now that the Old Man was dead and could no longer insist on his right of revolution, they could use the defense the Party lawyers had put forth for him at his trial. John Brown was simply an eccentric leader of a tiny organization to run off slaves. The arms he collected were for the protection of his party if they were attacked on the way out of Virginia. The infamous "Provisional Constitution" was merely a set of bylaws for the government of this "novel voluntary association."

Horace Greeley, present at the Republican caucus, was responsible for this clever formulation. He kept referring to Brown as "this private man," as if the Old Man and his friends had organized some typical New England charitable undertaking which had gone a little too far in its enthusiasm to uplift the fallen. Paradoxically, this did not reduce the Old Man's stature but enormously increased it, by ascribing to him the power of personally initiating, with little or no resources, an event destined to change the history of the nation and the world.

The cortege arrived in New York at 7 P.M., and the coffin was taken to an undertaker on lower Broadway. The Old Man's body had been placed in a rosewood casket, the only one available in Charlestown, but no plate had been put on it.

The corpse was now transferred into a plain pine box, and the rosewood casket was shipped back to Virginia. Brown's hanging clothes were taken off, and he was dressed in a pleated white shroud with a white cravat. Many people came to see him, and it was reported that his face was faintly flushed as if he were very much alive but that there was a nasty bruise on the left side of his neck where the knot had dug into it.

Since the next morning was Sunday, there were special sermons about him, some favorable, some critical. The two most notable were at the Church of the Puritans, where Doctor Cheever preached on "The Martyr's Death and the Martyr's Triumph," and the one preached by the Rev. Mrs. Antoinette Blackwell at Goldbeck's Music Hall. She appreciated fully his work in behalf of the slave, Mrs. Blackwell declared, but held up the higher, nonresistant opposition to slavery as dictated by the spirit of Christianity. She was happy, however, that the freedom-loving people of the North recognized Brown's greatness.

The New York *Herald,* the *Tribune,* and the Associated Press assigned reporters to go with the cortege to the burial at North Elba. Wendell Phillips and J. Miller McKim, leaders of the American Anti-Slavery Society, announced that they would accompany the body as escort, a gesture which informed the country that the Garrisonian Abolitionists claimed the Old Man as one of their own.

The funeral train, which was now taking on the importance of the cortege of a great statesman, with its entourage of reporters and official escorts, left New York early Monday morning and traveled up the Hudson to Troy, arriving there at two in the afternoon. Mrs. Brown was respectfully asked if the train should be stopped at stations where the people had gathered to watch it pass. She felt that this would be out of harmony with the Old Man's instructions to go straight from New York to the American House in Troy, a temperance hotel where he always stayed and where young Oliver had his final parting with Martha. There was an informal reception there, but Mrs. Brown did not want a procession held, and the train left for Rutland, Vermont, at four. The reporters began to marvel at the fact that all through this dignified and quietly solemn journey to the grave of a poverty-stricken hanged man, no courtesy was left out, and no bills were presented.

At noon that day, the thirty-sixth Congress met among predictions that this would be the last such meeting in the nation's history. The Senate assembled at noon, and the Chaplain, P. D. Gurley, D.D., immediately invoked the dreadful presence of John Brown, damning him soundly in the opening prayer. The first order of business was a resolution by James Mason of Virginia that a committee be appointed to inquire into the late invasion and seizure of the Armory and arsenal of the United States in Virginia and to report whether it was made under the color of any organization intended to subvert the United States government. And whether any citizens of the United States were accessory thereto, by contributions of money, arms, and munitions, and how same was obtained and transported to the place so invaded. And what legislation would be necessary to preserve the peace of the United States and its public property. Mason and the southerners were prepared for heavy resistance from the northern side to this, during which they could condemn the Republicans for trying to conceal the complicity of their leaders in the conspiracy.

But the Republicans had devised a very clever counterstroke. Lyman Trumbull, a moderate Republican from Illinois, rose and proposed an amendment to Mason's resolution, in virtually the same wording but proposing the investigation of the seizure of the U.S. arsenal in Liberty, Missouri, by the Border Ruffians in the Kansas Wars. For every accusation of treasonable and murderous invasion from the North to Virginia, the Republicans could raise an accusation against the South, citing chapter and verse from a prior investigation in the House of Representatives. This would allow the Republicans to defend themselves and the Old Man in the Kansas setting, where he was stronger and where the Party was most brutally abused. The South was taken by surprise, and debate was put over to the next day.

In the House of Representatives, too, to quote the *Tribune,* the members, before electing a Speaker, "insist on debating indefinitely (until the first of February) John Brown's Raid, Seward's 'Irrepressible Conflict,' and Helper's *Impending Crisis,*" a book warning the poor whites of the South that they had to take political power or perish. But it was especially in the Senate that the Old Man had his political resurrection. Every act of his life, every facet of his personality was revealed, attacked, and defended, between the hammer and the anvil of partisan debate. The pages of the *Congressional Globe* for December, 1859, exploded with the molecular juxtaposition of violent, hard-fought arguments, backed with voluminous research and inquiry.

With a weak President in the White House, the Senate was the ruling force in the government. Fifteen of the Senators had been Governors, and all had maintained close and immediate connections with their constituencies.

Seward and Sumner, the two most radical Republicans and therefore the most vulnerable to attack, were deliberately absent, and their places were taken by the two Republican bullyboys, Ben Wade of Ohio and Zack Chandler of Michigan. Wade had come to his desk in the last session carrying two loaded horse pistols, let them rest awhile on the top of the desk, and then, after glancing significantly at the other side, put them inside. They were there now. Wade had joined Senators Chandler and Cameron of Pennsylvania in a pact to "carry the quarrel to the coffin," letting their southern opponents know that they would not permit any more beatings to be given to their colleagues, like the one given Sumner, without resisting to the death.

From the first clash of the debate there rose the spirit of the Old Man, massive, omnipresent, erupting in venomous portraits by the southerners, softened, veiled, and removed from earthly judgments by the Republicans. Giant contradictions, the sure sign of the disintegration of an era, quickly became apparent. The defenders of an attack upon the government became the Constitutionalists. The accusers of the attackers became destroyers of the Constitution, confessing more sedition in debate than the government could prove against Brown himself.

For four days while the Old Man was above ground, and three days while his body lay, hard as granite, under the icy clumps and shards of the Adirondack earth, the South, then commanding a majority in the Senate, and with all the resources of governmental authority in their hands, saw the resistant spirit that the Old Man had shamed out of the North preparing to wrestle power daily from their weakening grasp.

On Tuesday, the Old Man's cortege left Rutland, Vermont, at 5 A.M. to travel to Vergennes. They arrived at 10 A.M., and there was the now usual informal reception of sympathizers at the temperance hotel. The next stage of the journey was to be by boat across ice-skimmed Lake Champlain. Carriages were provided for the party, and just before noon they set out for the lake. Along the bridge by Otter Creek, a group of admirers lined up on both sides, in military array, removing their hats in the driving sleet. When they reached the shore, the coffin was put on the boat, and the sails lifted to drive the cargo through the dark waters, fighting off the encroaching threat of the ice.

Precisely at this hour the debate opened in the U.S. Senate. Mason, a bluff, genial man, always dressed in a suit of gray, Virginia homespun, led off for the Democrats. Speaking in a low key and seemingly without rancor or exasperation, he asked for the ayes and nays on his resolution, which the Clerk had dutifully read. Lyman Trumbull rose and offered his amendment, first assuring the

Senate that he was anxious to vote for Mason's amendment "if any other persons than the twenty-two whose names are known to the country, are implicated in, or in any way are accessory to the seizure of Harper's Ferry, and the murder of citizens of Virginia, let us ascertain who they are, and let them be held responsible for their acts."

Trumbull was letting the other side know that all the Republicans would vote for the investigation. He knew where all the witnesses damaging to his side were. Howe, Sanborn, and Stearns were in Canada, Gerrit Smith was in an insane asylum, Theodore Parker was dying in Italy, Frederick Douglass was on his way to Liverpool, and Sumner and Seward were in Europe. And the Old Man had betrayed no one; he had never ceased to insist that the foray was "under the auspices of John Brown and no one else."

Trumbull was ideally suited for the Republican manager of the debate. He was born a Connecticut Yankee not far from the Old Man's birthplace at Torrington. He had become a schoolmaster at sixteen and, at twenty, headmaster of a school in Georgia. He moved from there to Illinois and brought with him a sound knowledge of the mores of both contending sections. He had a long, frail body and a small head, on which his hair was cut quite short. His mouth was tight, his voice high and light, and small, measuring, and reproving eyes glittered behind Pickwickian spectacles as he spoke with confident precision: "In regard to the misguided man who led the insurgents on that occasion, I have no remarks to make. He has already expiated on the gallows the crime he committed against the laws of his country, and to answer for his errors, or his virtues, whatever they may have been, he has gone fearlessly and willingly before that Judge who cannot err, therefore let him rest."

He then read a well-validated account of the take-over of the Missouri arsenal and commented, "Now, sir, there is a very striking similarity between the breaking into the arsenal and the attack upon the one at Harper's Ferry. The question of slavery had to do with both. The Arsenal in Missouri was broken into for the purpose of obtaining arms to force slavery on Kansas; the Arsenal at Harper's Ferry was taken possession of for the expelling of slavery from the state of Virginia, both unjustified, and both proper subjects to look into."

Mr. Mason replied that the Senator's amendment was obviously designed to hinder or embarrass the Harper's Ferry investigation, and he would not vote for it. As for the seizure of the arsenal at Liberty, it consisted simply in some wild, drunken Missourians breaking in without hurting its custodian, taking some guns, going to Kansas on a spree and then returning most of them to Liberty. For the Republicans to compare this spontaneous act of frontier hoodlumism to the apocalyptic terror at Harper's Ferry was a gross insult to their intelligence.

Davis of Mississippi introduced the southern demands with great dignity. If the federal government permitted war to be made against Virginia under "the immunities the Constitution secures" (freedom of speech and the right to bear arms), the southern states would be better off to become "foreign governments with police stations along each border and passports required, with such inquiry into the character of persons coming in as would secure immunity to peaceful women and children from the incendiary and the assassin." There had to be guarantees made to the South; they did not want more talk about slavery but for Republican leaders to go on platforms in the North and denounce John Brown as a ruffian, a thief, and a murderer.

The Republican whip, Henry Wilson, answered Davis. He deplored the deed at the Ferry, he had talked to no one in the North who had approved of it, but "The leader of the movement, by his bearing, his courage, had excited the sympathy of many men, and exhorted the admiration of all during his trial and during the scenes that have since taken place. I believe that to be the sentiment of the country generally. I believe that he was sincere, that he violated the law but that he had followed out his deepest convictions and was willing to take the consequences of his act."

Mr. Mason replied brutally: "I know nothing about the man except the notoriety he obtained as a ruffian, a thief, and a robber. He had been a vagrant for years, he had no resources of his own, but he brought resources for this insurrection costing a large sum of money. We want to know where that money was supplied, to get at those thousand rills which go to make up public sentiment and which resulted in furnishing an adequate treasure to send a ruffian with an armed band and arms enough at his command to place them in the hands of slaves, certainly to the amount of two thousand, within an hour after he had collected them. These are the facts we want to get at in the inquiry."

Mason's hard line was taken up by Iverson of Georgia, a seasoned old disunionist, soon to become a leader of the Confederacy. He said the intrusion of the Kansas matter was merely to break the force of the real investigation. "The Republican Senators say their people are opposed to Brown, then what means the ringing of bells in New Hampshire on the day Brown was hung?"

This brought John Hale of New Hampshire into the fray. "I have never said I had no sympathy for Brown. I said I did not approve his act, but John Brown displayed some high traits of character for which I have high sympathy."

"Who is John Brown," demanded Iverson angrily, "that he should excite the sympathy of any honorable man? A man who in Kansas for five years was engaged in no other business than theft, robbery, and murder, a man who in cold blood could take men out of their beds at night and in the presence of their children and wives, murder them on the spot—that is the man you have sympathy for?"

Iverson began to look hard at his northern Democrat colleagues, who had been notably silent since the raid. "It cannot be disguised that the northern heart sympathizes with Brown and his fate because he died in the cause of what they call liberty. All your political conduct proves that your intention is to excite insurrection in the South, so that slavery will become burdensome to the southern people and they will be compelled to give it up. I tell the Senators that the southern people are becoming aware of the intention of the Republican Party. I know how strong the party is. . . . I am afraid that too many of the Democratic Party of the North are going over to the Black Republicans, because the Black Republicans have exhibited more zeal and determination in their war against slavery than the Democratic Party itself has. I wish the Democratic Party was purer and better than it is. But, sir, the South will be able to take care of itself like Virginia. In the pride and power of her sovereignty she has spurned all assistance, and stands today vindicated as a sovereign state. We are able to protect ourselves and we intend to do it, and whatever may be your political action and course against the South and her institutions, we shall be prepared to defend ourselves to the last extremity, even at the sacrifice of the Union which you all pretend so much to revere."

Mr. Mason thought that this was a good time to call for the ayes and nays on his resolution but Mr. James F. Simmons, a Republican from Rhode Island, insisted he wanted to say a word or two on it, and so the Senate adjourned with no vote on the resolution.

On the opposite shore of the vast, dark tarn of winter waters, the funeral boat landed at Westport, New York. There was a heavy rain falling, sloshing away the snow, and wagons had to be substituted for the sleighs already provided. The Old Man was well known in this area, having taken prizes at the Essex County Fair with his fancy breed of sheep. A respectful group of mourners was waiting, and someone said that "they did not think, in the last extremity, that Virginia would do the bloody deed. They did not see how Governor Wise could have deliberately consented to the death of such a man."

The horses plodded on to Elizabethtown where it was decided to spend the night. The cortege was greeted by the county Sheriff, and everyone was invited to put up at his hotel next to the courthouse. He suggested that the body lie in state for the night in the large courtroom, and six young Republican lawyers volunteered to watched all night as a guard of honor. They were now within twenty-five miles of the North Elba farm, but the next day's journey was a difficult one, over a nearly impassable road up a high mountain. The Sheriff's son volunteered to ride his horse over the mountain that night and tell the family the Old Man was almost home. "Among the gentlemen who came to pay their respects at the courthouse were Judge Hall, the Honorable O. Kellogg, late Member of Congress, G. L. Nicholson, Esq., and others, irrespective of party."

With an even-tempered and purposeful obtuseness, the Republican Senators went on discussing the issue as if it were possible to separate the Old Man from his deed, and get the best out of both.

Mr. Simmons, in Wednesday's debate, spent more than an hour with this approach. "The acts of Brown are unaccountable, coming from a man of such characteristic virtue. His indomitable will, his unbending integrity, and the nervous truth with which he asserts everything, commands every man's respect . . . commanded the respect of the Governor of Virginia amidst the turmoil and strife of the conflict. These traits of character and everything we have read about John Brown in his prison and at his trial excited our sympathy. We cannot help it. There is not an act of kindness but what he has acknowledged, no matter from whom it came, and given with it his blessing that has more than satisfied the giver. He at first complained about the unfairness, or the prospect of unfairness of the trial: but after it was through, I dare say that the Senator from Virginia was gratified at his acknowledgment that he had a fair trial?"

Mr. Mason replied, tight-lipped. "Not in the least, sir, I was not at all gratified with it."

Mr. Simmons said he was gratified by it, and went on toying with the raging tempers of the southern members. Mr. William Fessenden of Maine gave a similar speech.

Finally, Mr. Iverson could stand it no longer and said, "The course the Republican Party is taking at this time warns the southern people of the danger under which we live in this Confederacy. They stand on the very brink of a volcano, and unless we take time by the forelock and provide for our safety before it is too late, that will be our condition. When the rights and equality of my section are disregarded then I think the Union is no longer worth preserving. I am for dissolving it, and as a distinguished man of my state has said, I would dissolve this Union tomorrow, as much upon an abstraction as I would upon a practical result."

The reply to this came hotly from Zack Chandler, a Republican fully as intransigent as the most violent southern separatist. "John Brown has been executed as a traitor to the state of Virginia, and I want it to go on the records of this Senate and to be held up as a warning to traitors, dare to raise your hand against this government, against our Constitution and our laws, and you hang! Sir, it is no small matter to dissolve the Union. It means a bloody revolution, or it means a halter. It means the successful overturning of this government or it means the fate of John Brown and I want that to go solemnly on the records of this Senate."

The members stirred uneasily. Chandler had finally broken through the crust of rhetoric and false sympathy covering the hot and deadly fires beneath. He did not let it rest there but went on to taunt the pride and dignity of the southern members. "Senators ask us why we have no sympathy for Virginia in this instance. Sir, we do not understand the case at all. Seventeen white men and five Negroes surrounded and captured a town of two thousand people with a United States Armory, any quantity of arms and ammunition, with three hundred men, as I am informed, employed in it under a civil officer, and held it for two days. These I understand are the facts in this case, and you ask why we have no sympathy? Why, sir, Governor Wise compared the people of Harper's Ferry to sheep. It is a libel, it is not true, for I never saw a flock of fifty or a hundred sheep in my life that did not have a belligerent ram among them. . . ."

Mr. Chesnut of South Carolina cried out at the ignominy with which the South was being treated by the North. "They constantly and without remission, taunt, abuse, irritate and disturb the people of the southern states . . . the thing must stop. We must keep armies on our borders, all the portals of our invasion and destruction are now thrown wide open. Call it treason, gentlemen, and make the best of it, but I tell you unless these things cease, it becomes our honor and our existence to maintain ourselves."

The moment had come when it looked as if the war would begin then and there. The northern Democrats began to plead with the Republicans to withdraw the Kansas amendment, or at least to adjourn without further comment. But Mr. Trumbull insisted on demanding from the South whether it was true that their policy was to withdraw from the Union and form a Southern Confederacy, "in case a certain individual is elected President, or in case the Republican party elected a President of the United States."

Chesnut wanted to know if the Senator wanted his answer now. Trumbull said yes. Chestnut confirmed the accusation. If any of the men in the Republican Party who supported the idea of an irrepressible conflict were nominated for the Presidency, the South would take it as a declaration of war.

The strategy of the Republican caucus was beginning to work. The baiting and the taunting, the excessive praise of the Old Man, was leading the South into making treasonable utterances. The debate was not half over, and the Old Man was still above ground when Ben Wade called for the day's adjournment.

The time had come for Horace Greeley to put to the country the question the Republican Party had been so successfully bringing to a head. "How is it that so many Statesmen of the Democratic Party have risen in their places to condemn and denounce the treason for which John Brown, a private man, trained to extreme courses by the adventures of merciless border warfare, was hanged, and not one thundered out an indignant reproof of open avowals of treasonable and revolutionary purposes uttered in both houses by the Congress?"

At dawn that morning, the cortege had begun the final stage of the journey home. The roads were so bad that oxen had to be provided at every steep grade. It took them more than two hours to travel eight miles to the town of Keene. Painfully, slipping back and surging forward in a breathless struggle for ascent, the cortege bested one peak after another. It was not until after sunset that they came to the Old Man's farm, where people carrying lanterns came wordlessly to meet them. Mary Brown was the first to get out as her carriage drew up to the little farmhouse door. "She alighted with difficulty, being much agitated. Instantly there was a sharp, low cry of 'Mother' and in answer, another in the same tone of mingled agony and tenderness, 'O Annie,' and the mother and daughter were locked in a long, convulsed embrace. Then followed the same scene with the next daughter, Sarah, and then Ellen, the little girl of five, was brought, and another burst of anguish and love ensued. Then came the daughter-in-law, Oliver's widow, and then Watson's, and there went up a wail, before which flint itself would have softened. It was a scene entirely beyond description."

This display of emotion, however, lasted only a minute or so, and the *Tribune* reporter continued: "The strangers were introduced to

John Brown's House at North Elba, New York

the family and supper was served. After a while, Mary Brown came to Miller McKim and Wendell Phillips to say the family was gathered in the parlor, 'anxious to hear a recital of what happened.' " Mr. McKim filled them in on all the details of their father's last hours, and then the Old Man's mourning children had the melancholy privilege of hearing Wendell Phillips explain his 'transfiguration' in the tenderest and most beautiful manner until all tears were wiped away. A holy pensive joy seemed to dispel grief and a becoming and filial and conjugal pride seemed to reconcile these stricken ones to their destiny." And so the hanged man came home.

The debate in the Senate on the burial day was largely a haggling over what everyone else had said and what they meant by it. Mr. Trumbull talked a lot about the wrongs done to the Free State settlers in Kansas. There seemed to be an uneasiness about saying too much, yet every facet of the slavery question was being examined, and every variance and abyss between the sections stood naked before the country. Jefferson Davis complained bitterly about the delay in taking the vote:

"A murderous raid was made into the state of Virginia. When

insurrection and rebellion against the government and the laws raise their ugly crest, it is no time to go into a disquisition on the abstract question of African servitude. A conspiracy has been formed, extending not only over a portion of the United States, but also into England. Money has been contributed at both places, it has been the work of years, a military leader was sent here from England, first to participate in the Kansas trouble, and then in this raid upon Virginia. If this is a fact, and there is surely enough to justify the suspicion of conspiracy, what Senator can decline to enter into the inquiry?"

Mr. Mason hoped the vote would be taken now, but Henry Wilson kept delaying the question, putting the burden of guilt on the South. "It may appear that Governor Wise has hung John Brown in 1859, for attempting to carry out a plan formed by him and his disunion compeers in 1856."

The southerners realized that they were not making progress; their strident accusations only seemed to inspire the Republicans to defend the Old Man more and more. Senator Albert G. Brown of Mississippi was moved to observe, with great psychological insight, that the sympathy in the North was "not for John Brown, heroic as you have said he was, but for the cause in which he was engaged. He came to levy war on a slave state, to murder slaveholders because they were slaveholders . . . disguise it as you will, there is throughout all the non-slaveholding states a secret, deep-seated sympathy with the object this man had in view. Men may recoil from it; they may almost shudder at feeling themselves that they sympathize with such conduct, and yet acts speak louder than words. Public acts will show what moves the heart of the private man."

Both the *Tribune* of the Republicans and the *Herald* of the Democrats produced powerfully moving accounts of the Old Man's burial. The day was clear and dazzling, the sky cloudless. The farmhouse was thin-boarded and weather-worn to a dingy black, just the sort of house that would be owned precariously by a farmer in straits and behind in his mortgage payments. Around it the towering masses and peaks of mountaintops hurled themselves in folds of dazzling white and deep purple against the sky, intolerant of the flat conformity of the tamed earth beneath. Their profiles rose in majestic solitude, and even the reporters were overwhelmed by the beauty of the scene. "Mr. Brown had expressed a desire that his body should be laid in the shadow of a great rock, not far from his house. It is a very striking and picturesque object and the recollection of it would not unnaturally suggest to the mind of Mr. Brown a place to lay his body."

The funeral took place at one o'clock. The coffin was placed on a table brought outside and put beside the door. When the lid was taken off, the Old Man's face appeared faintly flushed, almost radiant in the clear, wintry sunlight. The neighbors—about two hundred people were present—were invited to come forward and pay their last respects. Some of his black neighbors, who had been given land in North Elba by Gerrit Smith and were the reason that John Brown had settled in the area, sang his favorite hymn:

> Blow Ye the Trumpet Blow,
> the gladly solemn sound,
> let all the nations know,
> to earth's remotest bound,
> the year of Jubilee has come.

Mr. McKim offered a lengthy eulogy: "That John Brown was a brave, magnanimous, truthful, consistent man, rested not on the testimony of admiring friends, but was freely conceded by his open enemies." Mr. McKim knew this because he had escorted Mrs. Brown into Virginia. "Not only had he heard testimony borne in the South to the bravery and uprightness of the leader, but for Oliver Brown, Watson Brown, Dauphin Thompson, William Thompson . . ."

McKim looked out at the five grieving widows—the Old Man's, Oliver's and Watson's (both in their teens), and the widows of the Thompson boys. "Don't weep for them, the world will be debtor to them and history will embalm their memory. Of Copeland and Green we heard nothing at Harper's Ferry. This was eulogy. If they belong to the hated and oppressed race and if anything could be said to their disadvantage, we should have had it ere this."

A letter was read from poor Edwin Coppoc, awaiting his own hanging in Charlestown jail. "Some of Captain Brown's friends speak as if they regarded the result of Harper's Ferry a disaster. He has builded better than he knew. . . . He made such developments of the weakness, the imbecility and utter powerlessness of a slave-holding Commonwealth, as was certain to result in the extinction of the whole slave system."

"How feeble words seem here," Wendell Phillips exclaimed. "O Marvelous Old Man. . . . He has abolished slavery in Virginia. You may say this is too much? True, the slave is still there. So, when the tempest uproots a pine on your hill, it looks green for months . . . a year or two. . . . Still, it is timber, not a tree; John Brown has loosed the roots of the slave system . . . it does not live, hereafter. Insurrection was a harsh, horrid word to millions a month ago. John Brown went a whole generation beyond it, claiming the right for white men to help the slave to freedom by arms. Virginia is weak because each man's heart said amen to John Brown. His words . . . are stronger than his rifles, they have changed the thoughts of millions and will yet crush slavery. Harper's Ferry was no single hour, standing alone, taken out from a common life, it was the flowering of fifty years of single devotion. He must have lived wholly for one great idea when these who owe their being to him and these whom love has joined, group so harmoniously around him, each accepting serenely his or her part. We dare not say bless you, children of this home; you stand nearer to one whose lips God touched and we rather bend for your blessing. Men say, would that he had died in arms—God ordered better and granted to him and the slave those prison hours—that single hour of death, granted him a higher than a soldier's place, that of teacher: the echo of his rifles have died away in the hills, a million hearts guard his words."

Neighbors were invited to look for the last time on the Old Man's face. Mary Brown took the arm of Wendell Phillips and they began the walk to the shadow of the rock. Behind them came Oliver's widow and little Ellen Brown, holding the hand of Mr. McKim. Next came the widows of Watson, Dauphin and William Thompson, and the parents of the Thompson boys, then Brown's son Salmon, and young Sarah and Annie.

As the body descended into the frosty grave, a minister from Vergennes, famous for his stentorian voice, drowned out, with the strong words of scripture, the final gush of uncontrollable grief: "I have fought the good fight. I have finished my course. I have kept the faith."

The proof that Wendell Phillips was right and that the Old Man had touched the hearts and minds of millions, came in the last three days of the debate in the Senate. The southern bloc had abandoned its threat to walk out and retire to Richmond. Jefferson Davis, inadvertently during the session on the burial day, had given the reason. "In the South and West we have no manufactories for the construction of arms. Special arms, such as are employed by hunters, are those alone that we manufacture. Others are purchased in the North . . ."

The best they could do now was to try to frighten the timid Republicans and northern Democrats into revulsion against the Old Man and his supporters. While he remained a hero and a martyr to the masses in the North who voted Republican, the danger of another John Brown coming South and igniting the slaves would give them no peace. Soon they would withdraw within their own borders so that slavery could be contained, uncontaminated by the North, but they needed time to build up their supply of arms and materials of war. So long as the North deplored the *acts* of John Brown, neither declaring war nor establishing a peace between the sections, the South could take advantage of both positions. It "enables us," Davis pointed out in the secret counsels going on among the secessionists, "to make all necessary arrangements for public defense and the solidification of government more safely and cheaply."

The southerner's problem was to keep the overt secessionists from acting prematurely. Andrew Johnson, a Unionist slaveholder from a border state, was chosen to sum up the debate from the southern side. He began brilliantly with the restoration of motives behind Brown's act that would provide a logical connection with the Republican Party. Since Seward was known as an avid disciple of John Quincy Adams, Johnson reminded the Senate of Adams's well-known doctrine that if a slave insurrection broke out, the Federal Government, under the war power, could constitutionally end slavery.

"And do we not see the whole idea, to get up a foray, make a descent upon a southern state, establish a provisional government, and if the Federal Government is called upon to intervene, under the treaty-making power, we will emancipate all your slaves. This idea has been longer inculcated than many are willing to believe. The recent foray at Harper's Ferry was the legitimate result of the teachings to which I have referred, look at the provisional government which was framed by those who carried on the expedition; look at their idea of getting up stampedes and the expectation that when they struck the first blow, a portion of the white population and the blacks would flock to their standard, and then the Federal Government would be made an instrument for the overthrow of slavery."

It made Brown's planning, the details of which had been lost through the destruction of his papers, seem completely viable and sound. The Republicans, who up to this point had regarded the outcries of the South as part of the chronic anxieties of their repressive system, now could understand the terror Brown's operation had created. Johnson then went on, using government documents and a letter held in his excited hand, to create a vituperous image of the Old Man.

"Senators disclaim the acts of John Brown in one breath, in another they hold out apologies and excuses for the man, saying that he showed himself a model of endurance, a man of philosophy, a man of tact, a man of sense, and when we speak of him as a thief, as a robber and a murderer and traitor, they declare that we should not say such things about John Brown. Those may make him a god who will, and worship him who can. He is not my god, and I shall not worship at his shrine.

"Five innocent, unoffending men were taken out and in the midnight hours and in the forest and on the road fell victims to the insatiable thirst of John Brown for blood. John Brown and his companions, midnight assassins, with the weapons that were sent to them from the northern states, on May 24th, 1856, dragged the husband and two sons from the mother and inbrued their hands in their blood. These were his teachings, the shrieks of the mutilated and dying. That same night, when they took Wilkinson out and murdered him, they took his property and his only horse. Let us remember these facts and come to the old man as being a thief and a murderer. I want the modern fanatics who have adopted John Brown and his gallows as their Christ and their cross, to see who their Christ is. Now let the Republicans defend him, the murders, the infamy, the thieving, the treacherous conduct of this old man Brown, who was nothing more than a murderer, a robber, a thief and a traitor."

The South asked for an adjournment to let these terrible accusations sink in; next day the galleries were overflowing with southern sympathizers, confident that the Republicans could not answer this devastating attack. If this did not break Republican solidarity on the Kansas motion, nothing would.

Ben Wade spoke for the Republicans, calmly and simply: "I think I can explain the reason why many northern men have deeply sympathized with old John Brown. I ask you here, however, always to discriminate between the man and the act that he committed. Gentlemen seem incapable of drawing that line of discrimination. They run both together and they treat old John Brown as a common malefactor. They have a right to treat him so, but he will not go down to posterity in that light at all. I think I know why some considerable feeling and sympathy exist in the North for John Brown and it cannot be understood unless we go back for four years and see what was taking place in a distant territory of the United States and the part John Brown acted in that theatre.

"Sir, if the people of Virginia are excited almost to madness because a conspiracy has been formed and traitors have made a raid upon the sovereign state of Virginia, what do you suppose were the feelings of northern men, whose relations and friends had gone into a far distant territory, and formed colonies there, weak and feeble, scattered through a wilderness, when it was the deliberate purpose of a great, powerful and almost all-pervading party to drive them out, or to coerce them to subscribe to institutions which they abhorred from the bottom of their souls? Many were murdered in cold blood and others were driven out and their property was destroyed. They appealed to Congress but they got insult instead of sympathy. When I state this, I state what I know. My blood boiled then, in view of the oppression and tyranny that sacrificed that territory.

"In the darkest hour of Kansas, when your government failed to interpose its strong arm, then it was that Old John Brown appeared on the scene of action. Arming himself as well as he might, he commenced to do that justice to himself and his fellows that the government had denied. He went forth with a determination that carried terror into the hearts of the Border Ruffians and he hurled them from the territory and really conquered a peace. Now, sir, in order to understand northern sentiment, it is necessary fully to appreciate the feeling of those whose friends were stricken down in that defenseless territory. John Brown was their Champion."

Ben Wade was spokesman for his party, and his defense of the Old Man was designed to explain away sentiments that could prove politically embarrassing. But he was personally moved by John Brown and proceeded to say some things about him that went beyond the expediencies of the hour. "Old John Brown resided, for a long time, not far from that portion of the country from which I come. He was always reputed among the most honest and upright men in the community. There was nothing against his character. He is frequently spoken of as a common malefactor, a vulgar murderer, a robber. Sir, he proposed nothing for himself. His conduct was as disinterested as any man's conduct could ever be!"

Wade talked a while about the Declaration of Independence and its meaning, showing contempt for Johnson's racism. "The Senator from Tennessee said the Declaration of Independence applied only to white men. Will the Senator say a Negro has no right to life? If he has, he has just as great and inalienable a right to his liberty and his happiness. Sir, there is nothing more abhorrent to the mind of most northern men than the idea that one man was created as a serf to another . . ." Carefully, within the bounds of the Constitution, he hurled the challenge of the irrepressible conflict at the South.

"I know that I cannot touch the institution within the boundaries of the states where slavery is established by law, for there the Constitution does not enable me to reach it. But when you undertake to thrust it forth where it has no foothold, I meet you to contend, inch by inch. I would suffer my arm to fall from its socket before this accursed institution should invade one inch of territory now free.

"Now we are told by the hour that if we succeed in wresting this government from your hands and placing a constitutional man in that great office, you make this a contingency on which you will disrupt and destroy this government. Let me tell you, if a Republican President is elected to preside over you, mark you, preside he will. Who will prevent this? No man in the North is to be intimidated by these threats of disunion that are thrown into our teeth, daily.

"I tell you, if you wait until a Republican President is elected, you wait a day too late. I don't know what motive you have in preaching the dissolution of the Union, day by day. There is no law requiring that you should serve notice that you are going to dissolve the Union. Why don't you do it now, when you have the Government in your hand?"

The South, having exhausted every accusation and threat, called for a vote on the Kansas Amendment. It lost, but the solid front of Republican Senators remained unterrified of the taint of association with the Old Man.

If history could be honestly presented by the leap and freeze technique of time-lapse photography, we could glance next to that day a year and a month later when Henry Clay and Fitzpatrick of Alabama, Yelee of Florida, and Jefferson Davis of Mississippi rose and announced to the Senate that because their states had seceded from the Union, they were resigning from the Senate. At that moment the South surrendered to John Brown and his still multiplying sympathizers in the North. It was an abdication of power over the Army, the Navy, the Courts, Custom Houses, Embassies, and all its agents in the Bureaucracies, down to the postmaster in the tiniest village. They had threatened to do this if a Republican President were elected; he was, and they did it. Seward, the candidate with the most damning connection with the Old Man, was dropped, but Lincoln, a man the South felt was equally pledged to the irrepressible conflict, who had declared in 1858 that a house divided cannot stand, was nominated and elected.

All the attempts at peaceful adjustment, the Crittenden Compromise, the Peace Conference, the intricate Machiavellian accommodations of Seward and Company, all had failed. The issues remained the same as those raised in the Senate while the Old Man's body was in transit. "For the first time in history," Garrison's *Liberator* exulted, "the slave has chosen a president. John Brown was behind the curtain and the inauguration cannons of March 4 will only echo the rifles at Harper's Ferry."

The Republican radicals, the supporters of John Brown, took power. The South, in a final act of insanity, fired on Fort Sumter, forcing the masses of the North and West where they had been a little reluctant to go—behind a Free Soil President and a tight coterie of antislavery radicals pushing him into a revolutionary war. And once this war had started, it was inevitable that Charles Sumner would go to President Lincoln and tell him that "under the war power, the right had come to him to emancipate the slaves."

But the final maturing of John Brown's thrifty little coup, the giving of power to the powerless, did not take place until May 28, 1863, when Wendell Phillips and Garrison stood on the balcony of Phillips's house in Boston, watching the Fifty-fourth black Regiment march off to fight the slaveholders in Virginia. Garrison stood with his hand resting lightly on a marble bust of the Old Man. And when the black troops looked up and saw that, the band struck up "John Brown's Body," and the marching columns all sang and stamped to its cadence. They marched, as the Old Man had specified in his Provisional Constitution, under the flag which "shall be the same as our Fathers fought under in the Revolution."

A NOTE ON SOURCES   The sources from which this work has been constructed have been the testimonies of those who knew John Brown and fought either for or against him and thus could give, as Emerson puts it, "knowledge that cannot be abstractly imparted and which needs the combinations and complexities of social action to point it out."

They have appeared in the newspapers of the day, notably the New York *Herald* and the New York *Tribune,* and various government documents such as: The Report of the Invasion At Harper's Ferry, 1860; The Report of the Troubles in Kansas, 1856; and The Congressional Globe, Part One, 1859–1860.

Life at the Kennedy farm was intimately described by Osborn Anderson in *A Voice From Harper's Ferry* and by Annie Brown in letters to her father's biographers. The dialogue between Brown and Frederick Douglass was taken verbatim from Brown's Kansas letters and speeches and Douglass's autobiography and newspaper. The complicity of the Secret Six appears in the Thomas Wentworth Higginson Collection at the Boston Public Library and in the collections of the letters of John Brown.

The two modern books which I have used to support my general thesis are: *Coup d'Etat,* by Edward Luttwak, Knopf, 1969, and *Free Soil, Free Labor, Free Men,* by Eric Foner, Oxford, 1970.

www.ingramcontent.com/pod-product-compliance
Lightning Source LLC
Jackson TN
JSHW080102141224
75386JS00028B/838